The Politics of Authentic Engagement

Other Books by These Authors

The Politics of Authentic Engagement: Strategies for Engaging Stakeholders in Ensuring Student Success (2015)

The Politics of Authentic Engagement

Perspectives, Strategies, and Tools for Student Success

Kathy Leslie
with Judy Taccogna

Published in partnership with the
National School Public Relations Association

ROWMAN & LITTLEFIELD
Lanham • Boulder • New York • London

Published in partnership with the National School Public Relations Association

Published by Rowman & Littlefield
A wholly owned subsidary of The Rowman & Littlefield Publishing Group, Inc.
4501 Forbes Boulevard, Suite 200, Lanham, Maryland 20706
www.rowman.com

Unit A, Whitacre Mews, 26-34 Stannary Street, London SE11 4AB

British Library Cataloguing in Publication Information Available

Library of Congress Cataloging-in-Publication Data

Leslie, Kathy, 1942-
The politics of authentic engagement : perspectives, strategies, and tools for student success / Kathy Leslie with Judy Taccogna.
pages cm.
Includes bibliographical references and index.
ISBN 978-1-4758-1531-3 (cloth : alk. paper) -- ISBN 978-1-4758-1532-0 (pbk. : alk. paper) -- ISBN 978-1-4758-1533-7 (electronic)
1. Educational planning. 2. School management and organization. 3. Education--Parent participation. 4. Community and school. 5. Academic achievement. I. Title.
LC71.2.L46 2014
371.2--dc23
                                    2014043161

∞ ™ The paper used in this publication meets the minimum requirements of American National Standard for Information Sciences Permanence of Paper for Printed Library Materials, ANSI/NISO Z39.48-1992.

Printed in the United States of America

To all those who challenge my thinking and offer different perspectives so I may view life more fully and honestly: my friends and colleagues as well as each member of my large extended family, especially my children Lisa, Don, and Charlette; my grandchildren Hailey, Aimee, Taylor, and Patrick, and my husband Ed Arata.

Contents

Preface

I love whitewater rafting. Running the Deschutes, Rogue, Colorado, and many other rivers throughout this country has taught me many lessons about living natural systems that, if applied to human social systems, can create adaptive, resilient, and sustainable organizations. Rivers are complex and dynamic. Each river belongs to a larger river system, a river basin that includes tributaries and streams connecting and flowing together to form a whole. Over time, the river changes naturally, shifting to respond to the demands of the environment. Each element within the river system has an influence on the shifts occurring. The river adapts, self-organizes, adjusts, and emerges naturally so it can fulfill its noble purpose to support life and reach the ocean.

The principles of engagement outlined in this book come from what I have learned through years of experience working in schools as well as from rafting always-changing rivers. I find there are meaningful parallels between rafting a river in an evolving, living system and leading change in education—also a complex, dynamic system comprised of people with many views, beliefs, gifts, and talents, all needed to help students be successful so our democracy will advance.

Engagement processes increase chances that people can play an influential role in the evolution of an educational system. The energy and pressures from people within an adaptive schooling system will promote change in the entire system. To capitalize on those forces and ensure that the change contributes to the success of students, engagement strategies pull people in to influence the direction of modifications. Just as nearly all change occurs naturally in a river system, the most enduring and beneficial changes that can happen over time in an educational system are those nudged into place by participants within the system.

We cannot simply "do change" to the organization. Nor do we change people—they change themselves and therefore the system changes, just as the river system adjusts to meet its own needs. Engagement strategies lead to new understandings in people because they talk with one another and listen. The benefits from engaging families and communities are key to changing schooling and making a difference for young people.

However, citizens today are either not engaged or are fragmented, often working at cross-purposes and drowning each other out with loud, conflicting rhetoric. They seldom work together toward a common purpose. Citizens do not know they have an important role in ensuring student success, nor do they know the role others play. Further, they do not understand that everyone in society—not just teachers and administrators—is accountable for the success of the system and the students it supports.

Fragmented mechanistic thinking, power mongering, and lack of civility too often prevent the education system from moving toward a common purpose benefiting all, especially the students. Mechanistic thinkers do not see that systems are interrelated. They fight hard to devalue such thinking because they fear loss of control and power. They represent the *negative* politics of self-preservation. They value certainty, uniformity, and authority-driven decision-making.

On the river, however, such thinkers soon learn that a larger, more powerful, and integrated system takes over. Rafters must flow in and with the river. They must be present in every moment, responding to whatever emerges, watching carefully for river currents and patterns, looking for the *V* in the river where the energy will carry everyone forward. One lapse and rafters can hit a boulder, be thrown out, even die.

The living system and patterns of a river are much like those in other systems, as well—business, health, education, government, and social agencies. Success in any comprehensive organizational system involves nurturing trusting relationships—the *positive* side of politics—that guarantee a safe and successful journey for all and help participants deal with uncertainties of life, just as rafters must deal with the unexpected in the wild, natural river system.

I serve on Oregon's White Water Institute board. We teach participants in a classroom setting, combined with experiences on the river, how to work collaboratively across perceived boundaries. We help people learn and work together to address complex challenges by applying the fundamental principles of a living system to guide and navigate change. Participants from all segments of a community—whether a town, a school district, a government agency, an intergenerational group, or a community college—learn and practice tools for systemic thinking and empowering themselves, citizens, or stakeholders to fulfill the identified purpose, adapt, and make changes as needed.

As rafters, they quickly learn the value of systems thinking. They know everyone in the raft has a role to play. The river guide at the back of the boat has a complete picture of the river in her mind and uses an oar at the stern to manage the direction of the raft down the river. The paddlers listen and follow the direction of the guide but do the work making individual contributions that, taken together, get all the rafters down the river. They value relationships, diversity, uncertainty, and ambiguity. They learn the core value embedded in seeing and flowing with river patterns is abandoning individual agendas in favor of a collective, systems approach.

Similarly, facilitators of authentic engagement look for patterns and energy by listening deeply, casting away judgments, and being open to whatever thoughts, beliefs, or values emerge. They capitalize on associational politics of building trust and relationships. A lapse in listening to and exploring emerging ideas can jeopardize constituent trust in leadership, crumble the organization's reputation, or force leaders from their jobs—just as not reading the river correctly can result in disaster on the water.

As rapids on a river have various levels of difficulty, engagement work also presents varying levels of challenge, depending on the issues and the people engaged. I am writing this book to help you negotiate all of the challenges in your engagement work, no matter how difficult. The following official descriptions of the levels of rapids provide vocabulary in which you can also think about how to meet varying stages of challenge in your work. More difficult, challenging engagement efforts such as strategic planning and managing conflict require more skill and experience as well as use of the most appropriate tools. And sometimes, because the outcomes can be harmful, some engagement projects with some people should be avoided.

The international scale of river difficulty is a standardized scale used to rate the safety of a stretch of river or a single rapid. Rated from a Class 6 as the most challenging rapids, the grade reflects the technical difficulty and skill level required to negotiate that section of the river.

Class 1: Easy—Waves small, passages clear, no serious obstacles.

Class 2: Medium—Rapids of moderate difficulty with passages clear. Requires experience plus suitable outfit and boat.

Class 3: Difficult—Waves numerous; high, irregular rocks; eddies; rapids with passages clear though narrow; expertise in maneuvering. Requires good guide and boat.

Class 4: Long rapids; waves high; irregular; dangerous rocks; boiling eddies; best passages difficult to scout; scouting mandatory first time; complex and precise maneuvering required. Requires excellent guide, good boat, and quality equipment.

Class 5: Exceedingly difficult; long and violent rapids, following each other almost without interruption; extremely obstructed; big drops; violent current; very steep gradient; close study essential but often difficult. Requires excellent guide and paddlers, and a boat and outfit suited to the situation. All possible precautions must be taken.

Class 6: Unraftable—Nearly impossible and very dangerous. Involves risk to life.

My work with the White Water Institute grew from my lifelong love of rafting, and it has woven its way into my years as a public relations practitioner. In the mid-1970s, I believed my job was to develop award-winning publications and communication pieces targeted to specific audiences. I was convinced the power of persuasion, along with effective public speaking and writing, would move people to support public education, volunteer in the schools, and vote "yes" on bond or levy measures. I worked to put structures in place to ensure the educators' vision, beliefs, and values were protected.

In those early years, I served as a female administrator in the superintendent's cabinet in male-dominated central offices. Feeling fortunate to be an administrator and even have such a role within a man's world, I did not question my colleagues' thinking or decisions until much later.

Knowing it was important to hear the voices of constituents, I used surveys and public hearings to gather opinions. However, I also helped my superintendents control the outcomes on those measures by designing questions that elicited only the information educators wanted and needed. I believed in Eddie Bernays's "engineering of consent" model of public relations, supporting his notion of manipulating the thoughts, habits, and opinions of the public in order to support the organization.[1]

I supported the education world's school-relationship models in which constituents were asked to visit the school or district at the request of the educators. In those days, educators supported parental involvement but only to the extent that parents stayed out of the education business and simply cooperated with what the decision-makers—the superintendent, principals, and perhaps a few lead teachers—put in place. Before *A Nation at Risk* and No Child Left Behind, I did not think much about student achievement results because I believed schools were doing the best they could to ensure student success.[2]

Over the years, however, I began to understand that one-way communications did not consider adequately the needs, desires, and timelines of the recipients. The surveys we touted as giving us feedback from our communities were not truly representative of what families or groups of constituents were thinking, needing, or feeling. I moved, along with many other public relations practitioners, from being a public information officer and expert who provided information about the district and schools to embracing two-way systems of communication. I shifted from trying to engineer thinking to being a guide and facilitator who really listened, communicating the thinking of constituents into decision-making. In the language of the river, I moved to a place of knowing the entire system needed to be considered and honored, that our success in leading lay in moving with constituents, in listening to the surroundings and in engaging with the natural flow in order to come together, navigate rapids, and successfully generate new ideas and solutions.

I now believe *engaging* our stakeholders in talking, thinking, and deciding with us is key to improving our schools and, more importantly, student achievement. In authentic engagement work, challenges and obstacles will confront participants and the facilitator. Conflict will arise, misunderstandings will occur, and everyone will feel like they are in the rapids. I share ideas, strategies, and tools in this book that I have used often and found practical and effective. I hope they will help you learn to negotiate whatever difficulty level you encounter—be it a Class 1 or Class 5 engagement-rapid—using the natural energy and flow of a group. Depending on the rapid-class level, the politics of the moment, and the nature of the engagement issue you are addressing, you will need various levels of training expertise.

In this book, I want to inspire hope and provide tools and strategies that illustrate how changing your thinking about politics, listening deeply, and engaging stakeholders in meaningful dialogue will benefit students and address conflict and lack of civility. I frame the complexities in ways that simplify them and tell how you, your colleagues, and stakeholders can engage with each other authentically to help students be successful and build a strong democracy.

In creating such a tool, I am indebted to an extensive group of people who have informed my thinking over the years through conversations, their writings and speeches, or in our joint collaboration on various projects. A number of important thinkers in the areas of public relations and educational and organizational thinking have shaped my evolution as a practitioner of engagement. Many have provided helpful feedback on the process and content of my work with schools and districts.

I acknowledge the influence of Patrick Jackson, Gary Marx, William Banach, and Edward Bernays. Their work prompted the emergence of public relations itself, moving us from telling to listening, from marketing to collaborating. I thank James and Larissa Grunig in particular for taking time from their summer in Oregon to talk further with me about how their work and mine intersect.

I have had opportunities to participate with professionals and organizations on a number of projects that shaped my thinking. Two of the most influential organizations were the National School Public Relations Association (NSPRA) and KSA-Plus Communications. KSA provided opportunities for me to work with not only schools throughout the country, but with businesses, city and state governments, agencies, and other entities that influence education in a multitude of ways. This experience opened my eyes to the larger system of education beyond the classroom, school, and district.

Collaborating with colleagues such as Anne Henderson and working with the Prichard Committee for Academic Excellence and KSA deepened my understanding of parent engagement. Participating in several national issues' dialogues with the Kettering Foundation, Public Agenda, and the National Issues Forums deepened my conviction that engagement and dialogue generate understandings that create positive differences for communities. The Annenberg Institute for School Reform, in partnership with NSPRA, was seminal in grounding me in engagement work during our studying, exploring, and teaching of engagement strategies throughout the United States.

Superintendents Boyd Applegarth and Yvonne Katz were enduring supporters of my work with Beaverton (Oregon) School District's engagement efforts with families and the community. I learned from Dr. Applegarth the art of questioning to empower and from Dr. Katz visioning, strategic planning, and the value of fun, even when the work is overwhelming and very challenging.

I was privileged to teach graduate courses at Lewis and Clark College (Portland, Oregon) in public engagement, communication skills for administrators, and professional relationships. Students taking those classes have kept me current in what is happening in the trenches and have influenced the many strategies presented in this book.

Leaders of the work in organizational development have also played a role in the maturation of my thinking systemically: Peter Senge, David Bohm, Margaret Wheatley, William Isaacs, C. Otto Scharmer, David Matthews, Richard Krueger, Bob Chadwick, Joseph Jaworski, and Peter Block. Educational thinkers and skill developers such as The National School Reform Faculty, Thomas J. Sergiovanni, Lisa Delpit, Glen Singleton, and Michael Fullan have helped shape my approaches.

Some of the products and writings of these individuals and groups are listed as resources or appear in the reference list. However, while working over the years with their thinking, I acknowledge that I have incorporated their ideas so completely into my own practice that I can no longer directly identify the source of their influence. If I have spoken in these pages as though something is mine when it is actually not, please tell me so I can credit appropriately the valuable contributions of colleagues I respect and honor.

Several colleagues contributed to this book by reviewing the initial proposal, editing, contributing to selected chapters, and submitting perspectives for chapter 7: Rich Bagin, Sherre Calouri, Nora Carr, Patty Farrell, Harry Gamble, James and Laurie Grunig, Janet Hogue, Christine Jensen, Shelley King, Karen Kleinz, Marilyn Lane, Matt Leighninger, Steve Lynch, Jeanne Magmer, Gary Marx, Jane Lister Reis, Sylvia Soholt, Deborah Sommer, and Maureen Wheeler. I also appreciated Anne-Marie Chrisafis's keen editing skills, including her questions seeking clarification and her gentle way of saying something will not work.

Finally, I wish to thank my coauthor, Judy Taccogna, who first experienced engagement work as a principal in the same district in which I served as community engagement executive director. She insisted my work be documented and preserved so others may learn the strategies and tools I have been teaching and practicing over the years. During our joint writing process, she attended my lectures, studied my workshop materials and written articles, listened to my dictations, and did deep research on the subject herself. She then pulled everything together, wrote the initial chapter drafts, and managed all of the publisher's requirements for submitting manuscripts for two books I believe will be catalysts in helping schools become more committed to authentic engagement work. She brings the perspective of a teacher, counselor, principal, and curriculum director in school districts and as the education director at Search Institute, a national research organization focused on the success of young people.

In the quest to ensure success for our students and their families, and, more broadly, our communities and democracy, I hope your connections and dialogue with others deepen, and the creativity and sustainability of your collaborative efforts expand through your experience with these pages.

NOTES

1. Bernays, *Propaganda.*
2. Leslie, "I Used to Believe." Used with permission of the National School Public Relations Association (www.NSPRA.org).

Introduction

The Politics of Authentic Engagement was written to help educators and other interested leaders gain new understanding about how to engage stakeholders and act to ensure each child succeeds. A stakeholder is anyone who has an interest in education or would if they knew they could make a difference. Authentic engagement is empowering.

To improve the effectiveness of schools, educators and other leaders in both public and private schools must step up efforts to ensure all voices are heard, considered, and reflected in meaningful decision-making. Skills citizens learn through engaging with their schools can build confidence in their abilities to contribute opinions and voice concerns about issues and decision-making processes well beyond the walls of one school or the boundaries of a single district. In a range of group settings, parents, teachers, families, administrators, and community members inquiring, planning, dialoguing, and working together can make a remarkable difference in the education of children.

AUTHENTIC ENGAGEMENT: BRINGING PEOPLE TOGETHER TO DISCOVER COMMON GOALS

Engagement in Education and Democracy

Education in America has long been rooted in the core values underpinning our democracy. The Founding Fathers saw schooling as a way to develop a responsible citizenry capable of governing democratically. Without common skills and knowledge, chances were slim the new government could survive.

By the mid-twentieth century, however, it became clear that the quality of instruction and facilities for some populations, such as African American youth, were drastically less conducive to learning than those for the white population. Legislation of the 1950s through the 1970s led to improvements in opportunities for an even wider variety of young peo-

1

ple—those in poverty, with disabilities, with limited or no English language facility, or with cultural differences.

But the most revolutionary change was the shift in focus in the 1990s and early 2000s from merely working toward equal access and opportunity to ensuring *all* students make progress toward common standards and achievement gaps between populations be closed. The No Child Left Behind legislation of 2002 required schools to increase achievement scores of all students continuously, regardless of their demographics or special needs. The new goal became equal *outcomes* for all. The shift was intended to move K–12 education one step closer to realizing more democratic ideals.

Nonetheless, large segments of the nation's student population still remain underserved. Their communities feel the effects both socially and economically. Further, many parents and communities feel cut off from meaningful contact with schools and districts, some increasingly frustrated and angry with systems that do not listen to them or meet their students' needs. Strategies of authentic engagement help educators, families, and entire communities bridge the gaps in quality, opportunity, and access that still stand in the way of high achievement for each student. When educators are open to partnering with their stakeholders and stakeholders speak up with knowledge and skill, they can help close gaps in understanding so local communities and schools work toward common goals, become more inclusive, prepare students and their families to be active citizens, and improve economic and social conditions.

The Politics of Authentic Engagement

The word *engagement* no longer holds clear meaning. It has become so generalized that it is used in a wide variety of circumstances. People say they are engaged with the news, or with Facebook, or with crossword puzzles, or nearly any activity. As a facilitative process, authentic engagement is the practice of drawing multiple diverse voices into the processes of society, creating ways for everyone to participate in a dialogue about things meaningful in their lives, ensuring others truly hear those voices, and incorporating change into systems and structures.

It is not about education alone; it is about the whole of living together. Engagement goes beyond merely inviting a few folks to give feedback. It is asking citizens to be key contributors in thinking and problem-solving processes. It is the foundation of effective public decision-making, a basic skill and component of democracy that is critical to our schools' ability to build a healthy citizenry.

Authentic engagement is also integrally connected to politics. When asked what politics means to them, citizens usually say power, control, lobbyists, Democrats, Republicans, Libertarians, conservatives, or liberals. They most often see themselves participating by voting or sometimes expressing their opinions on issues and policies through surveys or in public hearings. This is what some refer to as aggregative or representative democracy. In this form of democracy, governing is a process of gathering and aggregating the preferences of citizens in order to select those who will represent them and for those elected officials to decide policy from among the preferences of the constituency. Those preferences are generally determined through polling.

This form of democracy does not require much citizen participation. Voting and sometimes stating opinions is about all that is needed from citizens in a representational governance model. Schools operating in this model of democracy ask citizens to vote for school board members who will represent the constituency, and they collect stakeholders' opinions through surveys and other forms of research. In addition, in most communities, citizens are asked from time to time to vote on funding measures.

This book does not dismiss the importance of aggregative democracy, but asks readers to expand their definition of democracy to include another form of governance called associative democracy. This form is distinct from aggregative democracy in that the politics focus on "relating to others," another definition for politics. This model calls for citizens of diverse interests and backgrounds to participate, deliberate, and dialogue among themselves to confront and solve complex problems.[1]

When the associative model of democracy exists in schools, families, other stakeholders, and educators become well-informed about educational issues, grapple with educational challenges, and engage in trust building, collective thinking, and collective leadership. Power is shared with stakeholders serving on task forces and committees to solve problems with others for the common good. As the federal government and states take on increased accountability for schools through the No Child Left Behind Act and Common Core Standards, responsible citizens must do more than vote: They must act by participating in decisions that affect their local schools.

If politics means the acquisition of power in order to bring about needed changes, then everyone needs to become educated on the issues they are interested in and exercise their citizen power by becoming authentically engaged in decisions that affect them. This responsibility belongs to more than just the elected officials and those in the dominant culture. Structures must be created so people of diverse populations and perceptions can participate. Citizens must know or learn how to think aloud, deliberate deeply, and manage conflict while considering all perspectives. With those skills, citizens can solve problems and improve life not only in schools but also in other areas of society. Becoming confident in working with people in a political sense is key to successfully bringing people together and moving agendas forward in the best interest of all.

Bridging differences to solve school and community problems for which there are as yet no answers is at the heart of the associative model of democracy. Being successful at such problem solving involves tackling other aspects of politics, as well—the politics of power and influence, diversity, and multiple points of view—and learning to shape the world in which people live to meet the needs of all. It means intentionally seeking to include diverse thinking and voices in dialogue and decision-making that promote and sustain viable change and academic achievement.

In the arena of authentic engagement, learning to "be political" does not have to mean taking a negative or aggressive stance. It can mean learning to bring people together. The strategies in this book are based on the need to maintain civil discourse to solve problems, create innovative pathways to achieve student success, and generate support for both the community and its schools. Building engagement skills in educators, parents, and community members alike will deepen understanding, enhance social capital, increase interaction, and sustain change. Learning the politics of engagement means accumulating the knowledge, skills, strategies, and processes to suspend personal judgment; listen and hear deeply; identify issues and concerns clearly; hold space for deliberative dialogue firmly; promote unanimity and create new options skillfully; and capitalize explicitly on the strengths and knowledge of everyone engaged.

Becoming political, with a positive and results-oriented focus, is a theme woven throughout the strategies in *The Politics of Authentic Engagement*. It promotes equity and opens opportunity. Being wise about and comfortable with political aspects of a leadership role will enhance understanding of the social landscape and help families and stakeholders deliberate through turbulent waters with circumspection and skill. Sensitivity to diversity of opinion and culture will rise along with skill in ensuring all voices are represented in the dialogue—all to the end of making decisions, solving challenging problems, and working together to design and implement strategies and programs that will support student success and meet the needs of constituents more effectively.

Engagement as an Avenue to Increased Achievement

By the late 1990s, the single issue both educators and community members were most concerned about was the level of student achievement on state and national assessments. Not only were overall test results disappointing, but disaggregated data revealed significant gaps in achievement between white and non-white populations.

A research review from the same period showed, for the first time, that meaningful family engagement has a positive impact on student achievement. Students get higher grades and test scores, attend school more regularly, demonstrate better social skills and behavior, and go on to higher education more frequently.[2] Newer data confirm these findings and suggest further that data hold true across all economic, racial/ethnic, and educational backgrounds.[3]

It is *meaningful family engagement* that makes the difference, however. Traditional involvement practices such as asking parents to help with preparation of classroom materials or to volunteer as a chaperone for field trips or dances are not enough. Particular kinds of family engagement with schools—those linked with learning tasks and development of specific student skills and knowledge—are the ones that result in improved academic achievement. In addition, improved relationships with families and communities create a great deal of buy-in from both groups for teachers and administrators when they need to change instructional methods to meet student needs more effectively.

Along with engaged families and communities, successful schools have high standards for all students, aligned instruction and assessments, effective leadership, quality instructional supervision, and focused professional development for staff. Engagement efforts cannot be limited solely to improving communication and dialogue with families and the community. Rather, engagement components must exist in all of a school's and district's instructional planning and overall improvement efforts. This book talks about how to embed engagement throughout school improvement initiatives, as well as assist families and communities in being more participatory in their young people's academic growth.

THE POLITICS OF AUTHENTIC ENGAGEMENT
AS A TOOL KIT FOR ENGAGING ALL STAKEHOLDERS

Using Engagement Concepts and Practices

Engaging people personally and deeply in the thinking, planning, and decision-making that affect them most closely will generate new approaches and solutions to what otherwise could be insurmountable issues. It is about listening in new ways and bringing others to the decision-making table. It is about helping families and entire communities, especially those traditionally disenfranchised, talk together using democratic processes so everyone can participate effectively. It is about ensuring underserved young people not only have equal access to quality educational opportunity, but equal opportunity to succeed in school and life—intellectually, emotionally, socially, and economically.

Educators are not the only ones capable of spearheading the efforts to bring people together to think and grapple with issues. The more people who are not directly employed by schools share this responsibility, the more they will learn. Engagement helps stakeholders find their voices, become good listeners, and think critically and deeply in order to become strong advocates for the best teaching and learning available.[4] Public relations practitioners, principals and superintendents, trained community members and parents, as well as other organizations that do community organizing can facilitate the training and structures to help all educational and community leaders promote a culture of engagement.

The two books of *The Politics of Authentic Engagement* provide practical approaches for leaders in a variety of roles to address the changing landscape of schooling, build dynamic relationships in support of schools, help parents/families support their children's achievement, and create a culture of engagement. Strategies described in the chapters of this book teach how to serve as a listener, teacher, leader, facilitator, and initiator in engaging others within professional settings to do real work. The strategies involve these skills:

- Listening: how to hold space for divergent views; how to manage conflict; how to build bridges and agreement; and how to hear and honor the stories of others
- Teaching educators: how to create excitement and build skills in teachers and other educators so they can successfully draw families and citizens in; how to listen to their perspectives and how to partner with them to boost student achievement
- Teaching families: how to help them understand their children and the educational environment; how to speak up to share their needs and concerns; and how to help their children at home with academic efforts
- Teaching ordinary citizens in the larger community: how to become leaders and advocates for children; and how to provide opportunities to dialogue, reach shared understandings, and solve problems together
- Leading: how to take initiative to work with the city, chamber of commerce, or county on projects such as organizing joint efforts to discuss education, solve problems, and meet needs affecting the wider community
- Facilitating: how to discover what families and other community members believe and value by providing opportunities for all voices in the school community to be heard; how to facilitate dialogue; and how to manage conflict
- Initiating: how to launch engagement efforts; how to help others become facilitative leaders; and how to incorporate diverse values, beliefs, and convictions within the culture of the school and district

The companion workbook, *The Politics of Authentic Engagement: Tools for Engaging Stakeholders in Ensuring Student Success*, supports leaders in helping others learn to engage by providing handouts, overheads, instructions, and other prompts to use in workshop settings.

Chapter Overviews of *The Politics of Authentic Engagement*

Chapter 1, "Discovering the Power of Authentic Engagement," provides a landscape view of the field of engagement. It emphasizes the importance of individual as well as collective responsibility for educational improvement. In sorting out what engagement is and is not, the chapter defines frequently used terms and describes the emergence of engagement from early practices of public relations. Strategies for thinking and working successfully across systems within a school and community are presented, and the significance of basing action plans on explicit assumptions and theory is discussed. The chapter includes a tool outlining the range of ways and the settings in which to engage others around schools and their communities.

Chapter 2, "Creating a Culture of Authentic Engagement," gets even more practical, describing in detail what authentic engagement in schools and communities looks like and how to take initial steps in creating a culture of engagement. Leslie articulates principles of authentic engagement that form the foundation for drawing people in to think together and collaborate toward sustainable solutions to complex issues. The chapter provides in-depth strategies for moving groups toward creative results and meaningful action, including building trust, using storytelling, balancing inquiry and advocacy, fostering deep dialogue, and using structures to hold process on a steady course.

Chapter 3, "Collecting and Using Stakeholder Research," outlines strategies for gathering and analyzing data from and about families, students, staff, and the local community in order to plan and make decisions, knowing what stakeholders need and desire. Techniques are explained for organizing and facilitating focus groups and for using the data gathered.

Chapter 4, "Engaging Families/Stakeholders and Schools," highlights how schools effectively engage families in their children's education. It contrasts traditional parent involvement with family engagement that more effectively supports academic achievement, including research-based strategies and models of engagement. A significant portion of the chapter presents strategies specifically designed to engage underserved populations—families of diverse cultures or those living in poverty, parents of special-needs children, and people who are angry or afraid. The chapter concludes by describing what families need and want to know about contemporary education and how they can best help their children succeed.

Chapter 5, "Facilitating Artfully," contains core strategies for working with groups in ways representing much more than routine levels of involvement. The chapter's goal is to enable group facilitators—both professional and emerging grassroots voices—to establish productive environments for families and community members to be included in planning and decision-making characterized by meaningful conversations and genuine listening. A key section of the chapter helps facilitators use various group structures such as public forums to generate meaningful dialogue around issues important to stakeholders, resulting in sustainable decisions that improve student learning. Discussing conflict management in depth, it provides models to help groups address and resolve complex issues with no easy answers.

Chapter 6, "Planning Strategically," describes twelve stages of strategic planning and how to engage stakeholders in the various processes. It helps readers lead change efforts through strategic district-wide or school planning efforts and provides a decision-making model, a stakeholder communication and engagement plan, and a process of visioning to create a new school.

Chapter 7, "Reflecting on the Journey: Inspiring Change," invites the reader to think more deeply about engagement, democracy, and leadership by reading perspectives from seven thoughtful, highly respected leaders experienced in developing cultures of authentic engagement. A parent, school board member, futurist, two public relations practitioners, a school administrator, and a business leader talk about the challenges they face and their hopes for a civil and open democracy where everyone is valued and heard.

How to Use This Book

This book is designed for leaders—public relations practitioners, superintendents, other district administrators, post-secondary instructors, teaching administrative candidates, school board members, principals, state education system officials, professional groups supporting educators (such as the National School Public Relations Association or the American Association of School Administrators), teachers, and parents. It is for people within schools as well as communities who are interested in schooling and in helping others understand and participate in deliberative decision-making on behalf of their children.

As a tool kit for those leaders, the book contains the following elements in each chapter:

TAKEAWAY MESSAGES FOR THIS CHAPTER

Important summarizing thoughts to take away appear at the end of each chapter for easy reference and review. For example, the messages from the Introduction are these:

- The politics of authentic engagement involves building trust and relationships to bring people together for the good of all.
- The approaches of authentic engagement include deeply embedded concepts and practices of a democracy.
- The practices of authentic engagement create a more effective educational and civic environment for families, students, educators, and the community.
- Engaging families directly in student learning makes a difference in the academic achievement of students.
- This book, along with its companion workbook, *The Politics of Authentic Engagement: Tools for Engaging Stakeholders in Ensuring Student Success,* containing workshop-ready materials appropriate for use in training others to engage, form a tool kit designed to help leaders in many roles understand and use strategies of authentic engagement.

Tools and How-To Elements

A variety of tools illustrating and condensing information appear in the companion workbook, *The Politics of Authentic Engagement: Tools for Engaging Stakeholders in Ensuring Student Success.* For easy coordination between the books, numbers, and titles of tools available in the workbook are referenced within the text of this book.

Helpful Resources Related to the Chapter

Broader resources helpful to engagement facilitators and instructors are described in a reference list at the end of each chapter. For example, resources relevant to this chapter are:

- Kathleen Knight Abowitz, *Publics for Public Schools: Legitimacy, Democracy, and Leadership,* is a scholarly analysis of how public schools can foster participative democracy by creating diverse publics who deliberate together, generating new thinking about and solutions for complex, perplexing educational issues.

- Anne Henderson and Nancy Berla, *A New Generation of Evidence: The Family Is Critical to Student Achievement*, is a 1994 review of research studies including not only a summary of the findings but actual descriptions of the studies from a variety of school sites. Schools and districts may find useful information within each of the site studies. Published by the Center for Law and Education, Washington, D.C., the review is available online at http://www.eric.ed.gov/PDFS/ED375968.pdf (last accessed May 28, 2011).
- Anne Henderson and Karen Mapp, *A New Wave of Evidence: The Impact of School, Family and Community Connections on Student Achievement*, is a 2002 review of fifty-one additional research studies presented in a format similar to *A New Generation of Evidence*. This review is available online from SEDL (Southwest Educational Development Laboratory) at http://www.sedl.org/pubs/catalog/items/fam33.html (last accessed May 28, 2011).

Complete bibliographical information for these resources is located in the reference list at the back of this book.

Notes

For easy reference, citations referencing the materials and extended thoughts of others who are quoted or have influenced Leslie's thinking and engagement work appear at the end of each chapter. Complete source data appear in the reference list at the end of the book.

NOTES

1. Based on Kathleen Knight Abowitz and Steven R. Thompson's *Publics for Public Schools*, 51–53.

2. Based on findings in Henderson and Berla, *A New Generation of Evidence*.

3. Henderson and Mapp, *A New Wave of Evidence*, 24–25, 37–38. Subsequent studies looked at the specific relationship of family engagement to student academic achievement, confirming a definite link between family and community engagement and higher student academic achievement. The newer data also that reveal students with engaged families are more likely to enroll in higher-level programs; earn more high school credits; graduate from high school and go on to higher education; adapt well to school; and demonstrate improved behavior and social skills at both school and home.

4. Leslie, "I Used to Believe." Used with permission of the National School Public Relations Association (www.NSPRA.org).

ONE

Discovering the Power of Authentic Engagement

Schools stand at a fork in the road. School/community relationships are often not what they could be, or worse, are destructive to student progress. Moving forward successfully means school and community leaders must choose the pathway that helps schools and districts learn to deal better with the pressures and challenges confronting them. Those who incorporate more effective ways of listening and relating to their stakeholders, which includes anyone who has an interest in education, will survive and thrive. Those who choose the status quo path of power, control, and disconnection will not. The strategies of authentic engagement raise not only the probability of surviving but also of making significant differences in the lives and achievement of students, helping to assure their future success as productive citizens.

The *politics* of authentic engagement involves building trust and relationships to bring people together for the common good. The *power* of authentic engagement moves people to talk and work together in ways that generate creative and sustainable solutions to issues and problems. The potential to generate such power lies in educators, families, and community members who are willing to learn how to hold space in their thinking for differing opinions, to listen without judging, to ask more questions to understand, and to speak from an awareness of multiple perspectives.

THE POWER OF AUTHENTIC ENGAGEMENT: A STORY OF SUCCESS

The board of a suburban San Francisco–area school district approved a multi-age education program (MAP), which included constructivist instruction, regular parental engagement, and expert teaching. One of the elementary schools incorporated the instructional approach into its overall program, running parallel with traditional single-grade classrooms. In the early months of MAP, excitement was high. However, it was not long before teachers and families of students in the traditional classrooms began to feel the MAP staff and students were receiving more than their fair share of resources and other support. They were frustrated and angry. The superintendent listened to their concerns and asked me to facilitate a process that would surface and address the deeper issues and discover a way both programs could coexist in peace serving children's unique needs successfully.

The participants—multi-age as well as single-age program families and staff—identified their hopes for the school, students, and staff. Themes representing common ground were evident in the range of hopes stated in their complete brainstorming list:

- *Our work will focus on what is best for children, and their needs will come first.*
- *Our school community will be a safe environment, practicing mutual respect and accepting differences.*
- *Our school will become "one great school" with blending and bridging of the entire community, including children, staff, and parents.*
- *Information will be transparent, and effective communication practices will become common practice.*
- *There will be internal support and advocacy for both programs.*
- *We will have the freedom to be unique.*
- *Parents/families will be happy with our recommendations and solutions.*
- *We will be open to change.*
- *We will effectively come to consensus about how two programs can coexist on one campus.*

A representative group of the school community and staff discussed both the short- and long-term implications for the traditional and MAP programs. They came away from their meeting with a better understanding of one another's concerns and clarified the short- and long-term issues. They also committed to improving communication, beginning with a joint letter from both programs pledging to gather input from the community in a future meeting.

With their common hopes in mind, subcommittees comprised of teachers, families, parent leaders, and administrators from both programs were formed to address the equity issues. The committees included Creating Equity, Parent Volunteers, Working and Playing Together, and Equity of Programs. Each group did research in their area of concern, developed proposals to address issues, and submitted them to the entire group for feedback.

All proposals were thoughtfully considered. Participants analyzed trade-offs and envisioned future scenarios given alternative decisions. The full group shaped final proposals and adopted them. Equity issues were resolved, and both programs—traditional and multi-age—now thrive within a single plan for student achievement.

"Our Best Hopes and Worst Fears" in chapter 5 of the companion workbook provides the protocol for surfacing hopes.

THE PATHWAY TO POWERFUL
SCHOOL/COMMUNITY RELATIONSHIPS

Changes in the School/Community Relationship

In the earliest days of the American colonies, school pioneers were the ultimate authority figures and communicators. They defined the parameters and rules and who was eligible to enter their doors, in most cases only discrete segments of the larger population. Citizens could choose to accept those boundaries or look elsewhere. Listening to constituents was of little or no importance to school leaders.

In nineteenth- and early twentieth-century schools, the teacher became the link to families and the community. People often used the school building as a gathering place. Connections were direct; conversations were immediate when student concerns surfaced. However, as land use changed from agricultural to urban and the economy from industrial to informational, the nature of parental and community involvement in schools shifted. Compulsory school laws proliferated, student enrollment mushroomed, and coordinating education within local areas grew more complex. The role of principal emerged to help run schools so teachers could focus on instruction, but school leaders often took on managerial duties with little leadership or communications training. Schools joined to form districts and districts merged to form county school systems, adding even more layers of administration that pushed families and the community further away from what was happening in schools. As the education system grew in complexity and in the number of students and employees, interpersonal communications became more difficult because not everyone possessed all of the information and because not everyone assumed responsibility for communications. Both educators and parents lost their earlier close connection.

School management practices often relegated the public to being an outsider where stakeholders did not feel included in discussions about how to best educate their children. Larger class sizes made it difficult for teachers to know the values and beliefs of families. Public concerns about declining test scores and the overall quality of education increased. When faced with trying to understand the many educational changes of recent decades, non-educators struggled to keep up, letting historically strong support for local schools diminish.

Ordinary citizens and families were blocked out of the system when an authoritative "we-know-best" leadership approach solidified in the late twentieth century. While many knew the voices of constituents were important, most educators continued to believe their professional training and experience fully prepared them for making decisions about the content and process of educating young people. Although they welcomed help from the community or families for funding special projects or contributing time, energy, and unique expertise to classroom or school projects, most teachers and administrators did not feel parents/families or other community members should tell them how to teach students or run schools.

More than not liking it, many educators became defensive when community or family members made suggestions for improvements or change. They failed to see that the strength of schools came from sharing responsibility and decision-making about the school and its students. Legislation of the 1980s and beyond that began to require schools and districts to involve citizens in planning and making decisions based on research was difficult for educators to embrace. It required changes in educators' belief systems and improvement in their skill sets for communicating with constituencies, engaging their participation, resolving conflict, managing change, and effecting measureable improvements in student achievement. The net effect has been too many communities, citizens, even parents and other family members, particularly those not in the dominant race, feeling alienated and unwelcome in public schools, the very entities founded to help people gain the knowledge and skills to participate effectively in a democratic society.

Shifts in Public Relations toward Engaging Constituents with Schools

From Publicity to Engagement

The twenty-first century offers new opportunities for educators, including school public relations practitioners, to improve the relationship between educational organizations and constituents. In the last century, districts looked for ways to tell good news about schools in an effort to market them, win budget elections, or get favorable media coverage. Increasingly, districts across the country recognized the need for someone in a specific role to help them communicate their work and gain the financial, political, and instructional support they needed. This resulted in the establishment of the National School Public Relations Association (NSPRA) in 1935, one of the first public relations organizations of any kind in the country. Over the past seventy-five years, the approaches public relations practitioners have used to communicate information about schools and generate support for their existence have changed as new needs emerged and their roles evolved. The work of these professionals broadened from telling, selling, and advertising to include listening and engaging.

Many early practitioners in the new public relations field worked within one of the earliest three of four models of public relations practice identified by James Grunig and Todd Hunt, in their theory of excellence, which also reflects the evolution of public relations over a 130-year period.[1] Next to the models of public relations identified by Grunig and Hunt are parallel terms used in this book. These descriptors, more commonly used today, identify contemporary models of public relations practice.

Until about 1950, most practitioners operated from the Press Agentry or Public Information one-way communication models. Although other approaches now exist, practitioners still use these models extensively today. Press Agentry and Public Information represent *craft* public relations that focus on the skills or craft of creating and sending clear one-way messages outward to the public.

Models of Public Relations*	Terms Used in this Book	Type of communication	Characteristics of Communication
Press Agentry/ Publicity model	Media Relations	One-way communication	Relies on publicity through media channels to win support for the organization or client.
Public Information model	Public Information	One-way communication	Uses one-way communication channels to distribute organizational information.
Two-Way Asymmetrical model	Persuasion	Two-way communication	Uses persuasion to influence stakeholders to behave as the organization desires. Uses research to determine where people are and then persuades them to change their minds.
Two-Way Symmetrical model	Engagement	Two-way communication & engagement	Relies on engagement and communication strategies to negotiate conflict, generate new ideas and solutions, and reach mutual understanding and respect between the organization and its stakeholders

* The names of the models of public relations are those of Grunig and Hunt, *Managing Public Relations*; the descriptors are those used by Leslie in her work with schools and communities.

The Press Agentry model has its roots in the nineteenth century. Press agents worked to influence the public by *creating* news. They strategized and focused their efforts on winning publicity for their client. This book renames that model Media Relations to reflect modern times. A school district working in a media relations model does not lie or make up stories as press agents once did, but it does concentrate the majority of its resources, including time and money, on gaining publicity through media channels. Practitioners count and compare positive and negative news stories, consider satisfaction surveys, and tally the number of events publicized and people attending. These data are used as primary sources to measure success.

The Public Information model focuses on developing messages that explain complicated facts to laypeople. Such public information efforts provide outsiders with accurate and positive organizational information but often omit unfavorable details. Further, it is a one-way delivery of the message—the facts as the organization sees them and as they want the public to perceive the organization. One-way communication is evident today in newsletters, podcasts, YouTube, Twitter, and speeches. A district trying to explain how a school program such as year-round school works through a pamphlet or e-newsletter uses this model.

The post-World War II Two-Way Asymmetrical model, which this book refers to as the Persuasion model, is similar to Edward L. Bernay's work. He introduced the use of propaganda, persuasion, and the engineering-of-consent model, all designed to motivate the public to think in a particular way and to persuade constituents to behave as the organization wanted them to.

This approach represents the first *two-way* communication model, but it still is not symmetrical or balanced in its methodology. The information sent from the organization outweighs the input coming in. Research by practitioners of this model is conducted to determine where the gaps exist between what people are thinking and what the organization wants people to think. Strategies are subsequently identified to persuade constituents to accept and support the organization's decisions. This approach also advocates telling constituents only what they might accept, hoping to readjust the thinking of the public to go with the status quo. Careful design of survey questions to bring responses of support and the subsequent use of those somewhat manipulated answers to persuade a district's constituents to make changes aligned with the superintendent's position reflects Bernays's approach.

The widespread use of the Persuasion model by businesses of all sorts has led to an enormous legacy of mistrust and lack of confidence in institutions. Advertisers rely on this model to sell their products. But school stakeholders usually do not want to be told and they do not want to be sold. Sometimes it is necessary to persuade people to move in a certain direction or accept a decision without extensive public involvement. However, when a culture of engagement has been created in which people know they can influence the direction of the organization meaningfully, the loss of trust coming from persuasion strategies is much less or nonexistent.

In contrast, the Two-Way Symmetrical model, which this book calls the Engagement model, seeks to understand both the organization's and stakeholders' points of view through practices that go beyond the craft to the *art* of working with people. The organization accomplishes such blending of perspectives by engaging participants rather than trying to persuade them. Communication flows in two directions. Engagement encourages acceptance of the thoughts and ideas of each voice as having merit. As a result, both the organization and the stakeholders become willing to change for the good of the organization and themselves. Examples of the Engagement model's more symmetrical and balanced approaches appear throughout the balance of the book.

Embracing Authentic Engagement

The engagement research conducted by James and Larissa Grunig stands today as the most important public relations research in the field regarding what brings results for the organization and what does not. The Grunigs claim that the Two-Way Symmetrical Engagement approach is the most effective way to build long-term relationships. For educators, it means proactively working to develop mutual understandings between schools or districts and their stakeholders that can change the attitudes and behaviors of educators as much as it prompts shifts in the views of stakeholders. Research done by practitioners is designed to learn how much the two groups understand each other so facilitators can plan next steps to find common ground.[2]

In an authentic engagement culture, public relations practitioners, educators, and other leaders have moved from seeing themselves as experts to viewing themselves as partners with stakeholders who also hold important insights and information. In the "expert" mode of communication dissemination, communicators assume all stakeholders are the same so they send one common message tailored to the organization's needs, having decided what stakeholders need to know. They communicate on their own time schedules and promote their own solutions based on what they believe is best for the organization. Messages are sent via impersonal forms (i.e., websites, e-newsletters, letters, or brochures) using impersonal formal language.

On the other hand, those communicating from a stakeholder orientation assume every stakeholder is unique with special needs and desires. They believe their constituents have valuable information and insights, and want to hear what they need to know. Sent on the stakeholders' need-to-know timelines, the messages have a "we" orientation and are sent using informal and personal forms, such as speaking face-to-face or using the social media popular with their stakeholders.

"1.1 Expert versus Stakeholder Orientation" in the companion workbook provides a useful handout that contrasts more traditional public relations and communication approaches with those consistent with engagement strategies. The tool contrasts a list of terms typical of the "expert" orientation when the organization is in a telling mode with behaviors representing the "stakeholder" orientation of authentic engagement that incorporates stakeholder voices and needs.

The case of one county school district, a system serving just over two hundred students across five small towns, illustrates the differences in perspective.

* * *

Making difficult economic adjustments, the district had closed schools in several small towns over the years. After receiving funding from local alternative energy project rebates, the school board decided to move the remaining elementary school onto the high school campus. The board announced its intention by putting a funding measure on the county ballot that would consolidate the elementary, middle, and high schools onto the high school campus. It was an impersonally delivered, source-oriented message—a message that generated intense anger. The school was the heart of the community in each of the towns, so the rhetoric surrounding the ballot proposal to take a school from one small town into another town was ugly. Voters defeated the measure soundly. Yet board members continued to contend they had "listened to everyone, let them come to our board meetings, and let them talk."

Board members explicitly said, "That's done. We do not want to go back and deal with that decision anymore." However, the board realized they did need to know what the community was currently thinking about their schools so they could plan the next steps. With board approval, the district asked me to facilitate a strategic planning committee and conduct an audit of the district's systems to accomplish the following goals:

- *identify strengths, challenges, and specific concerns*
- *identify educational priorities*
- *discuss options for spending alternative energy rebate dollars*
- *gather ideas for what students should know and be able to do when they graduate from high school*

- *develop a strategic plan*

In focus group meetings designed to gather information for the audit, it was obvious that the community would not let board members forget the election issue. It came up repeatedly in responses to audit questions. Nonetheless, when I reported the audit results, some board members were furious that school closures and consolidation were still issues.

To help the strategic planning committee (which included board members) move forward, I asked the board members to meet with constituents in small groups to put themselves in the stakeholder's shoes. Again, their frustration boiled over. They said, "We hired you to do our strategic plan, and now you are having us do it." Reluctantly, the board went into the community and listened. The district organized five small groups of stakeholders to meet with board members. When board members reported what they heard, their thinking had shifted. They said, "We can't believe how well this went. The people are appreciative and happy with us because we are listening to them." One board member protested, "But I told them what the bond was all about." The larger group of planning team members reminded him, "You can't just tell people what they're going to do." Even board members who were the most angry at the process in the beginning presented upbeat reports of community members who appreciated that the board was now listening to them.

One planning team member added, "The people who were so angry when they closed the first school changed their stance because they heard the school's teachers, who had been moved to other schools, say the educational programs at the merged sites were so much better." The teachers had reported they were able to teach better because classes were large enough to allow team teaching, students could participate in more interactive learning opportunities, and special education kids were better served. Once constituents heard the opinions of the teachers, they agreed the change was acceptable. But it was not until the school board had embraced a process of dialogue that attitudes shifted.

The planning team then formed three exploratory engagement teams: one team examined finance, another constituent engagement, and a third, curriculum. The engagement teams included strategic planning committee members and other citizens with specific knowledge or expertise, such as mayors from some of the towns and a representative from the county board of commissioners.

Getting all constituent voices in the room, hearing their opinions, and listening to their fears is powerful. It moves thinking forward. The process was unconventional for board members, but they learned that if they listen to people say what is on their minds, they can solve problems together. "2.8 Analysis of Intent: So Do You Mean?" in chapter 2 of the companion workbook provides an effective activity to help group members listen to one another.

Engagement involves more than simply delivering a message. As a bridging process, it includes listening, researching the dilemmas, and working to find agreement between the organization and stakeholders. It represents a way to increase collaboration, identify issues, solve problems, and develop strategies to improve schools. It nourishes a sense of ownership and responsibility in stakeholders who realize they have a say in the process. It builds trust in an organization, allowing ideas to emerge that are in the best interest of both the organization and its constituents. It promotes sustainability and can be an antidote to skepticism.

THE LANDSCAPE OF AUTHENTIC ENGAGEMENT

From Anger and Apathy to Responsibility

The educational terrain is familiar territory for most families and community members because almost all were former students. Many believe they know schooling well. However, understanding the big picture of today's educational establishment — the complexities of all the trade-offs, the challenges and intricacies of meeting the needs of all students, the difficulties inherent in balancing budgets to support systems — is difficult for non-educators.

Feeling heard by a principal, a superintendent, or a school board is often very challenging. Parents/families, in particular, find that navigating their way through school protocols and closed doors is an intimidating ordeal. Feeling shut out results in anger, apathy, or both. Wrath breaks out in tirades at school board meetings, threats to teachers and principals, and scathing indictments of the educational system as a whole. Alternatively, anger turns to apathy as those who feel powerless withdraw from even trying to affect a system in which they feel no sense of belonging.

People today are less trusting of organizations and resent being told to "just trust us." Although they know something is not working for them, they do want to understand how to improve conditions. They are quick to attack responses they believe represent stupidity, inconsistency, stonewalling, or incompetence. Many people have little respect for anyone in a position of authority, especially executives, administrators, and managers who they believe doesn't think citizens are smart enough to learn complex aspects of their organization or practices. Just understanding the maze of new educational approaches—instructional strategies, state and district standards, program funding—is daunting. But it *is* possible for constituents to grasp very difficult concepts fully if they are explained in plain language with pertinent examples.

*   *   *

For instance, engagement work in housing cooperatives in Newark, San Francisco, and Atlanta brought people together from culturally diverse environments. Families (parents, relatives, or surrogate parents) with little or no formal education and financially challenged with few resources of any kind were trying to raise children. The leadership of the housing association worked with me to get families living in the cooperatives—people who never had connected with their schools—to come to the gatherings we were organizing to help engage them with their children's education.

Our preliminary research, in conjunction with each school district, mapped out how children from the cooperatives were doing and showed families the achievement gaps that appeared in the data. Using several high-interest activities such as a learning-analysis game using cookies, families learned how their children's achievement was progressing, how adults at home could work with children to help them improve, and how the educational system operated. We talked about their expectations for their children and how the state academic standards helped their kids meet those expectations. Together we discovered ways to increase achievement by sharing examples of how that could be done. Families learned how to talk to and partner with school staff and how to help their children with learning activities at home such as cooking with their children using math and reading skills.

In spite of their inexperience with schooling, family members understood the ideas perfectly. They began to say things like, "I'm going to go to school and see how my child is doing." When these caring families knew what they were looking for in the data, they began to own the responsibility for helping their children succeed and were empowered to act on their own to get any answers and help they needed.

Not engaging families and communities fully in issues around children is costly in time and money to districts and schools, families and communities alike. Alienation of families, community, and business leaders has led to a loss of support and advocacy and, in some cases, funding for schools.

Although schools increasingly recognize they need parental and community support to institute new practices, many educators lack skills in diffusing anger, managing conflict, and marshaling the kind of staff and/or community dialogue that can generate new possibilities. Even the process of building trust and collaborative relationships seems challenging in the pressure-cooker atmosphere of the school day and year. With limited time, it comes down to how principals and other educators set their priorities and whether they will learn new skills that bring people together to solve complex problems.

In some communities, vibrant community/school and school/family relationships thrive. There are progressive practitioners embracing authentic engagement with great skill and success. However, fundamentally, little change has occurred over the past thirty-five years in the way most educators think about the roles of school, family, and community in the educational process, be that in public or private schools.

Educational change calls for stakeholder support, but people outside the educational establishment will take responsibility for helping such change happen only if they feel they have a say in the process. To that end, engagement initiatives need to promote inclusiveness, honor each voice, preserve what is working, focus on needed change, build consensus, and develop broad support leading to action. For change to stick, it must be rooted in an empowered community willing to collaborate and take responsibility, individually and collectively, for helping their vision materialize. The practices of engagement provide the structures and substance through which schools build social capacity within communities and families where all groups feel responsible for creating and sustaining strong schools.

> "When one has no stake in the way things are, when one's needs or opinions are provided no forum, when one sees oneself as the object of unilateral actions, it takes no particular wisdom to suggest that one would rather be elsewhere."
> —Seymour B. Sarason[3]

The enemy to battle most often in this frustrating drama of angry and disconnected constituents is not the lack of discipline, a dearth of role models, the questioning of standards, or even cuts in funding. It is the loss of stakeholder support as well as apathetic citizens. Schools must connect with their stakeholders or they will not survive.

It is up to educational and community leaders to initiate reconnections. Everyone now has to think, believe, and practice community—strong communities and families are the keys to strengthening education. Engagement strategies can provide structures needed to promote civility, shared responsibility, and an increased confidence that civil dialogue is possible in our society. Stakeholders engaged in such dialogue are more apt to recognize and accept individual and collective responsibility for moving agendas forward.[4] They adopt new ways of relating to one another, increase their ability to hear with hearts as well as ears and minds, and learn new approaches for facing and working through tough issues effectively.

The Nature of Genuine Community

The destiny of schools depends on the strength of the surrounding community structure. Strong community is evident when people feel they belong, participate in common practices, depend upon one another, and make decisions together. They identify themselves as part of something larger than the sum of their individual relationships. They commit themselves for the long term to their own, one another's, and the group's well-being.[5]

Intentionally building community is critical to improving schools. But most communities have internal differences in values and beliefs that make it difficult to coalesce around a common vision. Further, there is often a disconnect between schools and their communities at large. Even though the word *community* appears frequently in contexts such as the medical community, the school community, or the neighborhood community, members of those groups seldom know each other, let alone talk and solve problems together. Nor is community always synonymous with warmth and harmony. A community cannot speak with one voice until it thinks together, grapples with issues, and struggles with differences in values and ideas. A community must look without judgment at the perceptions of all and the ramifications of diverse approaches before it knows what it thinks or wants as a whole. True community is rare.[6]

What does it take to engage communities with educators and build a sense of common mission? What strategies do we use to nurture strong learning communities that will ensure all children are successful? What does that kind of thinking mean for educators? How does it change our practice?

Thomas Sergiovanni, professor of education at Trinity University in San Antonio, Texas, says groups must invent their own practice of community. He calls it finding a kinship of place and mind. It is a bonding together of people coming from shared understanding and commitment to a common goal. Sergiovanni explains that communities are organized around relationships and ideas. They are defined by their values, sentiments, and beliefs that provide the needed conditions for creating a sense of "we" from "I."[7]

In short, educators and others who redefine their role and lead as guides, facilitators, and builders of community are more successful when they are in touch with the values and beliefs of their stakeholders. They take on a "we" identity and help people speak up—give people voice and enable them to say what they are thinking, feeling, and believing. They empower others to contribute to the creation of a genuinely responsible community—divorced from special interests—focused on ensuring each child succeeds.

> We are changing behavior by making people step up and be responsible for education, for their local, social environment and their communities. The behavior we are after is to have everybody be a responsible, active partner in the life of community and the life of schools.
> —Karen Kleinz, associate director, National School Public Relations Association[8]

What Engagement Is and Is Not

The work of engagement involves patience, openness, honesty, understanding, and flexibility. It requires knowing that there is more than one right answer and exploring as many different viewpoints as possible. It necessitates mentally and emotionally holding space open for the views and concerns of others. It means creating opportunities for people to think about what they want, know, or believe. Authentic engagement is characterized by inclusive in-depth dialogue based on candor and trust.[9] While teaching people how to dialogue with respect, leaders have to also be open to divergent points of view, strong advocacy, and criticism. The process can be noisy, chaotic, and riddled with conflict. Handling it well requires managing oneself while thinking about others. Fostering clear thinking so people speak with awareness, sound reasoning, and measured emotion takes time and patience.

Engagement also requires significant shifts in thinking: from knower and judger to learner; from defensiveness to vulnerability; from arrogance to humility; and from critical observer to responsible participant.[10] It implies not weakness but a strength of mind and character that allows an individual to hold personal thoughts and beliefs in abeyance while hearing and learning from others. In a culture of engagement, participants learn to be more vulnerable and open to new, perhaps contradictory but useful information. It calls for a readiness to be influenced. Engagement practices promote progress in finding common ground by encouraging humility rather than arrogance in approaching a difficult conversation among fellow citizens. A core tenet is that an individual's active participation in dialogue around issues will better meet the community's needs in the end than his or her silence on the sidelines as a critical observer.

Principles of engagement include the concept that the organization needs to be as concerned for everyone as it is for itself—the symmetrical element. It needs to promote social responsibility, ethical practice, and diversity instead of focusing only on its own sustainability. There is no one clear formula for how to engage people because the process used depends on the needs of unique stakeholders. In each environment, the engager creates structures and opportunities within which people involved (the contributors) can influence the organization and, at the same time, realize and accept their own responsibility in the issues.[11]

The practices listed below distinguish authentic engagement from other forms of organizational connections with constituents. "1.2 The Practices of Authentic Engagement" in the companion workbook provides a useful annotated list of those practices for use as a handout.

- Using two-way communication
- Establishing equitable partnerships
- Providing opportunities for face-to-face interaction
- Using dialogue instead of debate or discussion
- Focusing on appreciative inquiry
- Designing opportunities for online dialogue

- Investing time to think deeply, reflect, and explore ideas, hopes, divergent perspectives, and options for improvement
- Trusting the power of process

Two-Way Communication

What happened in one small town's process is a prime example of the change that is possible when engagement practices are used. In this case, two-way communication was key.

* * *

The school district had tried three times to pass a bond to build a new school, each time publicizing what it wished to do through the media, principals' newsletters, and other one-way communication avenues. Each successive vote on the ballot measure failed miserably. Eventually, the superintendent asked me to help a committee strategize how to get a middle-school proposal approved by the voters.

After learning some strategies of engagement, planning committee members decided to host a community forum to hear what issues contributed to the bond's rejection. Committee members decided who would attend, how to invite participants, what materials participants would receive, and which processes to use at the meeting. Five hundred people, a sizeable group for a small town, gathered to consider several options the planning committee had identified for the location of a new middle school. Educators, students, and community members worked in small groups for an entire day weighing the options, sharing their opinions and ideas, and deciding which alternative to recommend to the board.

The top two preferences emerging were not at all what the district wanted, which explained part of the repeated failure of the district's ballot measures. People simply did not like the district's proposed location of the school. The community was not consulted in the development of the initial measure so, faced with an unworkable plan, they voted it down. The committee ultimately chose to move both final alternatives forward along with their rationale for each. When the board selected one of the suggested options and offered it to the voters, the measure passed with a large majority.

Had stakeholders of the rural school district not deliberated together in a community conversation, it is unlikely they could have articulated the common ground they found as they shared perspectives and ideas across small-group tables in the forum. Using a bottom-up process, the forum generated new thinking that resulted in more acceptable middle school location proposals.

This fundamental shift from one- to two-way communication reflects the movement of many public relations professionals and education leaders from the asymmetrical persuasive mode described earlier in this chapter to the symmetrical communication approach, balancing organization and stakeholder interests and needs. For example, instead of communicating "to" stakeholders via a public hearing, two-way communication involves deliberating "with" constituents in a community conversation.

The emphasis shifts from telling to sharing. Communications are not crafted to protect turf but rather to seek common ground. The goal is not to exercise authority but to help all stakeholders take responsibility for solutions to complex problems. It is not to influence people who already think in the same way the organization does but to involve those who do not have similar viewpoints in decision-making. It is a bottom-up communication style building a network of stakeholders engaged in processes rather than a top-down approach perpetuating a hierarchical decision-making system. "1.3 From One-Way Communication to Authentic Engagement" in the workbook illustrates these shifts in a handout useful in workshops.

Equitable Partnerships

Authentic engagement goes beyond traditional involvement to genuine partnership. It creates a sense of belonging to the school community and encourages responsibility in each stakeholder for educational outcomes. In classrooms, teachers can involve families in helping with bulletin boards or reading to students but engagement goes much deeper. The teacher who engages authentically invites parents/family to be active partners in a child's learning, sharing roles and responsibilities related to student learning with families. Teachers help families stay in touch with what is happening in class, teach them how to make a difference in their children's academic achievement, and invite interactions with other families.

At the school level, teachers and administrators often involve families in volunteer activities such as chaperoning dances or field trips and helping with school fund-raisers, but they rarely ask their opinions or fold parents' thinking into school decisions. A school engaging authentically provides structures for families, students, community members, and staff to influence and make decisions in a transparent manner. It offers interesting opportunities for participation on committees, helps families analyze school and student data collaboratively, coaches them in helping students with learning tasks, organizes ways to help families and teachers get to know one another, and shares information primarily in two-way communication modes either in face-to-face meetings or through social media.

For school or district administrators, engagement involves taking responsibility for breaking down the power barriers typically embedded in the district hierarchy. In a culture of authentic engagement, educators take the first step in creating an environment in which families and community members easily access information, ask questions freely, receive meaningful answers, express concerns, and request assistance. They first work internally with their own staff members to shift the nature of communications at all levels from a one-way to a two-way symmetrical model, demonstrating the desired behaviors of engagement, defining and loosening the power reins, and motivating their own teams to collaborate more effectively.

Face-to-Face and Social Media

Although face-to-face interaction continues to be the most effective way to interact with stakeholders, it is not the only avenue. Practitioners are successfully engaging stakeholders through social media. Events during the 2011–2012 Arab Spring demonstrated the power of electronic connections in marshaling masses of people to action. As social media continue to emerge and expand, there will be new ways to connect, inspire, and collaborate.

Beyond inspiring many to get involved, some engagement organizations have already created unique electronic processes to move dialogue forward in a larger online context in ways that preserve the unique characteristics of face-to-face authentic engagement. Digital media are evolving daily and offer a powerful forum for virtual dialogue leading to the discovery of innovative ideas and the generation of answers to unsolved complex problems. Because participants can engage on their own timelines and in their own spaces, the possibility for greater participation exists. Yet, while social media evolve to a more powerful role in connecting people, face-to-face interaction is even more important because people need to see facial expressions, see gestures, and hear tone of voice in order to understand deeper meanings and nuances. Both forms should be part of engagement work to build the kind of trust needed to make difficult decisions, resolve issues, and move forward together.

Dialogue, Not Debate or Discussion

A fundamental strategy in authentic engagement is providing opportunities for and capably facilitating genuine dialogue among participants in any group. The purpose of dialogue is to allow divergent points of view to be expressed and held respectfully on the table for consideration while everyone in the room has a chance to share and thoughtfully consider the frames of reference of others. People explain, argue, confront, explore, and think aloud together without jumping to conclusions or prejudging the ideas of others.

In contrast, the point of a debate is to win. Representatives of highly polarized pro-and-con stances present arguments, each seeking a monopoly on the truth, a correct position. Even though competitive debaters in high school or college switch positions and are required to represent convincingly the opposing point of view, the typical community debate process does not promote an environment safe enough for exploration of new ideas. It is not geared toward compromise or common ground, does not allow questioning of assumptions, and is increasingly uncivil.

Nor is discussion the answer. Although it does move groups toward decision-making and closure, it simply does not provide lasting resolution for complex issues. While open discussion allows a freer and possibly less contentious consideration of viewpoints than a debate, it is typically without a structure guaranteeing that all voices are heard. Although discussion can result in decision-making and closure, it does not resolve complex issues. Participants in a discussion strive to convince others of a stance or point by advocating for a particular position.[12] Though less competitive than a debate, a discussion's purpose of closure is still different from the creative synthesis of opposites possible through dialogue.

Dialogue is thinking aloud and collectively, through inquiry and temporary suspension of judgment or positions, allowing the exploration of issues. It acknowledges the value of others' multiple contributions—perceptions, experiences, ideas, and judgments—and develops a knowledge base greater than that of any one member.[13] Participants examine differences that surface and ask for more detail or clarification rather than simply telling or explaining a single point of view. Dialogue calls on people to reflect on what is happening as it is taking place. It is open to shifts in thinking as interaction proceeds, and it contributes to creating workable, sustainable, and actionable options. The structure of the dialogue process requires participants to suspend assumptions, and it creates a space in which collective thinking can emerge and common ground can be found.

From Inquiry to Breakthrough

In dialogue, inquiry encourages collaborative learning and discovery that can lead to disrupting and breaking through the existing order. Participants naturally bring their own beliefs and understandings to dialogue settings. They express them differently there, however, than in more traditional discussion or presentation formats in which group members advocate for particular stances. Engagement strategies help participants put their viewpoints as well as the reasoning behind those perspectives on the table and seek insights from others in order to refine thinking to help resolve a common issue of the group. Focusing on inquiry and advocating after deep inquiry involves a willingness on the part of all participants to listen, question in ways that seek understanding rather than challenge, and discover new information, including the thoughts of others. Asking others for their viewpoints rather than holding staunchly to one's position on issues promotes such inquiry.

Inquiry broadens the knowledge base in the room as participants respond to questions from others who seek more information or data, additional background, or added rationale for thinking. It moves the speaker from making an autocratic assertion to participating in a nonjudgmental exploration of the thoughts expressed—from a message-delivery position to a learning stance. It moves participants from being quiet bystanders to becoming questioners who seek clarification and explore the points of view and reasoning of others. In the end, such a balanced approach produces more creative thinking than discussion based solely on defending or challenging tightly held advocacy positions. It generates new ideas and creative ways to move toward sustainable solutions.

The Power of Process

In the earlier story of the school board trying to pass a bond measure to consolidate all schools onto one site, constituents were locked in disagreements with an educational establishment. With a soundly defeated financial measure as evidence, it was clear the board could not persuade constituents to accept their ideas. It took creating a structure of an informal conversation in which dialoguing face-to-face created enough safety so participants initially entrenched on each side of the argument could hear each other and begin to explore options for solutions together.

Granted, it takes time to allow such structures to work and courage to let dialogue emerge through group process. At moments of great urgency, there may not be enough time for shared decision-making. A leader simply must say, "For now, this is the way we need to go and this is why." This becomes much easier to accept on occasion when stakeholders are already participating in a culture of authentic engagement in which they understand some circumstances demand quick action that precludes their usual level of involvement. At those moments, they grant leadership the authority to make such decisions without feeling trust relationships have been compromised.

Structuring a process so thinking and decisions can evolve through dialogue is effective. It helps generate sustainability, the "stickiness" that keeps the results of interactions with and among constituents in place. Understandings and decisions emerging from stakeholders that drive next-step planning will be more powerful and sustainable than action based on what someone else persuaded them to adopt or required them to do. In authentic engagement, constituents also feel the organization hears them more deeply, prompting them to stay more connected and committed to the next stages of planning and action.

THINKING SYSTEMICALLY TO FIND UNDERLYING PATTERNS

The Place for Systems Thinking in Engagement

Effective decision-making in a school or district requires systems thinking on many levels. When considering a major change in a system, the engagement of those affected, including perhaps multiple organizations, different segments of the population, and subgroups, must be considered so implementation will go smoothly. A leader attempting to bridge systems has to think not only about how each group could be affected, but also about how groups can affect each other and—always—what the impact will be on student learning.

The success in creating a culture of engagement in a school or district depends on how the system is organized and what values are inherent within the system. Is the system closed or open? Controlled or adaptive? Self-organizing or organized externally? Planned or random? In a closed system there is little or no chaos, boundaries are clear and enforced, certainty is high, and everything is well planned. Short-term fixes based on "what is" prevail. Often there is only one right answer. The more controlled and closed a system is, the less likely it will succeed with engagement strategies that take into account the complexities of the real world. A closed, controlled system is less likely to be sustainable or develop successful long-term solutions.

On the other hand, engagement processes thrive in open, adaptive systems. An adaptive system is flexible and readjusts as the environment changes. It fosters diversity of thought and experience, encourages deep thinking, allows for uncertainties and chaos, and is open to knowledge beyond what it already possesses. While processes in an adaptive system take longer and require greater facilitation skills, adaptive systems are more likely to be sustainable while supporting people's aspirations.

Understanding and using the following five key concepts of systems thinking will help generate authentic engagement within schools and their communities and lead to more effective decision-making:

1. Schools as Complex Systems: School-related systems include many entities—the district, a school, department, team, family, community, neighborhood, professional organizations or unions, after-school programs, and a myriad of other structures with bearing on the work of schooling. Acknowledging those entities and engaging them in planning and decision-making enhances engagement and increases support for schools to meet needs of families.

2. Interrelatedness: When an event occurs in one area of the system, it is only part of the story. Like the tip of an iceberg, a single event or issue sits atop an unseen mass of deeper patterns and systemic structures. Such an invisible structure affects the system as well as the event. Understanding the underlying patterns and structure is critical to resolving issues and making good decisions in the organization.[14]

3. Pattern Awareness: Patterns and trends are always present in systems, though not always explicit. A pattern is an unspoken yet visible language. Within people and within organizations mental

models of deeply held assumptions, perceptions, and "reasons why" are patterns that can surface through dialogue and/or research (see chapter 3). Then there are process, structure, and paradigm patterns within organizational systems that if studied can help an organization see the entire picture with all the interrelated parts. Detecting unseen patterns in relationships, budgeting, equity, and curriculum and analyzing related events can reveal the systemic behaviors and variables at work, creating opportunities to identify potential and possibilities for the system.

4. Mental Models: People behave based on mental models they derive from beliefs, attitudes, and values—their theories about how the world works. Logical and realistic or not, the theories sometimes perpetuate unproductive interactions within systems. Discovering constituents' underlying attitudes and beliefs helps clarify rationales and promotes workable solutions to problems.

5. Feedback Loops: In a feedback loop perspective, the system is an interconnected set of circular relationships. It is different from a linear perspective where events are unidirectional cause-and-effect relationships: A causes B causes C, etc. With a feedback loop perspective, one observes the interrelationships between all events, seeing the patterns and systemic structures more easily. When the big picture is seen and understood, problems are more effectively addressed and solved. With a feedback loop perspective, reflection happens at higher than usual levels in which people intentionally review, reconsider, reconnect, and reframe:

   - *review* what is not working well and build on strengths of what is working;
   - *reconsider* basic assumptions and conclusions and the reasoning behind them;
   - *reconnect* to new practices and ideas from inside and outside educational settings; and
   - *reframe* new possibilities for approaching the issue.[15]

How systems thinking operates in engaging constituents appears in examples throughout the remaining chapters. Those examples will also serve as models to uncover beliefs, values, and assumptions in a variety of settings. "1.4 Systems Thinking and Engagement" in the workbook is a handout outlining how thinking systemically promotes better stakeholder engagement and problem solving.

Foundations in a Theory of Action

Systems thinking helps groups analyze the effects of particular actions on diverse individuals within the systems and on the sustainability of the organization as a whole. Careful analysis of the related systems within any issue and the plans formulated to address the issue will reveal the theory of action upon which any plan is based, including whether there are flaws in the theory that will doom the plan to failure. Developing customized theories about which approaches are likely to work in order to create a reliable action plan maximizes engagement implementation and success.

Consciously or unconsciously, people behave in ways consistent with their mental models. Likewise, decision-makers address issues and build action plans rooted in their models—in whatever theory they hold about why something works. The theories may or may not be founded on rational thinking or solid data. Further, individuals throughout the organization often suggest ideas for solving a problem or construct plans based on both spoken and unspoken assumptions held by individuals and the organization as a whole. Similarly, solutions are also based on beliefs, values, and mental models. Although action ultimately is the bottom line, taking time to understand the *theory* behind a chosen approach and the *assumptions* beneath the theories is basic to viable solutions or creating an effective plan.

It is therefore also critically important to help an organization examine its own assumptions and make explicit its underlying premises about how and why engaging constituents matters and how it fosters better thinking and results.[16] Making the organization's theory of action for engagement efforts conscious and visible will contribute to clarity in thinking together and in greater problem-solving capacity. A theory of action connects the goals and objectives to specific strategies and outcome neasures.

The theory of action for the engagement strategies in this book is: If schools authentically engage educators, parents/families, students, and the greater community in planning, solving problems, and breaking through obstacles that prevent the system from supporting improved learning, those engaged can and will determine how best to improve student learning and classroom instruction resulting in greater student success.

"1.5 A Theory of Action for Engagement Practice" in the workbook breaks down the theory of action for selecting engagement strategies. Using specific underlying assumptions, on which decisions about engagement actions are based, it then shows the theory of action for each, stating which particular approaches will be effective. It also identifies the possible weak links in local thinking or existing systems that need to be addressed for the engagement efforts to be successful.

Peeling back an organization's layers of thinking to identify the underlying assumptions can illuminate inconsistencies in values and practices held among individuals or employee groups and by the organization as a whole—insights that can be very useful in moving forward. It also follows that if weak links are addressed, success in the larger goal of engaging communities with schools is more likely to be consistent and, in turn, more effectively improve the bottom line of student achievement.

THE RANGE OF VEHICLES FOR ENGAGEMENT AND LEARNING

A number of professionals in the fields of engagement, public relations, and school/community partnerships identify a variety of engagement activities such as parent involvement, community partnerships, legislative advocacy, and standards implementation. This book categorizes strategies differently to reflect structural formats or vehicles through which authentic engagement is possible.

Each of the eight effective engagement or vehicle categories listed below can be configured in various venues or formats to achieve a variety of purposes. Choosing the vehicle and venue best matching an organization's purpose will result in deeper engagement and clearer identification of issues or problems, goals, plans, and actions.

Groups, Teams, and Task Forces

- Formal *focus groups* or what are sometimes called *listening sessions* provide settings for listening to stakeholder concerns, underlying beliefs, and thoughts on critical issues. They can be used to gather data about complex or highly emotional issues and strategies to handle them. They are effective in drawing information from groups with a variety of interests, cultural backgrounds, and values.

- *Dialogue groups* encourage the sharing of perspectives in a structured setting designed to ensure all voices are heard. These groups help generate new ideas and can provide sustainable options for resolving issues.
- *Tiger teams* or *strike teams* can address a critical issue quickly by identifying new options for action and ideas for modifying programs and practices or solving financial or other challenges. They can surface short-term tasks necessary to resolve dilemmas.
- *Problem-solving task forces, exploratory teams,* and *ad hoc advisory groups* can all help resolve district or school issues and challenges. They can develop longer-term plans to resolve dilemmas.

Large Public Gatherings

- *Community forum* is a process designed for participants to listen to many perspectives and gain a deeper understanding of the entire system, hear what the participants care about, and jointly decide on priorities. The hosting school, district, or other organization learns what their stakeholders value as well as their concerns. The topics of the meetings usually involve complex or priority issues affecting a wide range of stakeholders. The purpose is to gather data and receive immediate feedback on which issues to ask more questions about within the same meeting. While the facilitator shares common information about the concerns and issues with the full group at the beginning and periodically invites participants to report to the entire group throughout the meeting, participants are divided into small groups for several rounds of of conversations so everyone can be actively involved and heard.
- *Online conversations* can involve an even larger group of participants than forums. This venue provides instant and easy access for stakeholders to participate without the need to leave home, arrange child care, or find transportation. As in community forums, the purpose is to gather data by listening to concerns within the broad online setting and draw information from people representing a wide variety of interests and cultures.

Process Structures

- Many established and effective *process formats* are available in print and online: *Study Circles, Open Space Technology, World Café, Storytelling,* and *Appreciative Inquiry.*
- In most cases, the processes work with large gatherings of people by arranging participants in small groups for sharing. Organizers can host large numbers of people in ways that bring out a broad range of opinions as participants explore concerns and address complex issues, some involving conflict. The purpose of each process is to connect diverse perspectives; discover common ground; identify patterns, themes, and insights; and create innovative solutions. The group structure and processes also allow participants to develop action plans in a relatively short period. In turn, deep participant involvement promotes taking responsibility for aspects of the plans' implementation.

Governance Structures and Groups

- School boards and other board-appointed groups support engagement work by advocating for authentic engagement with stakeholders and making explicit the goals and decision-making processes of their work. They underscore the importance of transparency in engagement work.

Family/Student and Teacher Events

- Two venues are already regular occasions on school calendars: *family/student/teacher/ parent conferences* and *curriculum nights.*
- Both events provide opportunities to build relationships between families and school personnel. One specific way to do that is to enable and expect staff members to teach families in either venue how to advocate for their children and interact with their learning at home and at school.

Training

- Two forms of training are critical: *parent leadership training* and *staff orientation to engagement practices.*

- Learning to advocate for their children and interact with their learning at home and at school are skills many parents do not possess.
- Staff members can learn how to teach those skills to parents and, in the process, deepen their relationships with families of the children they serve.
- Staff training in how to reach families who are more difficult to draw into the school or classroom is also important.

Strategic Planning

- Three planning venues provide stakeholders opportunities to engage with schools and districts: *school- and district-level planning teams, strategic planning teams,* and *exploratory study teams.*
- All offer settings for listening to community or staff hopes and dreams or to perspectives on critical issues facing stakeholders.
- Each type of strategic planning team is usually involved with developing a mission and articulating a vision for their plan or project, as well as in developing strategies, action steps, indicators of success, and the budget necessary to accomplish their goals.

Partnerships and Coalitions

- These exist in various formats: *community partnerships for learning, school/district/ business partnerships,* and various *coalitions.*
- Partnerships and coalitions increase parent, family, and community engagement with student learning and promote joint responsibility for student success. Such collaborations help families and communities learn how to improve student achievement and create opportunities for community resources to help support teaching and learning. They also enhance the welcoming culture of a school environment and revitalize communities around the schools.

These eight categories or vehicles for community engagement can be tailored to meet local needs. Their purposes represent processes that are characteristic of deep engagement. Using an array of authentic engagement strategies will empower a school, district, and community to design and implement effective changes supporting young people in school, the families closest to them, and the communities around them. "1.6 Vehicles and Venues for Authentic Engagement Practice" in the workbook sum-

marizes these categories and characteristics as a handout useful in workshops.

BEST HOPES: REVITALIZING EDUCATION AND DEMOCRACY
THROUGH AUTHENTIC ENGAGEMENT

Changes in the educational system have usually come in periods of great
turmoil both within and outside of the educational establishment. Educators and constituents alike have debated which achievement results and
educational approaches are most appropriate. Although thinking on educational achievement as well as teaching practice has evolved, education
remains rooted in the need to develop an informed citizenry capable of
carrying on civil dialogue about new thinking and practices necessary to
meet educational, economic, political, and social needs.

In contemporary society, several shifts are occurring that make participation in the improvement of education a focal point for nurturing our
democracy through a period of change.

- Communities as well as educators have been creating more opportunities for public dialogue, collaboration, and participation supported by information and training materials from national networks such as Everyday Democracy, National Coalition for Dialogue and Deliberation, Deliberative Democracy Consortium, the
  Kettering Foundation, and Public Agenda. The development of
  Participedia, led by Archon Fung of the Ash Center for Democratic
  Governance and Innovation at Harvard and by Mark Warren at the
  University of British Columbia, is an open-source, Internet-based
  "participatory knowledge tool" that allows hundreds of researchers
  and practitioners to catalog and compare the performance of participatory political processes.
- Today's citizens are increasingly interested in issues closer to their
  hometowns, where they are more likely to work toward consensus
  and collaborate for changes locally. Education is an area where
  there is considerable local interest.
- Those who lead are becoming more creative about embedding local
  opportunities for decision-making and collaboration in social and
  cultural venues that attract everyday citizens more than traditional
  political arenas do.[17] The school district represents a core system in
  which to engage stakeholders.

- While citizens of today are more skeptical about government and less willing to be governed blindly, they are better at finding what they need to know and taking action based on that knowledge.[18]
- As constituencies have become more diverse, educational missions have become more inclusive.
- The technology of the twenty-first century compels the use of new ways to relate meaningfully to one another.

Acknowledging and capitalizing on societal shifts strengthens engagement planning efforts. In the process, a school or district can be the catalyst for more democratic participation beyond its boundaries. It is a win-win situation. A school district's use of authentic engagement calls for the community's and local government's assistance in the process. Engagement strategies open the door for collaboration in bringing all elements of the community together to influence and share decision-making. Helping to educate citizens and build community in order for schools, parents, families, and the community at large to support the academic achievement of students also enhances the democratic processes at work in local, state, and national governments.

Democracy ensures its survival by preparing the students of today for their emerging roles as citizens of the future. It is critically important to encourage and, in some cases, explicitly teach families and other constituents how to talk about their concerns, have their voices heard, participate proactively in the educational process, and exercise their role in democracy in practical and civil ways around the education of young people. Roles of educators and public relations practitioners have changed, as well. Incorporating new practices into leadership skill sets will make a positive difference in the revitalization and survival of schools.

Educators and community members alike can become effective change agents striving to improve student learning by engaging communities to support, encourage, and share responsibility for helping all children reach their potential. Research bears out the belief of engagement proponents that the bottom line of student achievement will show a positive difference when constituencies are engaged and their perspectives are folded meaningfully into decision-making about how to provide a better education for their community's children.

This book provides guidance to ensure organizations hear the voices of all stakeholders and bring them into decision-making processes. Embracing the wisdom, the politics, the processes, and the strategies for

engaging a school's and district's families and community is the beginning. Doing so will lower the rhetoric of blame and contention. It will
encourage interactions bringing diverse people together to address issues, solve problems, and create new futures. It will strengthen community and the democracy. It will allow new and powerful wisdom to
emerge for the benefit of all in our communities and society.

TAKEAWAY MESSAGES FROM THIS CHAPTER

- The power of authentic engagement is providing opportunities in
  which people talk and think together to make difficult decisions
  and solve thorny problems.
- The practices of authentic engagement reconnect families and citizens with their schools and empower their participation in student
  academic learning.
- The nature of public relations in school districts has evolved from
  merely providing information and trying to steer public opinion to
  engaging constituents in meaningful conversations and decision-
  making about education in local schools, districts, and communities.
- Authentic engagement gives voice to all constituents and generates
  dynamic family and community partnerships dedicated to improving schooling.
- Authentic engagement is characterized by inclusiveness, relation-
  ship-building, deep dialogue, honesty, transparency, trust, and
  partnership.
- Involvement and engagement are not the same; engagement is not
  the twentieth-century practice of inviting parents/families to help
  with bulletin boards, but rather bringing people together to solve
  problems and make decisions that will more likely lead to student
  success.
- Thinking systemically, making assumptions explicit, and generating a theory of action enhances efforts to plan and take productive
  action.
- The power of getting all constituent voices in the room, hearing
  their opinions, and learning what they think and fear moves thinking forward.

- Building strong communities is essential for improving and sustaining student achievement and schools as well as strengthening our democracy.
- Authentic engagement strategies and structures are useful in many settings in schools and school communities.

HELPFUL RESOURCES RELATED TO THIS CHAPTER

- Peter Senge and other contributing authors apply systems thinking to the school environment in *Schools That Learn: A Fifth Discipline Fieldbook for Educators, Parents, and Everyone Who Cares about Education*. Illustrations and charts help define key concepts of systems thinking undergirding authentic engagement practice.
- Chris Argyris defines theory of action concepts and provides a framework for moving from theory toward action in his book, *On Organizational Learning*.
- *The MetLife Survey of the American Teacher: Past, Present, and Future*. Since 1984, the MetLife Foundation has conducted annual surveys providing data about American education. Surveys are posted as ERIC documents or at http://www.metlife.com/about/corporate-profile/citizenship/metlife-foundation/metlife-survey-of-the-american-teacher.html (accessed November 18, 2011).
- Susan Clark and Woden Teachout in their book *Slow Democracy: Rediscovering Community* advocate democracy practiced at the local level through face-to-face, inclusive, thoughtful dialogue. The book includes many powerful stories of people reclaiming their power to make sustainable changes that benefit their communities—democracy working at the local level.

Complete bibliographical information for these resources is located in the reference list at the back of this book.

NOTES

1. Grunig and Hunt, *Managing Public Relations*, 304. The names of the models of public relations are those of Grunig and Hunt, *Managing Public Relations*; the descriptors are those used by Leslie in her work with schools and communities.

2. Grunig and Grunig, "Models of Public Relations and Communication," chap. 11 in *Excellence in Public Relations and Communications Management*, 307–319.

3. Sarason, *The Predictable Failure of Educational Reform*, 1990.

4. In spite of the anger and alienation that bubbles along, there is evidence of increased support for schools over recent years, perhaps indicating a greater acceptance of joint responsibility for educating children. In 2009, the *MetLife Survey of the American Teacher: Past, Present, and Future* published results of data collected from teachers, principals, and students. Teachers and principals believe parental and community support for schools has grown since the first survey on that topic twenty-five years ago, although urban schools still struggle to find the same levels of support as suburban counterparts. More teachers in the recent survey (67 percent) than in 1984 (54 percent) say parental and community support for their school is good or excellent. The report also verifies that responsibility for school change has moved from "the teacher alone to a broader responsibility for student achievement shared among teachers, principals, parents, communities, and students themselves." Recognizing and accepting such shared responsibility for schools is fostered by engaging families and communities more meaningfully.

5. Shaffer and Anundsen, *Creating Community Anywhere.*

6. Leslie, "Community Relations: Engaging the Public," chap. 14, 119–134, in *School Public Relations: Building Confidence in Education,* edited by Kenneth K. Muir. Used with permission of the National School Public Relations Association (www.NSPRA.org).

7. Sergiovanni speaks often of the importance of "we" versus "I" in building relationships (*Leadership for the Schoolhouse,* 47). He talks of it, as well, in *Building Community in Schools,* where he also emphasizes the concept of creating a kinship of mind and place.

8. Karen Kleinz (associate director, National School Public Relations Association), interviewed by Kathy Leslie.

9. Annenberg Institute for School Reform, *Reasons for Hope, Voices for Change,* 20–21.

10. Adapted from William Isaacs, *Dialogue and the Art of Thinking Together.*

11. James E. Grunig and Larissa L. Grunig, "Public Relations Excellence 2010."

12. Isaacs, *Dialogue and the Art of Thinking Together,* 41–43.

13. Rachael Kessler and Mark Gerzon of Mediators Ltd., "Forms of Discourse." Elements of the definitions of dialogue and debate are based on this workshop handout.

14. Senge, et al., *Schools That Learn: A Fifth Discipline Fieldbook for Educators, Parents, and Everyone Who Cares about Education,* 80.

15. Adapted from Cambron-McCabe and Dutton "The Wheels of Learning: The Rhythm of Learning and Learning to Learn," in *Schools That Learn: A Fifth Discipline Fieldbook for Educators, Parents, and Everyone Who Cares about Education,* edited by Senge et al., 93–98.

16. Theory of action concepts are based on the work of Chris Argyris, *On Organizational Learning.*

17. Leighninger and Levine, "Education in a Rapidly Changing Democracy."

18. Matt Leighninger, *Planning for Engagement.*

TWO

Creating a Culture of Authentic Engagement

People want to be connected and feel a sense of belonging to their schools. Most families want a voice in their children's education that they believe will help them succeed and, ultimately, contribute to society. However, many people don't know how to get involved with their school or support their children's learning. Sometimes families who are equipped to participate in their child's schooling encounter educators in power who will not let them in.

To create a culture of engagement and stakeholder influence in which people have a voice in how children are educated is to craft a system in which people know they belong, their ideas have value, and they share responsibility with educators for student success. It will not happen at a gathering to tell constituents how things will be done, or in a video explaining the district's plans, or even at a board meeting that includes public comment.

Authentic engagement moves far beyond events and information dissemination to creating opportunities for stakeholders to deliberate through dialogue and do meaningful work to improve the learning environment and promote improved student achievement. Ideas surfaced in ongoing, multi-tiered conversations with stakeholders and educators lead to new thinking about issues and sustainable solutions. Creating a living, sustained *culture of engagement*, deeply embedded in schools and local communities, is not easy but the benefits outweigh the investment.

The first part of this chapter captures the big picture of authentic engagement: what it looks like in action and how to build relationships and a foundation of trust. It includes the processes and structures to bring people together, address issues that matter to them, deliberate, and solve problems. The nuts and bolts of how to use a variety of approaches are introduced in the second part of this chapter. Chapter 2 in the companion workbook, *The Politics of Authentic Engagement: Tools for Engaging Stakeholders in Ensuring Student Success* contains ten tools useful as talking points, handouts, or workshop instructions.

UNDERSTANDING AUTHENTIC ENGAGEMENT: WHAT IT IS AND WHY DO IT

A Story of Success

It is quite evident that one urban middle school has been successful in improving the achievement of its students. The data are always in the news. A flag is flattened against the wall, pronouncing "School of Excellence. We reached our goal!" One look around the lobby, a visitor sees the priorities that got them there. In English, Korean, Chinese, and Spanish, a banner spells out the core school goal: "Working Together to Put Student Success First." The bulletin boards down the hallways are crowded with examples of student work showing what meeting a variety of academic standards looks like.

On their website is a schedule of meetings for parents, staff, and, in some cases, community members identifying various task forces working on different issues. Some of the issue groups are these: Creating a Sense of Belonging, Safety on the Athletic Field, Strategic Planning, and Carnival Planning.

A visiting mother, parent of a seventh-grade boy, does not even make it to the office before a greeter says hello and asks if he can help. The office is buzzing with adults, both employees and volunteers, assisting children and families with answers to questions and tending to their needs. Teachers work in partnership with families and with each other. They are not isolated in their classrooms teaching their own curriculum. Classroom doors are open to families, volunteers, and other partners who support student achievement in a variety of ways. The collective leadership model is at work here with churches providing English classes for families, tutoring for students at apartment complexes who need help with homework, and a clothes closet for students who do not have proper clothes for school. Rotary provides recycled library books and dental checks. SMART volunteers work one-on-one with students who struggle in reading, and senior citizens mentor students who do not have anyone to guide them in their everyday challenges.

This school is an A+ model of an open, adaptive, engaged system. There are other schools, however, where principals and teachers may work hard to create an open environment but are often prevented from reaching their goals because individual teachers run closed classrooms, inconsistent with the values established within the school. Those classrooms become mini-fortresses in schools that are otherwise striving to partner with their community in reaching educational goals.

In hundreds of focus groups, parents report that their children are in schools where they do not feel welcome as families, where their ideas are either not heard or ignored. In other cases, the leadership, teachers, and staff of entire schools and districts have a hunker-down mentality. They are convinced they alone have the knowledge, expertise, and experience to educate children. They do not want to hear from outsiders and, except for some token volunteer opportunities selected for parents, they rely solely upon themselves to get the job done. But do they?

Fragmentation and Thought

Evidence is clear when families *and citizens* partner with schools in educating students, young people achieve at higher levels and attend school more regularly with fewer discipline problems (see chapter 4). Why then do so many educators continue to shut the school and/or classroom door, giving families and others only cursory tasks?

Teachers in focus groups say parents do not know enough to influence educational decisions or help students in the classroom. They say students need to be independent of their families. Superintendents, principals, and teachers continue to hold sit-and-get meetings, back-to-school nights, parent/teacher conferences, and other activities in which families and community members do not have a way to influence the educational process, ask questions, or provide new thinking. Perhaps driven by egocentrism and fragmented thinking, many educators with good intentions believe the education of children will be hurt or slowed down if families, citizens, government, businesses, churches, and grant providers participate in the learning process and the business of education.

Too many educators see the world not as a system, but as fragments needing to be kept separate. Such individuals are mechanistic, fragmented thinkers who see things as distinct and disconnected. Most issues in schools are too complex and challenging to be solved using more of the same faulty thought processes.

A friend has a saying posted on her refrigerator admonishing, "Don't believe everything you think." David Bohm, theoretical physicist, claims there is a "systemic fault" in the whole of thought.[1] For example, when an educator says a parent does not have enough knowledge to assist in the education process, the educator fails to attribute his thinking to his own reasoning process, beliefs, and conclusions. Where did his thinking come from? What drove his conclusions? Was it a bad experience with a parent? Fear that says, "I do not have time to train anyone to do this right"? A belief that says, "I am the only one who knows how to do this"? These are examples of fragmented reasoning.

How does one know the difference between good and faulty thinking? Bad reasoning results from being stuck in a pattern of thinking about an issue in the same way one has always thought about it. Faulty thinking comes from not listening to others, not seeking new approaches, and not being open to new learning. Peter Senge contends that the most basic work of leaders is to create results, but not in isolation. Good reasoning, which may also be called *systemic thinking*, comes from seeking new knowledge and reflecting, both individually and with others, on the possibilities it creates.

Otto Scharmer, senior lecturer at MIT and author, asks people to consider why they create results nobody wants. He claims that the "current waves of disruptive change" require us to "suspend our judgments, redirect our attention, let go of the past, lean in to the future that wants to come, and let it come." He contends that these conditions require "a mindset on the part of decision makers that is more open, attentive, adaptive, and tuned in to emerging changes."[2]

Distinguishing Characteristics of Schools that Engage

The middle school story earlier in this chapter illustrates features of schools effectively engaging their constituencies—parents, families, students, and citizens in the greater community surrounding the schools. They are schools in which students, families, and citizens know they belong, have an important role to play in advancing student achievement, and are making a difference. Twelve characteristics distinguish such schools:

1. The school is welcoming.
2. Hope for each child and family is pervasive and alive.
3. The gifts and talents of each student and everyone connected to the school are recognized, honored, and accepted.
4. Families and teachers know each other and partner in many ways.
5. Collective leadership is fostered.
6. All stakeholders in the school, families, and community know they are members of the inside group.
7. A culture of trust, inclusiveness, and collaborative problem solving exists.
8. Achievement data are readily available and used in making decisions.
9. Many decision-making processes involve a wide range of stakeholders in deep conversations about issues.
10. An expectation exists for mutual responsibility in the community—among school staff, families, surrounding businesses, and residents—for the success of each student.
11. The capacity, supported by the district and community, for improving teaching and learning expands continuously, based on data collected about students, teachers, families, and the community.
12. People perceive their schools as "democracy at work."[3]

This list appears as "2.1 Characteristics Distinguishing Schools of Engagement" in the companion workbook. It can be a useful handout.

Other chapters will examine the twelve characteristics of schools that engage their stakeholders in specific settings. For now, the first item—the school is welcoming—is a good example of how easy it is to take steps toward achieving the remaining characteristics. Easy to address early on, it relates to the proliferation of literature in recent years about how school climate affects expectations for students as well as how they learn. Members of focus groups identified the items in "2.2 Is Your School a Welcoming School?" in the worlbook as having the greatest effects on improving their school's welcoming feel. The checklist can serve as a way to begin talking with others about what can be done together to improve the school's welcoming presence. Most suggestions are not only easy, they are relatively quick to achieve without a large financial outlay.

Principles of Authentic Engagement

What students, families, and communities want in their schools is not always clear and changes as new needs and issues arise. Through authentic engagement, what stakeholders want and what is possible becomes clear to everyone as issues are addressed. Although the look of engagement may vary from community to community, there are eight basic principles for success in creating an adaptive system of authentic engagement.

1. Those facilitating engagement work know themselves well.

    They know their own assumptions, beliefs, and biases and can suspend them when working with and listening to others.

2. Adaptive systems thinking is foundational to engagement work.

    Effective engagement processes work within systems. Schools are systems functioning within larger systems such as the district, which functions within a city and a state system—all of which are in a world system. What happens in any of these systems affects everyone and all other systems.

3. Influence is shared.

    Stakeholders know they have influence. Everyone in relationship with the organization has the possibility of influencing its decisions, and the organization genuinely cares about its stakeholders and their interests. A variety of formal and informal structures invite anyone to initiate conversations, submit ideas, or enter into dialogue to solve problems. Stakeholders see the results of their actions, thinking, and recommendations through feedback loops and in school and district policy, plans, and decisions.

4. Responsibility leads to accountability.

    Stakeholders assume more responsibility when they have a say in planning, goal setting, and solving problems. When they are engaged in addressing issues and providing innovative ideas and know their work is leading to improved student achievement, stakeholders will develop a strong sense of responsibility that will ultimately lead to accountability for the success of the school or the district.

5. Action emerges from theory.

   Practices of engagement are based on an explicit theory of action that culminates in steps designed to solve problems and produce results.

6. Engagement practices enhance democracy.

   Engagement practice epitomizes democracy in action by teaching the skills of living in a democracy and providing opportunities to use them locally. Responsible, well-informed citizens comprise a strong democracy. Engagement does not mean pandering to the citizens or popular opinion; it means responding to the informed collective public judgment of the stakeholders.

7. Authentic engagement embraces diversity.

   Engagement processes include diverse people—diversity of culture, ethnicity, religion, gender, sexual orientation, thought, style, and story.

8. Structures hold process and ensure civility.

   Authentic engagement uses process structures that integrate and enhance rather than block participation, promote deep listening, and encourage informed civil dialogue that will generate creative thinking and thoughtful solutions. Participants are trained how to listen without judgment and participate in dialogue through inquiry and advocacy.

"2.3 Putting the Principles of Authentic Engagement into Action" in the workbook summarizes these principles as a workshop handout.

NURTURING A CULTURE OF ENGAGEMENT

Contemporary society exists in an age of deep skepticism, suspicion, and mistrust of nearly everyone and everything. Many believe the public would not know the truth even if they were staring at it. The public believes organizational leaders would not tell the truth even if it benefited them. Public confidence in nearly every institution, government entity, and corporation is at an all-time low. Disillusionment exists both inside organizations and with constituents. How can organizations begin to build trust in such an environment?

Building Trust

Trust is the work of engagement. Building strong, authentic relationships is the first step. Yet trust is lacking in too many schools and communities. When people do not trust the organization, the facilitator, or the people to whom they must relate, it is difficult to address issues and find common ground. Examples of the lack of trust abound:

- The press release issued by the school district reporting only the positive scores on achievement measures, not calling attention to the differences in success levels between races, cultures, ability, or income and how the challenges are being addressed.
- The principal who does not seem to get around to implementing the new communication plan agreed upon in meetings with his community.
- The teacher who repeatedly demonstrates a lack of understanding about how students learn and confuses rather than supports them.
- The superintendent who speaks eloquently but whose words do not clearly define what she means, leaving constituents with additional questions.
- The school board that holds hearings but rarely listens deeply to or acts upon what stakeholders are saying if their opinions do not agree with board positions.

Trust is the foundation for building and maintaining people's commitment to any school or organization. Anthony Bryk and Barbara Schneider identify the *elements* of trust as being "open and honest, following through on promises, demonstrating competence, communicating clearly, and sharing decision-making."[4] In working to build trust, it is essential to begin where people are and move slowly.

*   *   *

For example, engagement work I facilitated with cooperative housing projects in Atlanta, Newark, and San Francisco often involved beginning a workshop with participants who had little or no trust in the outsider who was facilitating. They did not know me. Working on their turf, in their meeting rooms within the apartment complexes where they lived, I was often the only white person in the room. They were probably thinking, What is this white woman doing here?

She does not know anything about us. She thinks she is smarter than us. She has never nor will she ever walk in our shoes, live our way.

Nonetheless, I began by asking them what was on their minds. After some time—time in which they did most of the talking about their children and their challenges—I started very slowly to build a little trust. After a day of working together, learning how to read test scores, help their children with homework, and talk to teachers about their expectations for their children, they felt more confidence and talked more. At the end of the day, they knew how important their role was in helping their children succeed and were able to identify action steps and make commitments. Families and I slowly built trust and they took action from there.

Former governor of New Mexico and ambassador to the United Nations Bill Richardson once said, "You try to be nice to people and let them tell you how they see things, and you chip in with how you see it and kind of go slowly and try to work out a good friendship and start in from there."[5] Part of building such friendships involves being transparent with others. Secrecy destroys trust, so transparency is required in most everything.

* * *

For example, a group of concerned citizens from an elementary school approached the principal with questions about the district's budgeting process. They thought the district was misusing money and not budgeting correctly. The principal answered every question they had with all the knowledge she held. They wanted more. She advised them to meet with the superintendent of finance in the district office and helped them set the appointment and prepare for the meeting. District administrators decided to give them everything—the entire set of budget documents and all of the background materials, saying, "If you want any one of us to help explain anything, we are happy to do so, or you can get your own attorney to review our materials and process."

The parents chose to operate in isolation, without the district's help. After studying the materials for four months, they told the principal and the finance superintendent they could find nothing wrong. Further, they became strong supporters of the district, creating a formal group to advocate independently for the district, and worked tirelessly with the state legislature to secure funding and policy changes supporting all schools in the state.

Sometimes, of course, it does not go as well. People take things out of context, will not believe school and district administrators no matter how well intentioned they are, will misconstrue information or even lie using invalid information against the school or district. They will not give any official the benefit of the doubt—ever. Sometimes they discover incorrect information or see holes and missing facts in the material provided. Nevertheless, to gain trust, consistent transparency is vital, so it is important that the school or district furnish all information available and requested unless it is strictly confidential—for example, student records and employee files.

Six discrete *conditions* need to be in place to build such trust internally within an organization, as well as externally with the community or individual constituents.[6]

1. A fault-free environment

    The political environment is often one of blame and lack of responsibility. It is focused on finding fault, which results in people defending positions rather than solving problems. In a fault-free environment, it is much easier to generate new approaches to issues. The atmosphere is more open and transparent.

2. Accurate, free-flowing information

    Accurate and free-flowing information result from a fault-free, transparent environment. Public information is simply available up front to all constituents, not withheld or restricted. Transparency acknowledges the inability to control information—it gets out, no matter what. But a free flow of information sends the message that the organization has nothing to hide and can be trusted.

3. Opportunities for dialogue

    Opportunities for dialogue are needed both internally and externally. The process of dialogue involves getting beneath what is thought and said to surface the assumptions, beliefs, and values that drive thinking. By identifying attitudes and sharing them with others in meaningful conversation, participants begin to understand others better and learn what motivates them to think the way they do. Although there may not be universal agreement in the group, the level of trust rises, understanding deepens, and openness to influence emerges.

4. A clear understanding of roles

A person's role in a group or organization is frequently not clear. Distinctions or boundaries are drawn that do not exist in reality. Constituents often do not know their role or understand their responsibility. The question to address and answer is this: What is the role of the teacher, the principal, the student, the family, and the community in ensuring all students achieve? People in each role can discuss and define what are the roles and corresponding responsibilities. "4.5 Defining Roles and Responsibilities to Help Children Learn" in the workbook provides a helpful list.

5. Encouragement for taking risks

   Risk taking flourishes in a fault-free environment. People who feel safe try new things, are more creative, and explore other opportunities and options, creating a much stronger organization and serving students more effectively.

6. Unconditional warm regards

   Everyone wants the world to be gentler and kinder. People want to be given the benefit of the doubt. Everyone wants to be forgiven and loved in an environment where warm regards exist, barriers are broken down, and levels of openness and trust are raised.

Working to put these conditions for nurturing trust in place is consistent with what others say the *evidence of trust* looks like. In their research, Bryk and Schneider have identified factors indicating the existence of trust in an organization. Their four vital signs for identifying and assessing trust in schools are these:[7]

- Respect

   Do people acknowledge one another's dignity and ideas? Do they interact in a courteous way? Do they genuinely talk and listen to each other? Do they confront others with care and respect?

- Personal Regard

   Do people care about each other both professionally and personally? Are they willing to go beyond their formal roles and responsibilities, if necessary?

- Competence

   Do people believe in each other's ability and willingness to fulfill their responsibilities effectively? Do they address incompetence so it does not erode school-wide trust?

- Personal Integrity

Are people honest with themselves and others?[8]

"2.4 Conditions for Building Trust" in the workbook summarizes the six conditions in a workshop handout.

When constituents feel they are approached with respect for their thoughts, their trust, and their personal circumstances, they are more apt to share, engage, and solve problems together. The *strategies* in "2.5 Strategies for Building Trust" in the workbook are fundamental to building trust and to developing the indicators of the existence of trust. They are to be used continuously in both structured and unstructured settings where building relationships and talking genuinely with one another is important.

Strategies for Understanding Each Other

Trust is built in an environment where people can understand each other. Stakeholders who acknowledge divergent points of view while working to create change are crucial to improving the world. Too many people, however, have given away their power to politicians and other decision-makers because they think they do not have enough time, power, or knowledge to make a difference. But, community builder Peter Block says, "If it is true we are creating this world, then each of us has the power to heal its woundedness."[9] Citizens in their capacity to come together to make decisions and be accountable represent the best chance at making a difference. The vitality and connectedness of community will determine the strength of democracy.

Bringing constituents together to build the vital community about which Block speaks is at the core of authentic engagement. To that end, a number of strategies can be used to provide opportunities for dialogue and meaningful participation in decision-making: storytelling, examining inferences, analysis of the intent behind what is said, and going beyond advocacy to genuine inquiry into the viewpoints of others.

The Power of Story

Stories inspire by piquing interest and drawing people in. What do people remember about breaking news they just watched? Perhaps the compelling story of the unlikely Good Samaritan stopping to help the boy who slipped down the riverbank is the most memorable moment. What do people talk about when they meet colleagues at week's end?

They discuss the most outrageous workplace event. When do they feel closest to their friends? People feel united when sharing compassionate stories about their child's success or the pain of caring for a parent with dementia.

People want to hear stories—they relate to both the content and the emotion. In the end, each listener better understands the storyteller. So it is when strangers meet—stranded at the airport in a snowstorm, waiting in the long ski lift or grocery checkout line, learning the ropes at a new job, sitting among other families at the first parent meeting of the year—that stories break the ice. They provide a glimpse of what is meaningful, a view of what life is like for another person, often striking a resonant chord and suddenly building a bridge. Confusing concepts become clear because of the story told around them.

When people share stories with one another, they illuminate what is important in their lives. The stories reflect what a person knows and feels about a situation—their truth. The story reveals the color of the lens through which each person looks at the world and sees it slightly—or markedly—differently from someone else.

In addition to emotional impact, storytelling provides context. It is one thing to hear some families feel they cannot get the principal to listen, and quite another to hear a family member tell firsthand the story of how their child finally refused to go to school because three classmates taunted him incessantly in his middle school science classroom without his teacher intervening. Suddenly fellow group members understand the angst, the depth of a dilemma, or the issues involved. The group becomes a community that moves forward with greater understanding.

Group-process facilitator Christina Baldwin in *Storycatcher* captures the essence of storytelling:

> Storycatching is at its root an act of refuge, a place to turn, an offering that we will be listened to while we hold our hearts like a talking piece in our hands; and then we pay it forward—we become the listening ear for the next person, and the next. In this way, the skills of eliciting story, and the skills of receiving story, grow among us. Story makes community: communities make story.[10]

Storytelling is not simply an unstructured, open-ended, warm-fuzzy activity to relax people. It serves a much more significant role as the builder of a common language that will help people discover familiar threads in their disparate experiences. It can contribute to subtle or profound shifts in attitude and perceptions and can guide a group to the best way to accomplish something. Story creates the connections that make change possible. "2.6 Making Storytelling Happen" in the workbook helps facilitators promote such sharing of personal experience.

The Ladder of Inference

Understanding is also built through use of a strategy called the "ladder of inference." [11] People with varying backgrounds and experiences may perceive an event or set of data very differently from one another. The experience of looking at a line drawing or an inkblot often results in a variety of interpretations. In any group, participants may come to divergent conclusions because the assumptions driving their thinking are different from others in the room. Such assumptions may even cause some to focus on one element of objective data others gloss over as they select items more important to them for discussion.

Mentally and verbally climbing the ladder of inference together helps make visible the assumptions lurking behind what individuals think and say, sheds light on divergent meanings, and contributes to better understandings among people. The following rungs reflect what happens in the process of discussing anything with a group of people. [12] Explicitly analyzing thinking with a group as they work their way up the ladder of inference adds transparency to the thinking in the room (begin reading at ground level, reading up the ladder until the top rung is reached).

Rung 6: I take actions (based on my beliefs).

Rung 5: I adopt beliefs (about the world).

Rung 4: I draw conclusions (based on my assumptions).

Rung 3: I make assumptions (based on the meaning I give to data).

Rung 2: I add cultural and personal meanings (to data I observe and/ or select).

Rung 1: I select data (through my lens, based on my perceptions of what I observe).

Ground Level: I observe data and experiences (as a video/audio recorder might capture it).

"2.7 Climbing the Ladder of Inference" in the workbook includes these rungs of the ladder and provides an activity to help participants understand and negotiate each rung in a workshop setting.

Analysis of Intent

Revealing the whole story is another way to build trust, enhance relationships, and understand each other better. The person talking—the contributor in a dialogue—shares the whys prompting their position and the background information leading to their conclusions. The listener figures out what the speaker means instead of accepting their initial statements as fact. The listener looks for underlying intent and works to discover motivations and to understand perspectives of others. Overlooking the fact that someone's perspective has an underlying intent, a personally driven motivation, or a differing life view can cause misinterpretation, misrepresentation, and confusion. For example:

- Some listeners feel a speaker demonstrates *courage* in saying what s/he does to represent an opposite point of view from the prevailing opinion, while others think the same speaker is just *critical*. Does s/he represent an opposing view because of a life experience that altered his viewpoint? Or is it a core tenet in his religious or political beliefs? Or does s/he simply pose the contradicting opinion to generate discussion? Would listeners understand better if the speaker said why s/he thinks the way s/he does?
- A participant asks for *clarity*, but some listeners perceive the speaker coming across as *omnipotent* or *impatient*. Would more information about why the participant needs clarity be helpful?
- Someone speaks with *compassion* but comes across as *indecisive* or *overly accommodating*. Would knowing the life experiences of the speaker who expresses himself compassionately reduce the chance others perceive him/her incorrectly? Would knowing what compels the speaker to consider the softer side of relating to others by ensuring their well-being in difficult conversations be helpful?
- Another speaker is *self-reflective* but comes across as *silent* or *withdrawn* to some in the group. Would knowing more about the quiet nature of the speaker be helpful to others when they participate in conversation with him/her?

In each case, there may be a difference between the reality or intent of the contributor and the perceptions of the listener. Clarifying what is behind a statement or action leads to understanding by surfacing underlying motives and intentions.[13] While listeners certainly have an important role in ensuring people are heard, speakers are responsible for *clarifying*, as well—saying what is on their mind and heart, not just what they think listeners want to hear. Both the contributor and listener have a responsibility for promoting inquiry while respecting advocacy based on knowing someone's deeper story—the speaker in sharing more completely and the listener in considering the motivations and reasoning of others more deeply. These skills of listening and analyzing intent can be learned. "Analysis of Intent (So Do You Mean?)" in the workbook is a workshop activity designed to help group participants listen and analyze intent.

Incorporating the ladder of inference along with the "So Do You Mean?" exercise is another tangible, productive way to analyze intent behind statements. In any of the situations above, guiding a group starting on the ground level and climbing the ladder of inference could clarify the contributor's intent for himself as well as others. Flagging any negative or non-understanding responses to a contributor, such as those in the examples above, will help turn a contentious situation into one leading to better understanding. Using the opportunity to initiate a "ladder of inference" analysis into a variety of situations helps participants slow down their consideration of a contributor's words to investigate why the individual said what they said and to ask clarifying questions to understand someone's perspective better.

Inquiry and Advocacy

Inquiry is more effective in uncovering problems and revealing a more realistic picture of what is and which options will address the problems and issues than advocating for particular positions. People are good at arguing. They know how to debate and persuade. However, in this era of extreme polarization with little or no trust, advocating and convincing others of a position often does not lead to problem solving. In fact, people seem unable to solve most of the huge issues confronting them either individually or societally. Most people find it easy to advocate for a position. In fact, they believe they must. What is difficult is communicating a position thoughtfully with reasonable, nonthreatening passion and taking time to discover what others know and believe by asking questions. What is difficult is understanding and seeing others' well-informed thinking clearly and being open to influence.

Considering many options and proposals helps rid the bias toward one's own ideas and leads to thinking more deeply. Schools with open, adaptive systems foster collective inquiry and teach inquiry skills. They provide time for study and dialogue. Adaptive systems are constantly evolving and changing to meet the needs of the times. Inquiry never stops, so learning never stops. Because learning never stops, everyone in the adaptive system is flexible and open to influence.

Good thinking around decision-making calls for searching, reflecting, inferring, and more reflection by many. Searching includes carefully looking for evidence to support ideas, solutions, and emerging plans and taking time to explore the pros, cons, and trade-offs until settling on a sustainable direction. Educators often feel they do not have time to do engagement work because there are too many other tasks to accomplish. However, short-term fixes can generate suffering and long-term failure, as well as take much more time than the up-front time required to do the right thing. Often one has to go slow to go fast so time is not spent fighting unhappy stakeholders who reverse direction because they know a decision is unworkable.

What takes so much time to get to the point of action and implementation when engaging people in a change process? Unless the decision-makers or change agents begin with where the stakeholders are in their knowledge, experience, or thinking, it will be difficult—if not impossible—to engage on a level playing field. Sometimes this may require doing research to learn where the stakeholders are. Chapter 3, Collecting and Using Stakeholder Research, contains more about how to learn what various individuals and groups in the school and community are thinking and feeling.

The time it takes to move to action is much shorter when it is one individual making a shift, but much longer when an entire organization is collectively working together to implement an action. For an individual, the process involves these stages: reflection, connection, decision-making, and taking action. For an organization, each stage is more complex, involving public reflection, shared meaning, joint planning, and coordinated action. However, when a facilitator goes slowly in the planning and implementation processes, bringing everyone to agreement on the action to take, changes are much more apt to stick, work well, and be supported.

"2.9 The Wheel of Learning in a Community" in *The Politics of Authentic Engagement: Tools for Engaging Stakeholders in Ensuring Student Success* illustrates these differences in process for individuals and organizations. Subsequent chapters in that book provide the "how-to" in each step an individual and organizations go through in designing and implementing change.

Involving participants in deep inquiry is essential for shared meaning to develop when they are considering or involved in change. Participants move through a process of getting to deeper inquiry and greater understanding.

- Suspend or Defend

  The first critical choice a contributor in a conversation makes is to either suspend his judgment or defend his position. If participants can suspend judgment (listen without resistance), they can move to reflection and then generative dialogue—new thinking created as a result of dialogue.

- Reflect and Generate (if suspending is successful)

  If suspending is embraced, success in generating new ideas and solutions is possible. Participants who are able to do this can creatively problem solve and think together. On the other hand, if suspending judgment is not possible, the group will travel down a different road. They will either have a conversation or enter into debate.

- Defend and Converse (if suspending is not successful)

  If participants cannot suspend judgment and are stuck in defending positions, they can at best contribute to "skillful conversation" that is analytical, and may use hard data to get answers but simply represents reasoning made explicit. The conversation may be somewhat productive, but the interaction will not be particularly *creative*.

- Discuss and Debate (if suspending is not successful)

  At worst, defensiveness will have participants advocating and competing in "controlled discussion," perhaps moving into debate, which involves resolution by wearing each other down. Such interaction can rarely reach a creative or generative level.[14]

Simple, unobtrusive, but well-timed questions will help move a group from advocacy to inquiry when participants reach an impasse: "That's one opinion. What do the rest of you think?" Or just, "What do you think about that?" Or, "What other thoughts run through your head at this moment?" How to create effective questions and craft them so they are not invasive is part of the discussion to come in chapter 3 about running successful focus groups.

This picture of nurturing a culture of engagement describes authentic engagement: what it looks like in action and the foundational elements it needs to work well—trust and relationship building. Strong relationships are built on a foundation of trust that comes from listening without judgment, being willing to change one's mind, caring deeply about others' beliefs and values, and understanding all sides of an issue. Being open to learning and knowing both sides of an issue is a good strategy for understanding opposing perspectives. Knowing the trade-offs on all sides of an issue creates complexity that leads to deeper thinking and more sustainable solutions.

Chapter 4, Engaging Families/Stakeholders and Schools, includes concrete examples and approaches to help school and district facilitators design activities and structures for building trust and relationships and connecting with families, in particular, including engaging parents who typically would not connect readily with schools. It also provides suggestions for handling diverse needs of a variety of families.

PROMOTING GENERATIVE DIALOGUE: THE HEART OF COMMUNITY ENGAGEMENT

William Isaacs defines *dialogue* as a conversation with a center, not sides. It is a way of channeling the energy of our differences toward something never created before. Dialogue is exploratory. The key elements of dialogue are inquiry and reflection. Although the process serves as the foundation to decision-making, decisions are not made during dialogue. In "real dialogue," people do these things:

- come to the table as equals;
- think out loud together to learn one another's perspectives;
- uncover dissimilarities and examine them closely, appreciating the differences;
- explore pathways to common ground; and
- surface new insights through reflection.

* * *

A small group of people representing a Northwest coastal county decided to address low achievement outcomes for all learners in the area's public school system. They realized community support was essential to any significant change they sought. To that end, the group included a parent, two teachers, four administrators, one instructional assistant, a school board member, the Chamber of Commerce executive director, and representatives from a nearby Job Corps training center, the local community college, and the state commission on children and families. They called themselves the School Improvement Council.

During the following school year, the local council helped design a series of meetings to engage the community in a dialogue about school improvement. I facilitated a series of community forums, bringing about seventy participants together each time they met to answer these important questions:

1. *What does student success look like to you?*
2. *What should a high school graduate know and be able to do?*
3. *What are important skills all students should develop?*
4. *Of all we have talked about tonight, what is the heart of the matter for you?*
5. *What would have to be in place for students to succeed?*

In studying the written responses of small-group discussions at these sessions, the School Improvement Council identified common themes that consistently emerged. In the last forum stakeholders considered the themes, refined the work of the council, and prioritized the recommendations for what the district should measure to monitor progress. As a result of the opportunities for dialogue across stakeholder groups, the community reached understanding and agreements, helping the School Improvement Council meet the needs of the community's diverse populations. Without such intentional dialogue, the results might have been haphazard and ineffective.

Practices Promoting Success in Generative Dialogue

The following five practices foster success in generative dialogue:[15]

1. Respecting one another and listening to understand
   Respect for self and others includes embracing justice, compassion, and truth.
2. Suspending certainty
   When listening deeply, participants consider points of view with which they may not agree.
   Suspending the notion that a person's own position might be the only "right" thinking, will increase the ability for understanding.
3. Waiting for people to think

As people communicate their thoughts, listeners need time to think. The facilitator and participants need to embrace silence, providing time for connecting new ideas to old ones. The strategy of focusing people on listening helps them stop thinking about what they are going to say next while the current contributor is sharing thoughts. Sufficient time is needed for participants to inquire more deeply about what has been said to enhance their understanding.

4. Allowing space for differences

People come to any situation from divergent backgrounds and points of view. Building the expectation that ifferences in opinion will exist and are acceptable is part of the process.

5. Thinking and talking from awareness of many different perspectives

Paying attention to what other people are saying who may not agree with a personal point of view is a skill to be mastered. Visiting different places and people from other cultural and economic backgrounds in the community or traveling outside the country helps individuals learn about and better understand other cultures. Reading authors who hold different values than the reader expands understanding. There are many other ways to grow in awareness and speak with an underlying awareness of different perspectives.

Some learn to speak from awareness on the college debate team because they have to argue both sides of an issue. Others learn about different perspectives when they marry into families who see the world differently. When people know as much of the issue as possible, they can speak from awareness. Further, acknowledging that they may not have all the information, even that all the information may not be known, shows deep awareness.

"2.10 Practices Promoting Success in Generative Dialogue" in the workbook provides a bulleted handout of these practices for use in workshop settings.

Meeting the Challenges of Authentic Engagement

A partnership model among equals, engagement represents a major change in the historical relationship between educators and schools. It shifts power structures from the traditional hierarchy within an educational system to shared leadership. It builds ways to nurture leadership capacity among families and community members and enrich the organization's practices. It involves letting go of control and power in order to have it come back.

*   *   *

A large private school in the South struggled with those very power issues. The hierarchical structure fostered secrets and held tightly to control. In spite of parents who were enthusiastic about having their children at the school, the school administration did not perceive that the voice of parents or the teachers needed to be part of decision-making deliberations. Administrators felt teachers should teach, not make decisions outside of their classrooms, and parents should raise money but stay out of the classroom.

Eventually both parents and staff became dissatisfied with the ongoing status quo and their inability to effect changes they felt were needed. When the administrators were persuaded to conduct focus groups, they discovered that participants wanted a greater voice in the school. In response, they created a plan to engage parents, alumni, and teachers in their visioning and change process. They took the first steps in establishing a culture of engagement.

Moving forward with such a plan involves exploring ways to share power and decision-making in schools and districts. That can be threatening. The board, superintendent, principals, and teachers must recognize that they cannot fulfill their roles and meet their goals in isolation. Listening, valuing, and embracing the ideas of others fosters more participatory ways of deliberating and acting collaboratively.[16]

Skill-Building for Leaders and Participants

Successful engagement efforts develop leaders and ordinary citizens within diverse constituent groups who are thoughtful, knowledgeable, and able to see the larger picture. Often stakeholders simply do not know how to have conversations, do not know how to dialogue, and do not know how to inquire about the ideas of others or advocate successfully. It's important to teach specific skills, like how to listen without judging, ask questions to understand the perspectives of others, be comfortable with the silence in which people can think, trust the structure of group process, participate in deep dialogue, generate novel solutions, and plan for effective action. Building stakeholders' skills ensures engagement will be more deeply embedded in the culture rather than be closely held by privileged groups. Later chapters provide a number of specific skills to help both leaders and participants engage more effectively.

Action Orientation

Educators, families, and communities can create new futures together strategically and collaboratively. Authentic engagement processes generate new directions to realize those futures. The job of educational leaders is to innovate and integrate approaches designed and orchestrated to form alliances, coalitions, forums, and other structures to include all voices, build deep trust, and provide time for thoughtful deliberation and careful decision-making.[17] Planning and taking concrete action is the next step to change.

However, challenges to taking effective action are real. Tackling them methodically as part of a community planning process is essential. The following list reflects elements requiring concrete planning in even the earliest vision-building activities for engaging stakeholders so goal-oriented action can be undertaken in the end.

- Convincing citizens as well as educators that the work of authentic engagement can change the nature of schools and communities
- Building trust in hostile climates, increasing the civility of dialogue in the process
- Enhancing understanding by using strategies of engagement
- Finding ways to ensure everyone's voice is heard
- Implementing the practices of generative dialogue that can lead to creative solutions and effective action
- Being patient and listening deeply
- Creating an environment in which dialogue can occur
- Deepening relationships among diverse stakeholders
- Broadening and deepening the involvement of constituents in decision-making processes
- Breaking through walls of misunderstanding and ignorance by using effective protocols
- Ensuring stakeholder engagement results in action aligned with their insights and visions

- Supporting staff and stakeholder leaders as they incorporate engagement strategies into their own practices

The ensuing chapters elaborate on ways to overcome the challenges and succeed in engaging stakeholders authentically in dialogue to successfully move people toward action and making a difference.

TAKEAWAY MESSAGES FROM THIS CHAPTER

- Authentic engagement is powerful in connecting citizens to each other and to their schools.
- Twelve characteristics distinguish schools that engage families and their communities authentically.
- Eight principles of authentic engagement include mind-sets, practices, and structures that will ensure success in bringing everyone into the process of moving schools forward and participating in democracy.
- Creating a pervasive culture of engagement is based on building trust and developing relationships; six discrete conditions foster both.
- Ten strategies accessible to everyone involved are fundamental to building trust.
- The skills of sharing story; analyzing ideas to understand the inferences, assumptions, and intents within participants in any process; and being willing to inquire deeply into divergent perspectives will lead to better understanding, greater civility, and higher trust.
- The ability of a group to promote generative dialogue is fundamental to creating sustainable solutions to complex problems.
- Everyone needs specific skills in order to be successful in fostering authentic engagement.
- Dialogue leads to innovative ideas.

HELPFUL RESOURCES RELATED TO THIS CHAPTER

- William Isaacs's *Dialogue and the Art of Thinking Together* is a comprehensive look at the rationale, principles, and practices of dialogue. Practitioners who want a much deeper understanding of the process and applications of dialogue will find this book invaluable in refining their ability to convene dialogue.

- Bob Chadwick hosts consensus-building training for facilitators. His publications include many strategies for using circles, asking key questions, making collective statements, and managing change. His website at http://consensusinstitutes.co includes how to contact him and access his materials.

- In *Schools That Learn: A Fifth Discipline Fieldbook for Educators, Parents, and Everyone Who Cares about Education,* Peter Senge and his colleagues describe in detail, with illustrative graphics, the concepts and processes of using the ladder of inference and dialogue in the context of schools working more effectively on behalf of students.

- William Isaacs provides rich insights into the process of dialogue as part of Peter Senge's book called *The Fifth Discipline Fieldbook: Strategies and Tools for Building a Learning Organization.*

- Christina Baldwin and Ann Linnea present a sensitive look at the processes and practices of working in a circle format within a variety of school and corporate settings in *The Circle Way: A Leader in Every Chair.*

Complete bibliographical information for these resources is located in the reference list at the back of this book.

NOTES

1. Bohm, *Thought as a System.*
2. Scharmer and Kauder, *Leading from the Emerging Future,* 3, 5.
3. Adapted and extended from Annenberg Institute, *Reasons for Hope, Voices for Change,* 53.
4. Bryk and Schneider, *Trust in Schools,* 11, 22–26.
5. Bill Richardson, in a speech heard by Leslie on an unspecified occasion.
6. Leslie, "ABCs of Community Involvement," 3.
7. Bryk and Schneider suggest these four vital signs in *Trust in Schools,* 22–26.
8. The helpful questions to prompt reflection about Bryk and Schneider's four vital signs are by Cathy Fromme, "The Importance of Trust in Schools."
9. Block, *Community: The Structure of Belonging,* xi.
10. Baldwin, *Storycatcher,* 231.
11. Senge et al., *Schools That Learn,* 68–71.
12. The rungs of this ladder have been adapted from Senge and his coauthors, who included their ladder of inference in the "mental models" section of their book *Schools That Learn,* 71. The use of a mental model such as this is one of Senge's five disciplines.

13. Isaacs, *Dialogue and the Art of Thinking Together*, 199–202. The examples provided here are drawn from these pages in which Isaacs describes Kantor's "four-player actions" and how to listen for the underlying intentions or motives behind them.

14. Isaacs, *Dialogue and the Art of Thinking Together*, 41.

15. Adapted from Public Agenda, publicagenda.org.

16. Leighninger and Levine, "Education in a Rapidly Changing Democracy: Strengthening Civic Education for Citizens of All Ages." *School Administrator* 25–28.

17. Leslie, "I Used to Believe." Used with permission of the National School Public Relations Association (www.NSPRA.org).

THREE

Collecting and Using Stakeholder Research

ENGAGING STAKEHOLDERS IN ACTION RESEARCH

Effective research engages stakeholders deeply and authentically in sharing information that reveals what they are thinking and the reasons they think the way they do. Data gleaned from research projects can leverage action and move schools and communities forward in surprising ways. Research is also inherently political when it addresses value-laden issues such as race, social class, and ideology. It is used to advance political agendas, form policy, and make decisions about where students attend school, what curriculum content and instructional practices are implemented, why students drop out of school, how long a school day or year is, whether to hire directive or collaborative school leaders, how students are tested, how high standards are set, and how they will be measured.

As stated in the introduction, there are two models of democracy: representational aggregative democracy and participatory associational democracy. *Research* as described in this chapter is primarily a function of representational aggregative democracy because it is a method in which the desires, preferences, and concerns of the stakeholders are collected, measured, and considered by the administration and the representatives (school board or other governmental entities) of the population. However, one method of research called focus groups or listening sessions is a *process* of collecting information that is deliberative associational democracy. Participants associate with one another by dialoguing and deliberating over issues prompted by the facilitator. They participate by engaging with one another. The outcome of the dialogue is never certain, the participants control the dialogue, the questions do not lead, and new ways to approach an issue or problem may be generated as a result of the collective thinking.

Although collecting research can be an endeavor fraught with challenges, data can often be gathered quickly and make significant differences in outcomes.

*   *   *

For example, in one very fast-growing section of a suburban school district, the superintendent decided, without consultation, to bus kindergarten students from five schools to kindergarten centers to be located in less crowded schools in another part of the district. He believed it would temporarily alleviate the overcrowding situation until a new school could be built. He reasoned it would be less disruptive to fewer people, and the youngest children could adjust more easily because they were not yet attached to their schools. As soon as the proposed decision became public, angry families raised concerns. Newspapers and electronic media reported the outrage throughout the community and state. The superintendent was on the hot seat.

It was suggested focus groups be organized quickly to hear concerns and collect ideas for solving the problem. Within four days, twelve listening sessions/ focus groups were convened with no difficulty recruiting participants whose values were being challenged. Angry but reasonable participants said they would not send their children to schools across the district. They asked what "temporary" meant. Would their even younger babies still at home be subject to the same "idiotic" plan? They said they would rather transfer their children to private schools or keep them home than have very young children traveling on a bus up to forty-five minutes each way and be separated from their older brothers and sisters. Focus group participants said they would live with the crowded conditions until a new school was built and would organize and work to pass a bond measure. The superintendent smartly decided the children would not be bused. Families worked quickly and diligently to successfully pass a bond and build a new school.

> "The trouble with the world is the stupid are cocksure and the intelligent are full of doubt."
> —Bertrand Russell

This chapter presents a variety of research techniques facilitators use to gather information about local constituents, communities, staff members, and families. It focuses primarily on focus group research because this methodology engages participants through dialogue and challenges them to think more deeply. It describes how to plan for, organize, and conduct focus groups, as well as how to collect, analyze, and report the data.

The Importance of Research in Engagement Efforts

Too many times, people state opinions based on inferences, make broad generalizations or statements, are sure they are right, and have no tolerance for other ways or answers. But many of those conclusions or generalizations are not supported with data or substantiated with valid primary research. There are others who have well-researched information and understand an issue from many different perspectives but are slow to act because they are uncertain about what decision to make in light of all the data.

How can decision-makers become well informed and move forward with reasonable certainty? With very complex issues, it is unlikely they will have complete certainty. But it is possible for decision-makers to be well informed through a variety of methods and to take action, knowing they have the best information available at the time. Good decision-making results from collecting data; reading or listening to respected, successful experts and strategists; reviewing case studies; visiting successful programs; understanding and knowing the data in a sphere of influence; learning how others handle a similar situation; and asking stakeholders what they think and how they would address the issue. Once a decision is made, research can measure how well the decision is implemented and if the intended results are realized.

Before launching any research effort, it is necessary to understand how to communicate and use the results. Determining the answers to the following questions helps the organization decide how to proceed: Does my district want to *listen*, observe, learn, and be open to influence? Or is my district closed to feedback? Does my district want to *tell* stakeholders the way it is, make decisions in isolation, and do research to change others' points of view? Is my district an open system or a closed system? Unfortunately, some organizations conduct research only because they want people to think they are interested in them or care about them—a sure way to destroy trust.

What often angers participants who take part in research opportunities is an organization that does not report the results and does what it wants to do anyway. Focus group participants frequently say, "Well, I've told the district over and over but they just don't care what I think." Unfortunately, sometimes a district is unwilling to communicate research findings and/or use the findings in its planning or decision-making. Educators may not have liked the results, or they may believe the findings will not help them because they do not have confidence in the public's ideas.

There are other reasons why a district may not implement certain recommendations from participants in a research study, and it is important they understand why. It may be because the suggestion is not in agreement with what the majority of constituents want, it may be against the law, contradict proven research, or any number of reasons. Organizations build stakeholder trust by considering their opinions carefully, communicating the results of research studies affecting them, and stating why recommendations or ideas were or were not considered or implemented. It tells research respondents they matter and their ideas are important.

Researching what stakeholders think and desire is important to the long-term success of a school or district because schools belong to the families, students, staff, and the entire community. To be respected, credible, and successful, educators must be in sync with their stakeholders' interests, needs, and priorities. Demographics and public opinion change quickly and often, so it is useful to conduct studies on a regular basis. The community's concerns and interests keep educators from becoming complacent and resting on past accomplishments. However, the school/district cannot rely totally on public opinion when making decisions. Looking at the big picture and making good decisions calls for integrating many different sources of information and using a variety of research methodologies.

"3.1 Why Research?" in the companion workbook, *The Politics of Authentic Engagement: Tools for Engaging Stakeholders in Ensuring Student Success*, provides a handout containing rationale for doing research.

Choosing the Most Effective Research Methodology

To choose and shape the most effective research approach, project leaders ask essential questions in three categories:

1. Purpose and importance of the research

- What is the purpose of the study and what do you want to know?
- Who will use the information?
- Why do you want to know the information?

The research purpose defines the entire effort. Sometimes not everything planners want to know benefits the overall project in terms of eventual decision-making. Further, the answers to some questions can be detrimental to the project.

* * *

For example, in spite of being cautioned against asking such questions, the superintendent of one school district insisted focus group constituents be asked to rate their satisfaction with him as a superintendent and judge how well the district was managing money. When the responses were extremely negative, he refused to communicate the survey results. The superintendent's lack of transparency further generated a loss of confidence in him and in the district. It would have been better not to ask the questions in the first place.

2. Data-gathering sources and strategies

- What methodology do you want to use?
- Who do you want to participate in the study?
- When is the information needed?
- What is the best way to get the data, given the time frame?
- What degree of validity or reliability is desired in the results?
- What are the advantages and disadvantages of each research strategy under consideration?
- To what degree will any single form of research meet the organization's needs?
- To what degree will a combination of approaches better serve the needs?
- Who will write the questions?
- Who will interview the respondents?

Depending on what the organization wants to know, it may choose to survey, interview, hold focus groups, or a combination of these strategies. For example, if a district wants to find more time in a school day for instruction, a good starting place is a teacher survey. The survey could ask teachers how much time they spend on various duties such as preparing lessons, disciplining students, determining grades, checking homework, and transitioning from one activity to another. The survey results represent the current state that is crucial in weighing against potential alternatives.

They could also use a survey to measure support for or against various models to lengthen the school day. In this case, beginning with a survey would allow many teachers to provide baseline information, and using a different survey later in the process could help the district refine effective options. However, if the district wanted to go deeper to see how effective time allocation was and what the barriers might be to increasing time in school, focus groups would be more effective in surfacing those details.

*   *   *

An example of this approach occurred when a district chose to launch its study on lengthening the school day by asking teachers in focus groups how they were using time. Teachers said they needed more instructional time but thought it could be found within the current schedule. They expressed concern over too many initiatives and demands. They said existing instructional time was fragmented, particularly at the elementary level, by pull-out programs. They identified practices and conditions that could be redefined or eliminated in order to increase instructional time within existing schedules. Their ideas included these:

- *reduce class size*
- *hire more support staff*
- *reduce clerical or other duties for the teacher*
- *rely less on substitutes for staff training sessions or meetings*
- *eliminate or restructure SSR (Sustained Silent Reading)*
- *eliminate or reduce student advisory time*
- *provide more effective staff development for teachers*
- *examine the amount of time for and format of parent conferences*

In addition, participants responded to a number of possible scheduling modifica-tions (i.e., year-round school, extended day), considering both positive and nega-tive impacts. In this case, focus groups were the best way to obtain the needed information. Such groups provided an environment in which teachers thought together and bounced ideas off one another to create better ideas and solutions.

The time study in the school district continued for many months during which pros and cons were identified for various proposals and all stakeholder groups became engaged through additional focus groups, forums, surveys, and interviews. The district finally settled on a multipronged approach that was cost-effective and reflected the ideas and suggestions of all the groups. The sugges-tions teachers made in the initial focus groups were foundational to future work.

Study participants are randomly selected from all constituencies affected by the issue or served by the organization. If a community college wants to know what classes to offer, what time to offer them, and what the perceptions of the school are, its priority is to draw information from current and potential *students*. If it wants to measure how successful or unsuccessful classes have been, it would identify past students. If it wants to measure the general level of satisfaction of the college, it might survey current students, community members, colleges receiving the stu-dents, and employers hiring them. The required information determines the question format, as well: will an open-ended question format yield the results needed, or is it necessary to narrow possibilities to shorter, more controlled responses?

3. Usage and communication of results

- How will the results be compiled?
- How will the results be used?
- How will the results be communicated?

Regardless of the research strategy or strategies chosen, it is important for the researcher and organization to decide how to communicate the re-sults before beginning the research. The best approach for the school or district is to *share* the results with the community or, at the very least, the people who contributed to the data collected. As difficult as it is for an organization to face harsh feedback, sharing difficult results will help the research process raise the level of trust between stakeholders and the school or district.

Can all options proposed in multiple-choice question formats be implemented? Sometimes in multiple-choice questions, the district does not have the resources to implement an answer choice. If most respondents make that choice, the district creates a trust issue when it cannot make the choice happen. Raising expectations and then not meeting them breaks trust.

"3.2 Questions to Ask before Beginning Research" in the companion workbook contains a list of the essential research-related questions useful to planning teams.

Research Design

Determining the research design depends on the purpose, the stakeholder group, the data desired, time constraints, and budget. Below are three major designs most often used by schools.

1. *Historical research* is conducted to learn the context in which the issues and challenges under investigation arose. Especially when conducting a systems audit, it is important to know the cause, effects, and meaning of certain actions, as well as their applicability to the current study. Such static data are obtained by reviewing documentary sources or records such as test scores, policies, board testimony, past surveys and studies, curriculum development documents, and budgets. Historical research is most effective using primary sources.

2. *Observational/descriptive research* is a qualitative investigation describing a situation. It processes data taken in through observation. There are three ways to obtain descriptive research: personal observation, case study, and survey methods. Observational studies are often used in education to describe, for example, a classroom situation, citizen behavior at school board meetings, or participant dialogues. Other descriptive research is conducted through focus groups, interviews, and questionnaires. Descriptive statistics provide information such as sample size, demographics, and observations. Observational/descriptive research results, predominantly drawn from verbal exchanges as the products of inquiries, show trends and patterns that provide directional information on what exists now. The rich data obtained may form the basis for more detailed analytical investigations.

3. *Analytical survey research* is quantitative research that analyzes and measures the data collected. It tests statistically based hypotheses using statistical tools to infer deeper meaning, which lies hidden in the data. The research describes and answers why something exists. Educators may collect quantitative research to measure satisfaction levels among all stakeholder groups or to determine the extent to which there is support for a program, election measure, or new curriculum design.[1]

Strategies for Collecting Information

In an open-system district, research will have a high priority. To get the best results and most useful information, organizations use different data collection methods. Some involve more formal research and others more informal. For example, an electronic attitude survey can be combined with focus group research to probe more deeply into issues of interest emerging from the collected data. A *quantitative* attitude survey provides statistically valid information; whereas the *qualitative* data gathered from focus groups, soft soundings, and other descriptive research provides reasons and motivation behind opinions expressed in the analytical survey, thus enriching the total picture.

The following list briefly describes five relevant research techniques for schools and communities:

1. Soft soundings

    This qualitative research approach is the easiest and most readily available to use. It simply involves asking anyone—teachers in the staff room, family members visiting the school, constituents in the grocery checkout line—questions about how something is going for them or what they are thinking about a particular issue or question. Educators, students, parents, and community leaders can do soft soundings constantly whenever they are with another person or group of people by asking what they think and feel. It is an informal way to obtain information—as easy as asking, "What do you think about the levy the district is putting on the ballot?" This can also be done electronically through Twitter or other social media.

    Advantages: Soft soundings provide quick, easy directional information anyone can obtain. People asking questions hear many different perspectives, and their interest shows respondents their opinion is important. People enjoy sharing what they think.

Disadvantages: Soft soundings do not provide statistically valid information and may not provide clear direction.

2. Questionnaires

Questionnaires include either descriptive (qualitative) data or analytical (quantitative) data and can be distributed in person, through the mail, e-mail, or Web pages.

Advantages: Questionnaires are generally less costly than personal interviews. The question sequence is controlled, and respondents can look up information before they respond. Although not all respondents trust the surveyor's assurances, survey results can be submitted anonymously, often generating more candid and truthful responses.

Disadvantages: Because surveys are likely to be identified by the look of an envelope or declared as such by the surveyor online, they are often ignored, deleted, or tossed out, reducing response rates. Unless something directly impacts recipients or deals with an issue they really care about, they often do not even read what is inside the e-mail or envelope. Further, the task of keeping an e-mail database updated is challenging.

Obtaining scientifically valid and accurate results is not possible unless every member of the population in the study has an equal chance of participating. A representative sample of e-mail addresses is not usually possible to obtain because not everyone has e-mail and e-mail addresses are not public. Just as in telephone surveys, nonresponse bias influences the result, because people who are not interested do not respond to the Web or e-mail requests.

Questions on a survey can be answered out of order, causing confusion. As with all other prescriptive surveys, respondents may be limited in their answers by the choices given unless the survey provides space for open-ended questions. Respondents also cannot probe for more information or get answers to questions they have when filling out the survey, so misunderstandings cannot be clarified, potentially muddying the results.

3. Telephone survey

A telephone survey is a scripted set of questions about an issue used by an interviewer to gather responses from a selected audience via telephone.

Advantages: Phone surveys counter some of the disadvantages of mail, e-mail, or an online survey because the question order can be controlled and misunderstandings clarified on the spot before or while respondents answer. The questioner can also probe for deeper information as appropriate. It is less costly than doing personal interviews and can be completed quickly. Most important, phone surveys are considered more statistically valid than mail or electronic surveys because there is more control over the process.

Disadvantages: Obtaining a random sample of respondents is more difficult because answering machines and unlisted numbers introduce bias. People with caller ID often do not answer unknown phone numbers, or if messages are left, users simply delete them when they realize it is a survey call. Only people without those devices and services tend to answer calls, skewing the survey result. Valid and reliable results require costly and time-consuming interviewer training. In recent years, telephone surveys have become a much less useful tool, although research companies that conduct telephone surveys would not agree with this statement.

4. Personal interviews

A personal interview is a qualitative interaction appropriate to use with a limited number of respondents. It is a costly but efficient way to get information from a small targeted group such as media representatives, business leaders, or parents whose children dropped out of school. Highly skilled interviewers are an asset because they know how to compare and synthesize responses and highlight patterns. When interviewers are not trained, they are more apt to pick out anomalies—the startling odd comment just one person shares—because that is what catches their attention. Unfortunately, including such outlier information introduces interviewer bias into results.

Advantages: The interviewer can probe and clarify easily as questioning proceeds, use visual aids, and pick up nonverbal cues.

Disadvantages: Highly skilled interviewers are expected to obtain extensive and high-quality information. The amount of time needed to gather the data is more time-consuming and expensive.

5. Focus groups

   Focus groups are an increasingly popular way to capture real-life data in social settings. A carefully planned dialogue is held in a permissive, nonthreatening social environment. The study is designed to obtain data on perceptions in a defined area of interest. It includes a small number of invited participants (about eight to ten) who are interested in the issue or topic. It is conducted usually by a skilled facilitator and is most often an enjoyable experience for the participants. It differs in many ways from all of the data collection strategies identified above. Carefully designed questions and group dynamics stimulate conversation and deeper thinking. Participants influence one another, often changing their minds about issues as a result of the dialogue. Focus group research is a qualitative approach to gathering information that is both inductive and naturalistic.[2]

   Advantages: Using focus groups provides an opportunity to obtain more in-depth information including feelings, attitudes, beliefs, values, and the reasons and motivations for participants thinking, believing, and valuing what they do. Nonverbal gestures including facial expressions can be observed and recorded to determine if the spoken words are aligned with body language. Because participants exchange different viewpoints, focus groups can generate new ideas and solutions, which cannot occur with the other identified strategies. It is less costly than many other forms of data collection. The results can be obtained quickly and have high face validity. They identify trends and patterns in perceptions. Results are powerful and can lead to recommendations and change based on community values. The direct quotations included in the report often prompt decision-makers to action.

   Disadvantages: It is often difficult to recruit focus group members. They face differing work and family schedules, child-care needs, and transportation obstacles. Districts frequently offer incentives, such as a meal, games for children, cash, or a drawing for a gift certificate to attract focus group participants. The results are qualitative and, therefore, are not statistically valid, although valid trends and patterns can be identified. Even with a highly skilled moderator, groups can be dominated by strong personalities, leaving the facilitator with less control of the process. Differences in makeup among groups responding on the same topic can be troublesome. Data are more difficult and time-intensive to analyze because the data are verbal and observational. Often information recorded is transcribed in narrative form and can be coded by hand (most trusted method) or processed by a computer using a software program.[3]

While all five research approaches can play a role in gathering balanced information and may be used together to provide a more complete picture, focus groups engage participants in a more personal, meaningful way and often provide information uncovering the motivations and reasons why participants think and feel as they do. According to the late political consultant Lee Atwater, the conversations in focus groups "give you a sense of what makes people tick and a sense of what is going on with people's minds and lives that you simply can't get with survey data."

"3.3 Types of Data Collection: Advantages and Disadvantages" in the workbook provides a handout summarizing these five typically used techniques.

FOCUS GROUP PROCESSES AND STRATEGIES

A focus group is a set of individuals selected to provide feedback to an organization about a current issue, question, or proposal. Many groups can be formed on the same topic to provide a cross section of responses and ideas, ensuring greater sharing of perceptions.

Planning for Focus Groups

Successful focus groups share six common characteristics:

1. Nonthreatening environment

When people feel safe, they talk openly and freely, especially when discussing sensitive subjects. A safe environment means a comfortable social situation for group members. Often places other than the school setting, such as churches, community centers, apartment complexes, rooms, or other safe gathering places in their neighborhoods, are good places to conduct focus groups.

2. Homogeneity

Richer information is obtained when people of similar backgrounds, common interests, and the same status or socioeconomic level comprise a single focus group. Homogeneous groups have a more productive dialogue because participants feel safer. Other homogeneous categories to consider are occupation, educational level, age, family characteristics, and ethnicity. However, people selected to be included from each category do not have to *think* the same about issues. Including people who do not know each other is also helpful; the risk of sharing information is lower when a member believes s/he may never see other participants again. Although not always possible in small communities where everyone knows each other, it is the ideal.

*   *   *

For example, when we facilitated a comprehensive safety study in a district of great diversity and talked with parents of gay students, we made sure those parents were only with other parents of gay students. We invited parents of special education students to be in a group by themselves, each reflecting the differing ages of their children. Gifted students were in one group, and parents of gifted students in another. We talked with Hispanic girls separately from Hispanic boys, acknowledging that in that culture girls will not usually speak up when boys and girls are together. We organized Muslim groups similarly.

Without homogeneous group composition, results can be significantly skewed and group members may be intimidated by individuals who shut down the participation of anyone different from themselves.

*   *   *

I learned firsthand the importance of homogeneity and safety in a group when conducting focus groups on floating logging camps in Alaska. Local educators recruited all ten mothers in the camp to participate in the focus group. One mother was the wife of the foreman. I began by asking, "When I say education for your children on this floating log camp, what comes to your mind?" Before answering this and the remaining questions, all the mothers looked to the foreman's wife, making sure what they said was okay. I could not get them to disclose their feelings, concerns, or fears. They talked only about what was working. The foreman's wife's unspoken power was too threatening. Fortunately, the district let us conduct the focus group again, minus the foreman's wife. We discovered that many issues were not being addressed, primarily regarding children's safety.

3. Openness to influence

Participants influence each other as they respond to ideas and comments during dialogue. Though participants are in a homogeneous group, they hold different views on issues that contribute to generating new ideas and solutions. Focus groups are not designed to seek consensus on final solutions, but as perspectives are shared, participants influence each other and delve more deeply into the issues. This creates a healthy situation: it contributes to group members comparing and contrasting positions, or even shifting their viewpoints.

4. Powerful questions

The focus group process engages participants through verbal questions. Unlike most survey questions, focus group questions are open-ended and designed to stimulate dialogue and elicit many different responses. Questions are the heart of the focus group process and need to be carefully planned ahead of time. Because a focus group session lasts only one to two hours, the number of questions is limited to four or five. If designed correctly, one question may take up to an hour to discuss fully. Questions to avoid include prompts that can be answered with a "yes" or "no" because they cut off dialogue and questions that ask "why" because they can be seen as too invasive. Asking, "What happened?" or "What brought you to this conclusion?" or "How did you come to think this way?" invites participants to open up and talk more freely.

When planning, list all *potential* questions about the topic. Deciding on a question path is the next step, starting with where participants are in their understanding of the issue. It focuses participants on something very easy to talk about, moves from the past to the present, general to the specific, and starts within a very familiar context. For example, if a school's issue is teaching excellence, the first question could be, "Think of the best teacher you have had in all of your education and talk about what the teacher did to make you think he or she was excellent." The next question might be, "Now tell me what qualities you think teachers need today to ensure students are successful and prepared for the future."

A focus group is not a group interview in which questions are posed with the facilitator moving from one person to the next to obtain an answer. Rather, a question is placed before the group and participants discuss it among themselves. The emphasis during the session is on discussion and probing meaning rather than asking a series of questions.

"3.4 Guidelines for Asking Good Questions" in the workbook provides sample questions for each guideline. "3.5 Sample Questions for Focus Groups" gives facilitators some examples of possible questions.

5. Small size

Each group needs to be small enough to allow everyone to express opinions in the allotted time, say what they want to say, and participate in an interesting dialogue that generates helpful information for the organization. At the same time, groups need to be large enough to provide a *diversity* of opinions so the discussion will generate new thinking. Although experts say the best group size is seven to ten people, mini-focus groups of four to six people are possible. Groups of more than twelve participants, however, become fragmented and are difficult to moderate.

6. Skillful facilitator

Selecting a moderator who has the ability to create a safe, receptive environment quickly and move participants through well-designed questions is essential to getting useful information for decision-makers. Determining whether the facilitator should be a third party or an employee of the organization is a consideration. To reduce costs a district may decide to use employees or volunteers to facilitate. For example, if the school or district wants to gather information from a disenfranchised group, it is preferable for the facilitator to be of the same culture, gender, or sexual preference, or is in some other way representative of a particular group, though not someone in a power position within the school system.

A public relations person usually has a good understanding of group dynamics, may already have experience in facilitation, or can be trained. Others who can be coached to facilitate include parent leaders, teachers, or students—anyone who has experience working with groups, listens well, and can record what people are saying. Though not ideal, getting useful basic information is still possible without using a professional, paid facilitator if s/he is well trained in moderating groups and processing data.

In addition to creating good questions for group participants to consider, a capable, well-trained facilitator plays a key role in the success of the focus group process. Demonstrating these effective facilitator behaviors is essential:

- Be a good *listener* who can quickly establish an invitational rapport with the group;
- Be familiar and comfortable with *group processes*;
- Exercise mild *gentle control* over the group, which involves sensing when to be silent and listen, when to let the group go where it will go, and when to transition to other content;
- Make *transitions* to keep the discussion moving by summarizing periodically and moving people on;
- Maintain *group enthusiasm* by using humor and making eye contact with people;
- Have adequate *background knowledge* of the issue, its context, and organizational priorities;
- *Remain neutral* by avoiding sharing any personal points of view and not using gestures such as head nodding or facial expressions able to be construed as agreement with one person's opinion over another;
- *Avoid correcting* any inaccurate information unless the group corrects it spontaneously;
- *Resist becoming engaged* in any way in a conversation with participants;
- *Deflect questions* group members may ask to engage the facilitator; and
- Still *come across as human*, caring, and interested to learn what people have to say.

The companion workbook includes two helpful tools related to these questions and planning for focus groups. "3.6 Questions to Ask before You Start Focus Groups" presents the full list of questions. "3.7 Focus Group Timeline and Responsibilities" provides an easy-to-use checklist to ensure all focus group planning steps are accomplished.

Inviting Focus Group Participants

Many stakeholders were trying to remove the superintendent and people were angry. I had completed all the focus groups when a group of teachers showed up—uninvited. They asked if they could talk with me, saying, "We are the people who are very unhappy and you have not heard from us. We decided you needed to." It was an eye-opening session. It uncovered many issues and feelings that had not been surfaced in other focus groups. Although I had to put the information in context with the rest of what I had heard from others, it gave me an entirely different perspective. In order to protect themselves, district administrators had organized the focus groups without including this group.

One of the hardest steps in the process of conducting focus groups is recruiting participants and getting them there. Sometimes schools pick the people who are most active and supportive. Selecting most participants randomly will net better results. Existing lists (parents, community leaders, volunteer lists) can be used as a basis, choosing every fifth name, for example, so friends or supportive individuals are not the only people chosen.

Although initial selection of a random group is important, it may also be essential—especially when doing research on complex issues—to invite a few others who know the topic more deeply, can verbalize and express opinions well, and serve as catalysts in moving conversation forward. Unless the focus group is designed to gather information from administrators specifically, they should not participate in or even listen in on a group made up of staff, family, or community members.

When the research calls for meeting with constituents, such as senior citizens, preschool parents, or businesspeople, organizations in the community can identify potential research participants. The Chamber of Commerce, senior citizen groups, churches, social service agencies, political parties, mental health organizations, business partners, and housing cooperatives are a few examples. Asking each of those entities to suggest names or organize groups to participate in the study will make the recruitment process easier.

Although some research recommends using four separate focus groups for each homogeneous category identified, fewer groups done well can generate sound data. Sometimes two groups from the same category will be so different in their thinking that a third group from the same category may be needed to clarify themes. Because there are so many different stakeholder groups in a district, leaders sometimes want up to twenty or more focus groups. However, most districts can afford closer to twelve sessions. Large national research organizations do this kind of work with only five focus groups across the country and still collect good qualitative data. It depends on what the district wants to know and from whom.

Once participants have been identified, invitations are sent out so they are received about three weeks before the session. For ten to twelve people to attend, at least twenty invitations are needed. The invitation list needs to include correct spelling of names, addresses (e-mail and home), and phone numbers. The invitation includes the purpose of the study, when and where the session will be held, descriptions of any incentives to be offered for attending, and a phone number and/or e-mail address to which to respond. In addition, those invited need to receive background information so they can talk intelligently when they arrive at the group session. Letters still carry more weight than e-mail, but if invitees have shared other preferred ways to receive the information, those desires should be met. In all cases, the invitations and information sheets should be in the language of the recipients.

To encourage attendance, invitees must be contacted eight to ten days after the invitations are sent, thanking those who have responded and asking those who have not if they received the letter and can attend. A call or e-mail to all participants the day before the session will remind them of the date and time of the session and ensure greater participation.

"3.8 Sample Invitation and Messages" in the workbook includes a sample letter, adaptable to local situations.

Facilitating Focus Groups

Facilitating focus groups is a straightforward process: the facilitator creates an atmosphere in which a conversation among participants draws out perceptions, information, and feelings about the topic at hand. In a compact time frame, the skilled facilitator uses time judiciously. To start the group, the facilitator sets a friendly and accepting tone, introduces him/herself, outlines ground rules, and gives a brief overview of the session. Facilitators vary in whether they prefer to have participants introduce themselves. Not doing so sometimes preserves a greater sense of anonymity; if group members do use names, it is first names only.

Introduce the topic of interest to the participants, the purpose of the focus groups, and definitions of any key words in the purpose statement. Next, the well-crafted set of questions leads respondents gently down a logical pathway to elicit conversation among participants. At times, the

facilitator pursues deeper information and follows new directions generated by the discussion.

Ground Rules for Focus Groups

As a focus group session begins, it is important to share rules, processes, and rationale for collecting information and make agreements for how
everyone will relate to one another. Elements to address include these:

- Confidentiality: Talking about the need for confidentiality raises
  participants' feelings of safety in the environment. Letting group
  members know the that facilitator will not attribute any remarks to
  particular people is the first step, followed by communicating that
  the same expectation exists for participants. Asking for and observing a head nod from each person individually around the table or
  circle to confirm they will observe these rules of confidentiality is
  critical, whether or not the session is being recorded.
- Side conversations: None are permitted while another group member is speaking.
- Interruptions: None are permitted while someone is speaking.
- Questions: Facilitators are not experts on the subject; in focus
  groups they listen only. They refrain from answering questions
  from participants during the process except in the introduction,
  when participants may ask questions about the process itself. The
  moderator may record the questions and have someone get back to
  the participants who asked.
- Time frame: Reaffirming the beginning and ending time reinforces
  the effort to stay on track. The facilitator's role includes moving the
  discussion along, keeping members from dominating the conversation, and ending the session on time.
- Speaking with candor: Honest statements about perceptions and
  feelings on the issues are welcome.

Resources for Focus Groups

- A *recording device* is essential to create a record of each member's
  contributions to the group. Drawn from the recording, verbatim
  quotations are often powerful messages to include in the focus
  group report. Although companies frequently videotape focus
  groups, some facilitators believe video reduces trust levels with the

loss of anonymity. It is important that whatever tools are in the room do not compromise the level of trust necessary for frank conversation.

- Not every facilitator can do all the tasks of questioning, recording, and monitoring, as well as keeping the group moving. Although not usually necessary, an *assistant facilitator* can be helpful in several ways as long as s/he has a specific role to play and abides by the confidentiality rules. One important role the assistant facilitator can serve is to be of the same affinity group, such as gender or race, as members of the homogeneous group identified for research, especially if the facilitator is not. The assistant facilitator can also take notes, watch for nonverbal responses, and do other tasks so they are not viewed as only a silent observer. That individual can be anybody who is trusted—a parent, community member, or even a teacher. Another role filled by an assistant facilitator is serving as a translator interpreting for group members who speak other languages.
- "3.9 Focus Group Facilitator Script" in the workbook provides a model for facilitating the processes of a focus group.
- "3.10 A Focus Group Script for Students" is also available there.

Additional Facilitation Skills

Four skills a good focus group facilitator uses are: probing for more information, maintaining mild control over the group, possessing a good sense of timing, and being comfortable with silence.

1. *Probing* for more information is only necessary if participants have strayed off course, have merely covered the surface, or have stalled in their conversation. Questions and statements can stimulate conversation: Please explain further. Can you give me an example? Is there anything else? I'm not sure I understand. That's one opinion. Let's hear from someone else. Let me briefly summarize what I think I heard you say is . . . is that correct? What have I missed?

2. *Exercising mild, unobtrusive control* over the group involves either drawing out or managing some group members. To aid the facilitator it is helpful to place a name tag—a large index card folded in half—with first names in front of each person. Permitting participants to use a name other than their own helps and reinforces the

confidentiality of what is being said. These unique challenges can be present:

- The shy participant: At least two or three times in a ninety-minute period, asking quiet members to say something can encourage their participation. If they still do not want to voice an opinion, let them remain silent.
- The expert: Oftentimes in focus groups, an individual will say, "I've been here for twenty years and I know that this is not the way it happens." At an appropriate time not insulting to the one speaking, the facilitator can say, "That's one opinion; let's hear from someone else." The facilitator remains quiet until a participant speaks. If after five seconds no one responds, move on or ask someone specifically by name what s/he thinks.
- The dominant talker: The person who rambles on consumes valuable time and sometimes disrupts the flow of the discussion. As part of the instructions before beginning the focus group, let the group know the cues to stop talking: "We share airtime. If I see you are talking for a long time, I may stop looking at you. That is a cue you have talked long enough. If you miss that cue, as soon as you take a breath, I'm going to say, 'Let's hear from someone else.'" Using humor to send the message will help.
- The fearful participant: At times people say, "Could you turn off the recorder now?" because they are going to say something sensitive. It is appropriate to do so. Even though the facilitator has stated ahead of time that no names are linked with anything said, participants can still feel vulnerable.

3. Facilitators with a good *sense of timing* know when to allow the discussion to continue, when to move on, and how much time to spend on each question. They honor the time frame and the participants by starting and finishing on time.

4. Knowing when *silence* is needed and being comfortable with it comes with experience. Silence fosters thinking and encourages quieter individuals to enter the conversation. The "five-second pause" is an important technique to give people time to think.

Someone will almost always talk within five seconds (see chapter 5 for more on skilled facilitation).

"3.11 What a Facilitator Should and Should Not Do" in the workbook provides a list of effective practices facilitators can use, along with actions that detract from good group process.

EFFECTIVE USE OF DATA

Data Analysis

The process of analyzing focus group data begins with raw data, moves to a series of summary statements about the comments participants made, and ends with an interpretation of meaning for the organization to consider. The qualitative data from focus groups is more difficult to analyze because it cannot readily be processed by entering it into a computer and having it all reappear in neat numerical values. Raw data (all information recorded or taken as notes) is processed by hand. Although software does exist to process such qualitative data, the firsthand ability of the facilitator to analyze it adds credibility to the reporting process and reduces costs.

After creating transcripts of the exact participants' statements and subsequently reading through all the data, the facilitator/researcher organizes it into themes, and then calculates the number of responses supporting each theme. The analysis provides reliable directional results and identifies trends and patterns. When narrative focus group data collected is meticulously transcribed and analyzed in this way and is later tested using a statistically valid research method, the two sets of results are very often in sync. Rarely is the data skewed when the analysis and reporting protocols recommended in the section below are used.

Organizing the Data

Using the verbatim transcripts from each focus group sessions, the steps in the data organization process are these: examine all data collected, categorize the data, tabulate frequencies, and recombine it into themes.

The number of comments under each theme is the frequency indicator, showing the importance of the area to participants. Those themes can then be rank ordered within and across focus groups.

Information emerging from these small-group sessions is highly sensitive. When analyzing data, the facilitator deletes names attached to comments, demonstrating the value the organization places on confidentiality and anonymous participant contributions, as well as avoiding difficult backlash from breaches in the confidentiality assurances.

Interpreting the Data

Interpreting data gathered from qualitative research involves looking at what participants have said in the transcripts (the raw data) and how many times they stated similar ideas. Descriptive written statements, based on notes taken during sessions about facial expressions and other nonverbal body language, are also considered. In addition, transitional remarks made by the facilitator and included in the transcripts may be important in identifying on-the-spot feedback about observations and conclusions made during the session. From those sources, the facilitator draws meaning and develops the report.

In some situations, facilitators need to summarize information from a focus group session directly after the meeting. "3.12 Focus Group Response Sheet" in the workbook provides a format for recording first impressions and other feedback.

Reporting the Data

Copies of the full report or condensed versions of it are communicated to the target stakeholders as well as to the organization, per the agreements established between the facilitator and the school or district.

Typically, the full report includes these components:

- Introduction and methodology: An overview of the research's purpose and context, acknowledgment of people assisting with or underwriting the efforts, the researcher's background, an overview of qualitative research and the focus group processes used in the study, and an outline of the report's contents.
- Executive summary: A narrative or bulleted summary of the process, findings, and any recommendations that may be proposed.
- Findings: An in-depth account of all relevant findings, listing a few of the participants' statements, which support the themes. Participants' actual words can influence people receiving the reports, of-

ten moving them to action. It is hard to ignore verbatim statements from individuals who contributed to the process.

- Interpretations: From participant comments and additional nonverbal cues observed during sessions, the facilitator will provide interpretations based on what participants shared and their significant interactions during sessions. This section may also identify key trends or dilemmas.
- Recommendations: This section of the report includes the researcher's conclusions in narrative format about what is needed in the short term as well as over time to address the issues raised.
- Next steps: The final content section includes a brief one-page summary of the facilitator's thoughts on the next steps the school or district could take to move ahead in addressing the study's findings and recommendations, possibly reiterating the agreements about full disclosure of results to participants and the community.
- Information about the researcher: The report closes with background and contact information about the researcher(s) who conducted the focus groups, analyzed the results, and compiled the final report.

While data reports include these common elements, one unique form is known as an audit report. Audits use a variety of strategies to examine an organization's work in a specific area or to look at an entire system. Providing a snapshot of needs, policies, capabilities, and activities and programs, audit reports can include a review of materials the district or school is using, the gathering of information from focus groups, feedback received in other venues such as public meetings, and the collecting of historical research about a particular issue or the entire system.

Using an Audit

Two forms of audits most useful in engagement practice are the *communications and engagement audit* focusing on the communications and engagement systems of an organization and a more comprehensive *general systems audit* looking at all aspects of the school or district.

- Communications and engagement audit

    A *communications and/or engagement audit* is a study of the communication system and engagement practices within a school or district to determine how people perceive communication practices, what they know, what they want to know, how they want to receive information, how they are engaged, how they want to be engaged, and what issues they care about.

The methodology may include focus groups, surveys, personal interviews, reviews of historical data, observations of both formal and informal meetings, and a review of electronic and printed communication pieces to determine what messages a district is sending, if the material is understandable, and if it is relevant and focused on teaching and learning. The researcher can conduct a gap analysis to determine if people hear and understand the district's communication. Through observations of meetings, study groups, and other engagement activities, the study may also report who is engaged, how they are engaged, if they grapple with real issues, how they are making decisions, if they are doing meaningful work, and if it is making a difference.

- General systems audit

  A general systems audit is a process of collecting and assessing evidence in order to give the school or district a full picture of how it is doing. It is a comprehensive study of an entire organization and all or some of the systems within it.

  As a research project, it looks at all aspects of an organization rather than just one area. It is an examination of many elements and systems in a school or district. The audit's scope depends on what the district or school wants to know. It could include historical, analytical, and descriptive research. Depending on the scope of the project, documents appropriate for study in a general systems audit include survey results from previous years, reviews of the current budget and budget history, current and past achievement scores, strategic plans, technology plans, policies, and any other organizational documents.

  A systems audit can provide a picture of policy and budget capabilities, curriculum strengths and challenges, facility needs, community assets, and barriers to student success. The methodologies used in a general systems audit are the same as those used in a communications and engagement audit.

TAKEAWAY MESSAGES FROM THIS CHAPTER

- Engaging stakeholders in research—allowing them to express their hopes, desires, opinions, and issues and to deliberate about them—can lay the foundation for meaningful change.
- Research designs and practices engaging stakeholders well can be facilitated by professionals or can be learned by others within a school or district.
- While many research approaches can play a role in gathering balanced information, focus group methodology supports a culture of authentic engagement because stakeholders generate new information, learn from each other, and provide insights explaining the motivations and reasons why they think and feel as they do.
- Analyzing and reporting data including insights from stakeholders can often compel further meaningful discussion toward better supporting families and students.

HELPFUL RESOURCE RELATED TO THIS CHAPTER

- Richard Krueger and Mary Anne Casey's *Focus Groups: A Practical Guide for Applied Research* (third or fourth edition) is an excellent resource available for helping facilitators understand, organize, conduct, analyze, and report on focus groups.

Complete bibliographical information for this resource is located in the reference list at the back of this book.

NOTES

1. Adapted from Paul Leedy, *Practical Research*.
2. Adapted from Krueger and Casey, *Focus Groups*.
3. As of the publication date of this book, three such programs are Ethnograph, NUD*IST, or NVivo.

FOUR

Engaging Families/Stakeholders and Schools

Today's school leaders know the truth—closing the stubborn achievement gap and ensuring each child is successful requires a high-quality staff, high expectations, a focus on learning, results, and engaged families and communities. Decades of educational research clearly reveal the positive influence family/stakeholder engagement has on student achievement. The strategies for gathering local research introduced in the previous chapter combined with understanding validated national research about the effects of parent engagement provide a solid foundation for taking specific steps to improve student achievement. Educators want to turn this knowledge into action. This chapter will describe how to draw families/stakeholders in to design effective and sustainable solutions together.

WHAT A PARTNERSHIP SCHOOL LOOKS LIKE IN ACTION . . . AND WHAT IT DOESN'T

The first step toward building a school environment where family engagement thrives is to determine if the local school exhibits characteristics of a *partnership* school. A helpful starting point is knowing what a school that effectively engages families and communities looks like.

A self-assessment for families, developed by KSA-Plus Communications based on content from engagement leader Anne Henderson and others, defines what a partnership school looks like. Available as "4.1

101

Partnership School Self-Assessment" in the companion workbook, *The Politics of Authentic Engagement: Tools for Engaging Stakeholders in Ensuring Student Success*, the assessment allows respondents to evaluate their school along a continuum of practice including four types of schools: the *fortress* school, the *come-if-we-call* school, the *open-door* school, and the *partnership* school. Most schools fall somewhere between the come-if-we-call and the open-door school on the scale. Many have a number of programs to engage families in some way but fall short in other areas.

The goal of the *fortress school* is *protection*. The principal might say, "We are doing a great job with kids who want to learn. If students are not meeting standards, it's because their families don't support them at home." Educators in a fortress school believe families belong at home, not at school. Parents are afraid to complain because "they will take it out on my kid." The role of teachers is to teach the prescribed curriculum. Communication is one-way, from school to home. The school handpicks parent association members, who are usually white, middle class, and wealthy, from a group of active and supportive families. Decisions and educational practice protect school power and project an image of the educator as an expert in all educational matters. The school prides itself on keeping students in line and sends the message it needs little help from the outside. Classroom doors are closed, and teachers run their classrooms as they see fit although abiding by state and federal laws.

The come-if-we-call school strives for *shared values*. Although the school does not differ significantly from the fortress school, the principal and parents agree the families' role is to help their children at home and to support what happens at school. One-way communication prevails with a student handbook and the principal's newsletter. The expanded role of teachers includes parent/teacher conferences and open houses as a means to let parents know what goes on in the classroom. The principal and teachers plan, communicate, and execute parent events. Parent groups remain a group of hand-selected individuals who listen to the principal and nod in agreement. The principal and lead teachers make most of the decisions.

The open-door school focuses on *enrichment*. Families and community members are welcome at school as helpers and advocates. The principal, who works hard to include parents in discussions regarding school problems, usually makes the final decisions. Teachers contact families at least once a year, and the school has a paid parent coordinator or enlists a volunteer to answer families' questions. Parents receive information about their children's progress via regularly sent folders of student work, but schools do not share standardized test data unless required. The school sponsors curriculum nights several times a year, but educators lead all of the sessions. Non-English-speaking parents may or may not have translators available. A site council is composed of the principal, teachers, elected or appointed family members, and other school personnel. The educators heavily influence the council's decisions. Teachers and the principals believe they are the experts in the schooling of the students. The school makes little effort to include the disenfranchised, silent, or non-English-speaking populations.

In a *partnership school*, families and other stakeholders participate in concert with the school to do whatever it takes to ensure all students learn and succeed. There are clearly defined roles and responsibilities for teachers, administrators, students, community members, and families. The school knows how to engage with all families. There is a home visit to every new family and subsequent visits when needed. Translators are available for all non-English-speaking families. Parents and teachers look at test results together and decide how to address challenges. There is a democratic and open problem-solving process. Families and educators research issues together, dialogue, and jointly discover and implement solutions to problems such as bullying, high absenteeism, and academic tracking. The school uses technology to its advantage, employing simple e-mail or a family portal to communicate regularly and frequently with families about their children's progress. Online discussion groups address current school issues. School computers are available for families without home access to connect to the portal and other school information. Staff works with local community leaders to improve the school and the neighborhood. The school provides family leadership and school partnership training. Families know they carry as much responsibility as educators for the success of each student. Partnership schools have moved from parent involvement to *family engagement*.

BEYOND PARENT INVOLVEMENT TO FAMILY ENGAGEMENT

For years, educators have spoken of the need to "involve" parents. However, schools often live in the mind-set of getting parents to come to school events, contribute to school projects, help a bit in some classrooms, and sign the form saying they have seen and understood the quarterly grade report students bring home. Traditional means of home-to-school communication such as parent/teacher conferences, open houses, science fairs, newsletters, and parent meetings offer only one kind of involvement. Parents are more passive than active; educators speak and parents listen. There are no avenues for parents to make suggestions, express their opinions, or work with educators to make changes.

Parent *involvement* is typical in come-if-we-call and open-door schools. In partnership schools, however, parents, extended families, and community members are actively *engaged* in the school because there are expectations everyone is responsible for the success of students. Teachers and administrators are evaluated on how well they engage communities and families. Structures support two-way communication, participation in student learning, consideration and accommodation of family needs, and joint family/school decision-making processes. Families and educators agree on a decision-making process including who will make what decisions. Specific attention is given to engaging marginalized families who may be resistant to participating because they are not comfortable with the dominant culture, may not think they are smart enough to participate, have tried in the past and have been silenced, or think it is not safe in the school environment.

Leaders developing a range of family engagement strategies could experience pushback from both educators and parents as each group becomes comfortable with new roles. Given the diversity of cultures, socioeconomic levels, sexual identities, and education levels—the great pluralism in most schools—there will be conflict as people express their interests and advocate for their beliefs. Conflict is a sign of authentic engagement. A discussion on managing the conflict is in chapter 5. Integrating a partnership practice and philosophy into everyday work is challenging. In time, the initial efforts requiring hard work, time, and patience will pay off with more time available for educators to focus on teaching and greater student success. To ask educators, families, and communities to do more by actively engaging with one another, there must be a high ratio of benefits-to-time expended. The benefits will be worth the effort—student achievement will improve.

What the Research Says about Engaging Families

The Student Achievement Link

Today's research provides clear evidence that if families are partners with their school and are engaged in their children's academics and learning, everyone benefits.[1]

Students with meaningfully engaged families earn higher grades and test scores, take more challenging courses, and, more often, earn a high school diploma. After high school, a greater percentage of these students enroll in community colleges, trade schools, and universities. However, the benefits to students are more than just improved academic performance. Because engaged families insist their children attend school regularly, these youth are less likely to become involved in destructive behavior, both in their school years and throughout their lives. They tend to exhibit better social skills, resulting in greater professional success and satisfaction in their personal lives. Furthermore, these benefits accrue to *all* students regardless of their economic, religious, ethnic, or educational background.

Families also benefit. When families feel they are working as partners with their children's schools, they are more confident in helping their children achieve. They have a better understanding of the curriculum and standards and tend to hold higher expectations for their children. As parents increase their ability to support their children's learning, their own self-confidence increases. Their heightened self-respect creates a stronger bond between teachers and parents, resulting in improved communication. Supporting student learning does not mean meddling in all the details of a child's education program or doing the child's homework. It does mean understanding what students should know and be able to do, holding high expectations for accomplishment, and encouraging children to do their best.

For *educators and schools*, the benefits come down to one thing: appropriately engaged families. If that were the only benefit, it would certainly be worth the effort. However, there are so many more reasons for building family/school partnerships.

Communities also benefit from partnership schools. Families and other community members who actively participate in local schools—even receive special training to do so—bring their experience to their neighborhoods and local governments. They are more willing to serve on citizen

boards and commissions. They possess solid communication and decision-making skills and they understand the need for cooperation and
teamwork among all the government and nonprofit entities that serve
their area. Communities are also more likely to enjoy citizen financial
support for school facility improvement and curriculum enhancements.

According to *A New Wave of Evidence: The Impact of School, Family, and
Community Connections on Student Achievement*, family engagement programs linked to student learning increase the correlation between engagement work and greater student achievement. Further, families will
know their involvement with their child's learning is producing results
because the school consciously makes connections to learning. Educators
engage families in six areas:

- Learning Standards: by helping families understand standards and
  their relation to what is happening in their children's classrooms
- Grade-level Activities: by showing the relationship between class-
  room-based activities and learning standards
- Skill-Building Workshops: by encouraging family members to help
  with learning at home, including reinforcing homework and using
  effective discipline methods
- School/Family Communications: by expecting staff to connect regularly with families and hosting opportunities to assist students,
  even at high school, where families can help with academic planning to increase the probability of graduates getting jobs and entering higher education
- School-level Transitions: by arranging ways to ease transitions for
  students—as well as their families—to the next level of schooling
- Partnerships with Afterschool Programs and Services: by making
  connections and developing partners in the community who can
  help with learning by coordinating their offerings and supporting
  the learning happening in schools

"4.2 Engaging Families and Other Partners Effectively with Student
Learning" in the companion workbook provides more specific strategies
for creating effective linkages in these six important areas.

Parental and Family Interests around Schooling

Families want to know how to help their children succeed. They want
to learn proven techniques so they feel capable of making a difference. At

the same time, they want teachers to know about their families and children. Families want school principals and teachers to see that they love their children and want what is best for them. They want teachers to get to know their children deeply: who they are and how they learn. In turn, they are not satisfied with general feedback that only says, "Everything's going okay." Families want to know how their children are getting along with others, what academic challenges their children are facing, and how they can help.

They also want teachers to know that family life is complex, busy, and sometimes impacted significantly by economic conditions. Time is valuable to families, but finding and enjoying time together can be difficult when excessive homework requirements interfere. Families who understand teacher and school expectations can support their children better, though they often need suggestions about how to guide children in doing homework.

Clear, open, and frequent communication with families is imperative. E-mail can be an effective and immediate channel for sharing, along with home visits or phone calls for those without Internet access. Where available, a family portal within the school or district website enables direct and immediate contact between teachers or administrators and families, keeping everyone informed of the students' progress and/or issues. Both school staff and family members can initiate conversations.

"4.3 Ten Things Families Want Teachers to Know . . . and the Questions They Want to Ask" in the workbook is a useful handout.

Roles and Responsibilities of Families at School

One way to begin a conversation about roles and responsibilities is to offer families a *family engagement assessment* as part of a workshop covering activities at home, participation at school, and home-to-school communications. "4.4 The Family Engagement Checklist" in the workbook opens up many opportunities for discussion among groups of families or workshop participants. One use of the checklist is to gauge how effective school workshops have been in helping families understand student report cards, attend family/teacher conferences, or volunteer at school.

While it is important to engage families in a variety of ways in teaching and learning, it is also important to clarify areas of responsibility. Everyone needs to know and understand expectations and boundaries. Asking questions to determine the role of each person—parent, teacher, administrator, and student—can begin the process of identifying those roles and responsibilities. Listing roles on a chart keeps everyone focused on their own tasks. "4.5 Defining Roles and Responsibilities to Help Children Learn" in the workbook can be used in a workshop to lead participants in thinking through their responsibilities. One version is for parents or other adults working with the students; the second set of instructions is for an educator session.

Families and community partners who work closely with educators begin to understand the complexity of the learning process. They learn what it takes to reach standards of achievement in a complex educational system. Family and citizen partners are more likely to take leadership roles in helping other stakeholders and decision-makers, including federal and state elected officials, understand and support students and schools when they have participated in learning opportunities and understand curriculum issues, how schools are funded, and how they spend their money. When well-informed education partners deliberate and dialogue with confidence, they become mentors; liaisons to other families; tutors for math, reading, and other subjects; and managers of special academic projects. Family partners become key communicators within the school community and in their neighborhoods, towns, and cities.

Families take on responsibilities in relation to their children's learning and their school.[2]

- As *teachers*, families provide discipline, instill good values and habits, and demonstrate respect for teachers. They take time to understand homework expectations so they can unobtrusively oversee homework and read with children at home. They provide learning activities at home and in the community to reinforce classroom work. A variety of teaching roles are open to families and community members. It takes a village to educate children.

* * *

For example, the Spring Branch School District's award-winning mentoring program in Houston, Texas, serves nearly six hundred students on thirty campuses. The Springboard program has more than two dozen partners including businesses, alumni organizations, and faith groups. Springboard's goal is to increase significantly the college readiness, aware-

ness, and college-going rates of students who are "on the brink of success." The program aims to improve these characteristics of students: levels of academic achievement, attitudes toward school, self-confidence and pride in achievement, recognition of schooling's importance for a successful future, and self-image as college-bound students.

The program recognizes not all low-income parents have time to work adequately with their children because they are often struggling to survive. They may be exhausted from working long hours, holding two or more jobs, commuting long distances, and worrying if there will be enough food or adequate medical care for their children. There are also those children whose parents are ill, mentally challenged, on drugs, or incarcerated. Children do not get to choose their parents, but with good mentors their chances of achieving in school increase significantly.

- As *supporters*, families ensure their children are well nourished, rested, and ready to learn. They attend school activities to connect with other families, encourage their children as they make academic progress, and contribute to the school by volunteering. They demonstrate positive attitudes toward learning and schooling by showing that they are learning new things themselves. Family members can learn how to read achievement data, how to become partners with the school, how to help with student homework, and how to work on committees studying complex issues in order to solve problems. Schools need families and community members to fill many supporting roles.

- As *advocates*, families attend family/teacher conferences to learn about their children's progress and advocate for them, when needed. They ask questions and seek answers from educators at the school as well as from outside sources to understand their children's challenges and address issues and dilemmas in the learning process. Families help educators better understand their children's learning styles and personalities. They also work on election issues and lobby lawmakers to pass laws supporting all aspects of education, including funding. A perspective submitted by parent Janet Hogue (see chapter 7) identifies several roles for advocates in the story about how her district lobbied and won funding for schools throughout the state.

- As *advisers* and *decision-makers*, families join groups to study and resolve school issues, provide opinions and insights to school and district staff, and participate in formal school advisory and decision-making groups. They may assume leadership roles aimed at solving educational problems or improving education. While many parents and community members do not have time to serve in these roles, those who do find the work rewarding and greatly beneficial for all students.

The Political View of Partnerships with Families

Not all families can take an active role at a school. However, they can fulfill the responsibilities of a parent or family member as teachers and supporters at home. School/family partnerships are an important component of a thriving community. National research affirms that effective family/school partnerships raise student achievement. Convinced such partnerships would make a difference, the federal government passed legislation in the last decade to foster important school/family links.

The No Child Left Behind Act (NCLB), also called the Elementary and Secondary Education Act (ESEA), mandates that Title I schools engage families in their child's learning. Although parental involvement has always been a centerpiece of Title I, it now has a specific statutory definition for the first time in the history of the ESEA. The statute defines parental involvement as the participation of parents in regular, two-way, meaningful communication about student academic learning and other school activities, including ensuring these elements:

- parents play an integral role in assisting their child's learning
- parents are encouraged to be actively involved in their child's education at school
- parents are full partners in their child's education and are included, as appropriate, in decision-making and on advisory committees to assist in the education of their child

Unfortunately, there are no accountability measures for this mandate and it applies only to Title I schools. If the Title I provisions were implemented in all schools, there is no doubt student achievement would improve. The Act offers several opportunities for family engagement that any school can do without much difficulty.

Opportunity #1: Developing a School/Parent Involvement Policy

NCLB requires each school to develop and approve a parent involvement policy. The policy identifies how to engage families and make decisions about the family/parent engagement program. Schools update the parent involvement policy regularly to reflect the changing concerns of families.

Questions schools and families can ask include:

- Does your school have a family engagement policy?
- Is it updated regularly?
- Does it address family concerns and issues?
- Does it address how to engage marginalized families?
- Are all families engaged in developing the policy and updating it?
- Does it address how all families and staff can work together to improve student learning?

Opportunity #2: Participating in a School/Parent Compact

A compact describes how educators and families will build a partnership to improve student achievement. It is an agreement negotiated between the school and its families, not just a laundry list of what parents and teachers will do. It includes items such as family/teacher responsibilities (attendance at parent/teacher conferences, for example), access to school staff, reports to parents, and what families and staff will do to ensure student success. The compact includes details on school/home communication.

Questions schools and families can ask include:

- What do students need to be successful?
- What extra help is needed?
- How will teachers keep families informed of student progress?
- How will teachers and families work together?
- What are families' expectations?
- What are teachers' expectations?
- How can families assist teachers?
- When will the principal meet with families?

Some schools have also used "4.4 The Family Engagement Checklist" in the workbook to develop a parent/family compact. In that process, families note the items on the checklist they currently do routinely to help their child succeed in school. They sign a compact with the school stating that they agree to continue doing those things. Then families identify actions they do not do and/or do not know how to do, and school educators or family volunteers agree to help them develop those skills. Families agree to learn and use the new skills.

Opportunity #3: Developing a District/Parent Engagement Policy

Just as a Title I school is required to have a parent involvement policy, districts need a policy to guide and support schools in working with families to create their individual policies. A school's parent involvement or engagement policy is usually more specific but follows the intent and spirit of the district's work. Parents and educators develop the district's engagement policy jointly and regularly reevaluate it to meet the needs of schools and families.

Questions to ask include:

- How are families engaged in developing and approving the policy?
- Is the policy available in a language and communication process all families will understand?
- How will families receive the policy?
- How will all families (including families who do not speak English) be engaged in the policy review and improvement?

Opportunity #4: Using District Report Cards

All districts must distribute report cards including data showing how each school and the district as a whole are performing. The district report card must also break down achievement data by subgroups and graduation rates.

Questions to ask about district report cards include:

- Does each school's improvement plan address the data in the school report card?
- Is the district or school report card designed and written so it is understandable?
- Does the school/district provide training for families, teachers, and principals on how to use the report cards?

Getting Started with Strategies for Bringing People Together

Efforts to change thinking about *engaging families* rather than merely paying lip service to getting *parents involved* in old traditional ways requires a fundamental shift in trying to understand families. Seeing and listening to parents and other family members in new ways generates fresh approaches to get them interested in and confident about becoming partners with the school. Making the fundamental assumption that families love their children, share an emotional bond with them, and want to connect with their lives is a good place to begin. Knowing most families want to participate—even partner with the school if they knew how—helps educators look for and appreciate what they can share in terms of strengths, insights, and useful ideas.

Understanding a Wide Range of Basic Needs

To move educators to new strategies, it is critical that they understand what level of needs each family is attempting to fill. Abraham Maslow's theory of motivation suggests there is a hierarchy of needs that must be met before an individual can be productive, creative, and fulfilled—and be motivated to attend to higher levels of satisfaction.[3]

1. Physiological Needs

    Physiological needs of having enough food, water, shelter, and warmth form the broad base of the pyramid often used to illustrate how one progresses through the five levels. People at this lowest level are trying to fulfill their most basic needs. When families are coping with challenges at this level, it is not surprising that they cannot pay much attention to their children's education. They are scrambling to survive from day to day. Educators can support struggling families by sharing information about and connections to resource people who can help meet their basic needs.

2. Safety

    The next most basic level includes the need to feel safe—feeling secure, having a sense of stability, and being free from fears. Maslow talks about related conditions that also ensure this feeling of safety, including the opportunity to speak and act freely (so long as it does not harm others), seek information, and defend oneself. He contends the lack of safe conditions can cause defensiveness and alienation. When families perceive that educators are discounting them or not listening to their desires and fears, they are not motivated to engage with their children's education.

Steady employment provides other measures of safety, such as financial and physiological security, contributing to a sense of stability. Fears of needing to relocate, of being at risk of harm in a housing location, or of children being bullied at school or in the neighborhood, all detract from families focusing on school achievement.

3. Belonging and Love

The third level of human needs is belonging—being seen, being valued, and being heard. Families with unmet social needs often feel isolated from the school community. They may not feel that they will be accepted or needed. When schools provide opportunities for families to meet each other at social and recreational events, they begin to make friends and feel a higher level of acceptance. Some schools have been successful in creating a buddy system where more involved parents form liaisons with members of less involved families and invite them to attend school activities.

Family liaison programs designed to connect schools with the least-connected families, such as those who do not speak English or for other reasons are not comfortable in schools, create a sense of belonging.

* * *

The Niles Township High School District in Illinois has an effective family-liaison program. All district families feel connected to their school and know how to help their children succeed academically. The program hires family liaisons as hourly employees who are qualified translators, live in the community, and know or will learn the district's priorities and goals. The liaisons welcome families, encourage them to attend school activities, help them understand how to support their children's success in school, provide translation services, attend meetings, and do whatever they can to help families partner with the school in helping their children succeed.

4. Self-Esteem

The next higher level of human needs is achieving mastery and feeling recognized and respected. Feeling capable of making a valuable contribution helps build self-esteem, but individuals can only contribute meaningfully when opportunities are opened to them by school personnel. In turn, high self-esteem in family members results in their willingness to volunteer their time and talents at school as well as learn how to help their children with academic tasks at home. Educators foster and encourage engagement by recognizing family members for their work. Schools teaming with community agencies can help families gain access to services supporting self-esteem development such as language or parenting classes, counseling, and job training.

Schools can also provide training opportunities for families. One school district offered computer classes so parents could learn to access information on their child's academic progress. Parents filled every class. To start, schools ask families what they need to become a school partner.

5. Self-Actualization

The peak of Maslow's pyramid of human needs represents the state of feeling fulfilled as someone who appreciates oneself and is motivated to pursue inner talents and express creativity. Family members operating at this level want engagement opportunities where their contributions have long-term impacts, such as participation in decision-making, school improvement planning, and goal setting. Schools providing leadership training for adults receive a rich cadre of people able to lead committees, serve on school boards, and motivate others to participate.

Spending time attending to the lower levels of needs on the pyramid could seem unrelated to school success. In the past, such attention was considered outside the realm of school responsibility. However, if Maslow's theory is accurate, helping family members as well as staff meet lower-level needs so they can ultimately operate at successively higher levels of well-being can directly influence the quality of family engagement.

Levels of student achievement increase when more families move up Maslow's hierarchy. However, schools cannot do it alone. They can initiate partnerships with others in helping meet families' lower-level needs. The motivation for educators to partner with others in the community is to realize the common goal of raising academic achievement and increasing success for children.

*   *   *

For example, the Beaverton School District in Oregon recently launched a WE campaign. The district believes in helping Beaverton students lead full and successful lives. To that end, its goal is to engage everyone, including the more than 70 percent of the community who do not have children in school. Each school is required to organize a Community Engagement Team to promote and assist with developing collaborative school-based community outreach, engagement efforts, and volunteer activities among parents, nonparents, businesses, faith communities, and community organizations. Each school team meets regularly to assess school needs and collaboratively and strategically set measurable goals, plan activities, track progress, and evaluate outcomes.

As a result of the WE campaign, several parents from higher socioeconomic schools self-organized through the Internet to assist schools in reaching out to less affluent families. These more affluent parents met with the principals of the lower-income schools to assess their families' needs. They learned in one winter month there was a great need for warm clothing. Within two weeks, they collected, cleaned, and distributed six hundred coats. Through word of mouth and the Internet, the core group's membership increased to about 350 parents and continues to grow. The group has formed partnerships with churches, businesses, social service agencies, and many other community groups. Working independently of the school district but in cooperation with the principals of several schools, they lobby for increased school funding, advocate for all students, launch projects to serve low-income children, and serve as a model for what is possible when people engage with their schools and community for children. In one recent project, they collected 6,000 books for a community library that distributes them to children who do not have access to books at home.

Meeting Diverse Needs and Expectations of Families

Meeting diverse needs not only means considering personal and family needs on a continuum such as Maslow's, but it also means addressing families from diverse cultures, those struggling in poverty, those with special needs children, those relegated to a minority status involuntarily, and those just angry at or afraid of the educational system.

Families of Diverse Cultures. William Demmert, one of the founders of the National Indian Education Association, once said, "Culture shapes minds. It provides us with a toolkit by which we construct not only our worlds, but our very conceptions of ourselves and our powers. Learning, remembering, talking, and imagining: All of them are made possible by participating in a culture."[4] The difficulty arises when others do not recognize or understand the ways differing cultures have shaped the lives and perceptions of children and families.

Today's schools, especially in urban and suburban areas, serve a highly diverse population. Everyone better meets the needs of students and their families when they know and understand the history and cultural norms of local diverse groups. Too many times educators are unaware of cultural norms, have lower expectations for some cultures, and do not create a sense of belonging for those outside of the dominant culture. The words of students from an elementary school in a large suburban school district capture the issue:

* * *

- *"Kids bully the Nepalese and make fun of them and call them Indian. 'Use more English, you Nepalese.'"*
- *"Kids hang around and talk in Spanish, cussing at us in their language."*
- *"We need a Spanish-speaking teacher on the playground to listen."*

From parents of the same school:

- *"Our kids need to learn about their heritage, study about Mexico and who they are and why they came here. Everybody needs to study the various cultures, not just the immigrants. It is important to learn about your parents and your families."*
- *"We have a majority of non-English-speaking parents who are not as involved, so the remainder of the parents that don't have language barriers have to bear the weight of volunteering and participating in activities."*
- *"I was one of those parents who came from a non-English-speaking family. A lot of it is their culture because parents are not involved in their home countries in schools. So it is a culture shock to them. A lot of them don't read or write and aren't able to understand the letters that come home with their children. I have seen it because as a tri-lingual person I have had to help interpret newsletters for some parents."*

- *"Everybody has a dream. The reason we came to U.S. is so our kids can get a good education and be good citizens."*
- *"I go to parent club meetings, not a lot of parents attend; they always speak English so I don't know what's going on."*
- *"They only speak English; they think I am dumb for not understanding English. I can't depend on the meeting working for me."*

If educators are to move families beyond parent involvement to *family engagement*, they must become culturally competent. Teachers, administrators, and other staff members need to work intentionally to increase their understanding of local families and the cultures they represent in order to meet the needs of students with wide-ranging backgrounds, experiences, and languages. Training to understand the specific cultures within any single school or district is necessary; it is an ongoing learning process for adults as well as students.

Educators and others who work with first- and second-generation immigrants must strive toward understanding their own cultural identity and its relationship to others. Building a diverse network of colleagues and partners helps in the effort, as does engaging in ongoing learning opportunities, such as diversity workshops and classes. Identifying and addressing issues relevant to particular groups of people in their local workplace or school is also important, so cultural history, learning styles, language, communication, gender roles, and value systems are considered in meeting needs of families and children in schools. "4.6 Action Ideas for Increasing One's Own Cultural Competency" in the workbook provides concrete ideas for examining personal perceptions of diversity.

Connecting consciously and intentionally with those of other cultures, even if mandated in a school plan designed collectively by staff and others, can be challenging. It includes addressing situations perceived as unsafe by students of other backgrounds, engaging classroom volunteers of diverse cultures, making more phone calls to establish personal relationships with families, asking non-English-speaking family members to help with translations of materials, or eliciting suggestions for culturally appropriate family activities to reinforce school learning at home.

It involves recognizing that parents from other cultures often do not take the initiative to ask questions because they do not know what or how to ask or they feel unsafe in the dominant culture. Teachers help when they communicate specifically how students are and are not progressing. Teachers who are willing to personalize planning with families can identify specific ways they can assist their children with challenging learning tasks at home.

Two tools available in the workbook provide specific approaches for school staff to connect with families: "4.7 Helping Families of Diverse Cultures Interact with the School" and "4.8 Key Questions for Conversations with Staff or Families." The latter could also be helpful in writing school plans to address diversity.

For parents and families, a chance to sit down, talk, and share stories with families of other cultures can begin to bridge a gap of common misunderstandings. Translators break through the language barrier. Hosting cultural nights at school featuring cross-cultural activities such as folk dancing, food preparation, singing, and games helps people become acquainted. Schools can also weave cultural activities into the fabric of the school day to attract families to visit and share.

Building cultural competency can generate a very desirable shared culture in which everyone focuses on high achievement for all students. This happens when structures are in place to promote shared power and voice, when the school community designs staffing and leadership patterns to benefit students through intentional diversity, and when no one is satisfied until every child meets or exceeds academic standards in all subjects. There are additional groups with special needs that also require understanding and unique approaches.

Families in Poverty. Deeper understanding of what it means to be in poverty is essential for educators. It begins with knowing families well and the challenges they face. Approximately 21 percent of school-age children are from families living in poverty. The children may be living in a shelter, a car, or a home without heat, with little food, and with no money for medical support. Their parents may be working two jobs, be medically fragile, or be mentally ill. Families represent all cultures, education levels, and ability levels. With few exceptions, all want their children to succeed.

When families struggling to meet their own basic physiological needs consider connecting with their children's schools, they might respond to a different set of approaches and incentives. When these families build trust with their child's teachers and school, it will be easier to encourage them to acquire skills they can use to help their child succeed in school. For example, the barrier of inconvenient meeting times can be broken by hosting a "museum" meeting format, with school open from 6:00–9:00

p.m., when families come and go as they wish, taking in what they see as interesting.

Educators will be more successful in engaging families by meeting with them in places family members consider safe, such as a church social hall, the recreation area at their apartment complex, or their own homes, which may be a shelter or an automobile. Often it is more effective if students are present with their families. Once there, families can share stories and be assured their concerns are heard. Asking gentle questions begins to build trust. Addressing each parent as Mr. or Mrs. communicates respect and moves participants toward reaching better understandings. Using humor, when appropriate, relaxes people. Delivering bad news about a child's behavior or lack of academic progress through a story rather than an accusation about a child keeps a discussion productive and positive.

Incentives are another useful tool to encourage engagement. Providing babysitting and a meal during school meetings helps meet basic family needs. Giving away school supplies and games at the conclusion of the gathering encourages attendance and participation. Local businesses may provide coupons for free or discounted goods, services, and groceries.

Unfortunately, too many educators and others stereotype students and families different from themselves, often targeting those in poverty by believing they are lazy, do not care about school or their children, are not motivated, and may be violent. While those beliefs may be true about a few people, they are not true for most. The reality is that low-income and wealthy families hold the same attitudes about education.

Low-income parents are less likely than their wealthier peers to attend school functions or volunteer in their children's classrooms—not because they care less about education, but because they have less *access* to school involvement than others. They are more likely to work multiple jobs, to work evenings, to have jobs without paid leave, and to be unable to afford child care and public transportation.

People in poverty do not have weaker work ethics or lower levels of motivation than wealthier people. Although society stereotypes poor people as lazy, 83 percent of children from low-income families have at least one employed parent; close to 60 percent have at least one parent who works full-time and year-round. In fact, the severe shortage of living-wage jobs means many poor adults must work two, three, or four jobs. According to the Economic Policy Institute, poor working adults spend more hours working each week than their wealthier counterparts.[5]

These additional ideas can help schools relate better to families in poverty:

- Examine how the school may be reinforcing classism through such practices as tracking, ability grouping, and setting school boundaries.

- Become more aware of classism when it occurs either because of personal invisible prejudices and lack of knowledge or by the views of others toward those in poverty.

- Hold listening sessions with students. For example, high school students living in poverty who spoke in a focus group about their sense of belonging said they do anything they can to fit in: work extra jobs and go without eating so they can buy an iPod or go to Goodwill and secondhand stores to purchase name-brand clothes. One student said, "We have no heat in our house but nobody knows that 'cause I make sure my clothes, always 'hand-me-downs,' fit in. And I make sure I am always clean and neat."

- Make people aware when they exhibit prejudices and stereotypical beliefs about poverty.

- Provide workshops on current primary research concerning poverty in order to surface and change misperceptions.

Involuntary Minorities. Involuntary minorities are people transported by force to this country or taken over and relegated to a minority status. African Americans, Mexican Americans, Native Americans, and Native Hawaiians are part of this country because of slavery, colonization, or conquest. Some of them believe the social, political, and economic barriers they face are permanent—that hard work and education will not change their situations. Many have less positive beliefs about the dominant society than voluntary minorities. Some distrust white Americans or display minimal effort in school so as not to "look white." Involuntary minorities are likely to place equal value on education, common sense, and their street smarts. Further, many feel education will not help them get ahead so they must choose between academic achievement and maintaining their culture. Most local schools do not incorporate the cultural needs of involuntary minorities.

When educators try to engage involuntary minority families, it is important to understand "white privilege" and to recognize and accept any anger, even if it is not evident. Trust and relationship building may go very slowly. Knowing and understanding the culture and working within it will help.

A review of hard-core hip-hop music lyrics from artists such as Dead Prez in "They Schools" points to the deep anger and resentment of black students who believe they are regarded with disdain and no compassion. They believe they are taught not to their learning styles but to the styles of the dominant white race. The duo rappers refer to teachers who lack understanding of who black students are, what they need, and what matters to them. They rap about students like themselves who learn by observation and participation rather than through books, even though they may want to be doctors or dentists, which no teachers would expect of them. Lyrically they claim the school brainwashes them and say that if black students disagree with a teacher, they are taken away in handcuffs or expelled. They speak of schools only teaching students how to be slaves for white people, the principal serving as a warden, security guards conducting searches of lockers and backpacks of black students for weapons and drugs. Their lyrics are harsh but reflect what black students are repeating in similar words over and over again in focus groups throughout this country when asked about their sense of belonging in the schools they attend.[6]

Anger is difficult to receive under any circumstance. However, accepting the anger and significant challenges of involuntary minorities, trying to understand their life situations, and creating conditions of safety at school for them could help lower their animosity. Going slowly and working within their cultures to identify points of pride and the legacies of their heritage can provide a basis for relationships. Building in many opportunities for open and honest discussions regarding the curriculum, standards, and expectations for children will provide opportunities for deeper understanding.

A mismatch of goals can make working together with a single focus difficult, but it is not easy to modify culturally held expectations. In fact, some attempts by students to conform to the dominant culture can put them or their families at risk from others of their own culture chastising them for trying to conform to the majority expectations. It is complicated for both the dominant and the minority cultures.

Yet some family members from these groups do want to serve on decision-making committees where their opinions and ideas are valued. Since these families also believe collective efforts are the best means to achieving upward mobility, increasing the numbers of parents from these groups will motivate more group members to follow.

Parents of Special Needs Children. Parents of children with special needs are some of the strongest advocates for their children. Many parents are tired, frustrated, and afraid for their children and for their own future. Many times parents of special needs children are angry and do not know what to do. They believe they have tried everything with no success. Our local and state systems do not serve the parents of mentally ill children well. Educators who work with these students are most often dedicated and patient as well as trained in working with mentally ill children. However, educators are not always successful, and parents may not believe what educators are doing is right for their child. Organizing parents into learning teams has worked in many schools as an avenue to learn the newest research and strategies from members of the medical profession and educators in the field. Communicating about available resources and providing time for the parents to talk with one another and share their stories and ideas for working with their children is most helpful.

Parents Who Are Angry or Afraid. What causes parents/families to become angry or afraid? It can be as simple as educational jargon or as complex as a cultural misunderstanding or a terrible, unforgotten experience that occurred months or years earlier. In focus groups, participants share what makes them angry: broken promises, defensiveness, stereotyping, making incorrect assumptions, stonewalling, patronizing, rudeness, dishonesty, an unwillingness to admit mistakes and apologize, a failure to communicate, lack of respect for family members and students, low expectations of students and families, lack of professionalism, being asked for advice but having it ignored, and failure to communicate.

When confronted by an angry parent or family member, slowing down and breathing are essential. The old adage, "Seek first to understand before trying to be understood" is never more important than at the moment of confrontation with an angry person. Managing a difficult person means managing oneself. It is necessary to hold a space for a different point of view. All parties in a confrontation or conflict carry some part of the truth. Conflict is normal but can only be normalized when it is acknowledged. People are less trusting today and will not automatically trust new people, ideas, or institutions. Many have no respect for anyone, especially those in positions of power. Actions taken and words spoken affect the ability to build trust.

As seen in Maslow's theory of motivation, listening to and understanding the needs of families that fall within any of these broad categories—being culturally different; living in poverty; being an involuntary minority; parenting a special needs child; or being angry and afraid—are fundamental to helping families become more confident and assertive in relating to schools. Listening to representatives of diverse groups and understanding their needs can also result in engaging families in the local school or district's decision-making processes and in fostering other kinds of meaningful support for their children in classrooms.

"4.9 Beaverton Inclusive School Scan" in the workbook is a self-reflective tool for leaders to consider as they create and maintain an inclusive learning environment for all students and families regardless of their background, culture, socioeconomic level, ability, or gender.

Using Stories to Build Bridges

Storytelling is a powerful tool for educators to understand members of diverse groups. Families sharing stories of their history, school experiences, families, religion, and values not only brings people closer together but also helps enhance sensitivity to how others see the world. Educators who give families an opportunity to share their stories empower them to create personal and group identities.

Getting stakeholders to think through who they are brings change and forward movement. For example, asking contributors to identify a difficult situation they have faced and explain how they solved it can help them learn about the kind of thinker or person they are, especially if others show interest in their response. Asking participants to tell the story of their life is powerful. The storytellers each share their family history or the migration of their family, identifying where they came from, how they arrived at their current location, who they left behind, and what they are presently doing. Powerful connections to self and others are made through stories and voices.

Once a foundation of trust is built, parents and other family members can be easily encouraged to talk about the expectations they have for their children—their hopes and dreams. It is easier for educators to construct effective family engagement opportunities that empower families to find their voice and become full partners with the school in helping their children succeed when educators know about a child's family.

Overcoming Obstacles to Family/School/Teacher Relationships

To bridge the achievement gap for economically disadvantaged students and children of a range of cultures and simultaneously increase academic achievement for all students, it is important to ask families what needs to be in place for them to be partners in their child's education. Families frequently do not engage because they do not believe they have anything to contribute. In other cases, they do not have the skills they need, such as language, understanding of school curricula, ability to work in bilingual settings, or the social skills of the primary culture. School or community groups, social services agencies, or churches can often provide information and skill-building opportunities through classes and workshops. "4.10 Overcoming Obstacles to Family Engagement" in the workbook includes a number of practical solutions to removing roadblocks in the way of schools connecting with families.

Breaking through Barriers to Involvement and Engagement

Across the country, educators and families alike identified the following as the barriers keeping families from participating in their children's schools: lack of time; lack of fundamental trust for teachers and institutions; uncertainty about what to do; personal educational experiences; cultural and language differences; and lack of a safe, supportive environment to do so. Some families say they are not involved because they do not feel welcome at school. One adult participant in a focus group said the only time his parents came to school was when he was in trouble. "My mother figured if she didn't come to school, I hadn't beat anybody up. I don't think she much liked going to school only to get beat up by the principal." He inherited his feelings about parental involvement in schools from his mother, and there wasn't a reason to change his mind.

Teachers are often uncomfortable talking to families—especially teachers younger than their students' parents. Others are simply not skilled at building relationships and not culturally competent. Further, not all teachers are willing to accept parents as equal partners. Staff members who believe there is just one way to do something create barriers.

Even time becomes an enormous hurdle. It is difficult for many families to meet if child care is not available or too costly. Sometimes families need to meet at different times of the day because they may work a shift that does not permit them to come to school without loss of wages.

All of these barriers beg for training opportunities in which school employees—administrators, teachers, and support staff—learn how to foster transparent and open communications, build cultural competency, and feel comfortable with families. In turn, educators can help families feel like valuable members of the school community. With appropriate training and resources in their own languages, family members can work with their children at home.

One way to break the "unwelcome" barrier is to get to know families off school grounds.

*   *   *

My first year of teaching was at a middle school in Hawaii. All of the seventh graders in my classroom faced both economic and academic challenges. Each year the students passed from grade to grade based solely on their age. Not one child could read. After the first few weeks, it became obvious why: school was simply not a priority for any of the students or their families. When the Pacific surf was up, the kids were surfing. If I was going to get them to come to school every day, I was going to need their parents' cooperation. Unfortunately, most strategies I tried to get parents to school failed, as did many attempts I made to visit them at home.

I had to meet them on their turf—the Friday night cockfights. Although illegal now, cockfighting has a long cultural history on the island. Participants who raised the roosters spent hours studying the bloodlines of various breeds. Gambling on the fight's outcome was the thrill of the evening. As distasteful as I found those Friday evenings at the fights, I kept attending them week after week. Eventually, by talking informally to parents on their turf, expressing an interest in what they were doing, and tipping a few cans of Primo beer, I gained their trust.

I believe the weekly fights paid off because I showed families that I cared about them and their children and wanted them to succeed. I also recognized that these parents were highly unlikely candidates for active participation in school activities, committees, or events. I knew I had to tailor my requests for participation so families would feel they were doable. Since reading was an important goal, I asked each parent to do two things: (1) watch their child read for fifteen minutes a day and (2) encourage their child to bring home books from the library. By the end of the school year, every child in the class was reading—some better than others, but all were reading.

Some school districts have been successful holding family meetings in apartment complexes, neighborhood churches, or community centers—all places where families felt safe. Once families feel comfortable talking with educators on their own turf, they are more likely to feel comfortable coming to school for a family/teacher conference or helping a teacher prepare a science project. Schools with successful family/school partnerships frequently offer experiences that make it worthwhile for families to "go to school." Opportunities to use free computer labs, take English as a Second Language classes, or take Spanish classes for English speakers can entice families to begin a partnership with their school.

Some families say they feel uncomfortable at school because they do not speak English. In communities where many do not speak English, schools should translate all written and oral communications into the main languages spoken by their families. Too many schools rely on students telling their families about family/teacher conferences, parent meetings, science fairs, and other school activities. The messages remain undelivered. When educators communicate to families in their native language, it demonstrates respect and acknowledges that families play an important role in their child's education.

* * *

For example, one primarily Hispanic suburban school district with a large migrant population recruited parent leaders from the community and formed a district migrant-parent advisory committee. These parents served as advocates for non-English-speaking families and helped develop a program to increase parental participation in their children's education. The school district also created and expanded its Office of Hispanic Outreach to support parent involvement and build parent leadership throughout the district.

Another school district received a grant to provide training sessions on partnering with the school and helping their children be successful in school for families who did not speak English. The district also invited parents of special-

needs students and of children struggling in school. Families from many cultures came to the trainings.

To build trust and a sense of belonging, instructors encouraged participants to tell stories. Rich descriptions of their struggles as parents and their desires to help their children succeed in school built a strong community of support, even though not all spoke the same language. Interpreters and microphones made language a nonissue. The parents talked about the values of each of their cultures.

In turn, participants in other diverse groups gained respect for the Hispanics' deep sense of family, the United States population's strong desire for independence and freedom, the Asian culture's respect for their elders, and Russian participants' valuing of hard work and suffering. Together these parents identified ways to help their children succeed in school, including setting a schedule of walking the halls of the middle and high schools, where discipline was a challenge due to staffing reductions. Staff found the presence of family members at school helped teachers and administrators focus more on educating students. Bridging diverse groups of families led to a deeper understanding of other cultures, an appreciation for the differences, and a synergy that led to action. Schools felt supported in meeting their goals of improving student achievement and narrowing achievement gaps.

Recruiting and Motivating All Populations to Participate

There are no surefire methods for recruiting and motivating families to participate in events, committees, study groups, parenting classes, or other activities. Although each school population is different, a personal invitation, face-to-face or on the phone, is the best strategy. Helping families understand there are certain things they should expect from their child's school often helps them feel more legitimate in asking questions or seeking help. Finding ways to communicate that the school values their expectations can motivate some families to participate. "4.11 What Families Should Expect from their School" in the workbook lists twelve expectations parents should have of their children's school.

Building Social and Political Capital

Families of diverse cultures or those living in poverty often do not have much social or political capital within the dominant cultural system. Social capital refers to the relationships, connections, trust, and shared understandings and behaviors holding together members of a network or community.[7] An example of having social capital is a person knowing someone who knows someone else at a company where they want to work. Such capital is the glue that not only makes cooperative action possible, but it also helps families move up the economic ladder.

It follows that political capital for a family is the network of connections they develop to feel they have worth within a community and can carry influence within a political system. Social and political capital are important elements for engaging and empowering families within a school and community. Encouraging families to engage with school happens in many ways and builds such capital at the same time. Sometimes both educators and interested parents feel they cannot improve a school. However, if families collaborate with other parents and organizations, they can make a difference. There is, indeed, power in numbers. This list illustrates with humor and much truth how the responses of school personnel often change as many—versus just a few—parents advocate for their children and school:

1 parent = A fruitcake
2 parents = A fruitcake and a friend
3 parents = Troublemakers
5 parents = Let's have a meeting.
10 parents = We'd better listen.
25 parents = Our dear friends . . .
50 parents = A powerful organization![8]

One recent study examined how family social capital and school social capital affects academic achievement. Researchers defined family social capital as the bonds between parents and children (factors such as trust, open communication, and engagement in their children's academic learning). They defined school social capital as the school's ability to be a positive place for learning (factors such as student involvement in extracurricular activities and the ability of teachers to meet individual student needs). While the study found a school having social capital was important, *family social capital* was actually more critical to student achievement. It bears out family engagement as essential to a child's academic success.[9] "4.12 Building Social and Political Capital in Families" in the workbook provides activities for helping staff understand the issues of social and political capital.

WHAT FAMILIES NEED TO KNOW ABOUT EDUCATION

At an ethnically and economically diverse suburban elementary school, the staff asked parents what they needed to know in order to help their children succeed. Families said they wanted to know the "why" behind learning expectations and how homework assignments help students meet academic standards. Families are hungry for information about how the educational system works and how they can help their children achieve in school. Educators, however, often use terminology families are not familiar with, such as "standards" and "accountability measures." Further, families may not even understand their child's report card. The more families learn about education, the curriculum, academic expectations, report cards, and other concepts unique to education, the more competent they will feel and the more effective they will be in helping their child succeed in school.

Contemporary Education Systems and Practices

> "My vision for family engagement is ambitious. . . . I want to have too many parents demanding excellence in their schools. I want all parents to be real partners in education with their children's teachers, from cradle to career. In this partnership, students and parents should feel connected—and teachers should feel supported. When parents demand change and better options for their children they become the real accountability backstop for the education system."[10]
> —Arne Duncan, U.S. Secretary of Education, May 3, 2010

Educational systems and practices evolve continuously. Community members, parents, and other adult family members often think of their own school experiences as the way teaching still ought to look today. Families who attended school in other countries are likely to have radically different perceptions of what their children's school in this country should look like. It is, therefore, important to provide explicit information about a wide range of current educational practices. Information needs to be tailored to each diverse set of families in order to engage them in the school and in helping their children learn.

The following six education-related topics and concepts are critical for families to understand. Language and details appropriate to use in facilitating a parent workshop are included as "4.13 Helping Families Understand Contemporary Education" in the workbook, along with a companion handout of workshop content highlights as "4.14 Contemporary Education Systems and Practices."

1. Education in the United States

    The United States was the first country to provide free publicly funded education for all children, although initially it was not mandatory and did not extend past thirteen years of age. By 1965, however, legislation under the Elementary and Secondary Education Act (ESEA) required the education provided to all children — even those in poverty — be of equal *quality*. Today, the No Child Left Behind (NCLB) law, which is part of ESEA, requires schools receiving federal Title I funds to ensure all students meet challenging academic standards.

2. Benefits of Family Engagement

    Engaging families in their children's schooling provides many benefits for a variety of people and organizations. When families participate, research shows that *students* get higher grades and test scores and *families* gain confidence in both the school system and in themselves. *Teachers* experience higher morale because students are succeeding and they are receiving more support from families and the community. *Communities* benefit because the schools are of higher quality, attracting new residents and employees, and their school-engaged stakeholders have greater skills in decision-making processes.

3. Standards

    Educational standards are clear but broad statements about what students should achieve at various grades, ensuring students in one school learn the same content and skills as students in another. Standards identify the knowledge and related skills students should have by the time they graduate from high school to succeed in entry-level, credit-bearing, academic courses in college, in workforce training programs, and/or in jobs. The more consistent the standards and expectations are, the better prepared students will be to work and compete in a global economy. Although teachers and school districts do maintain choices of curriculum materials and instructional approaches, common standards establish high expectations for *all* students across the country.

4. Measurement of Progress

Schools measure progress annually by giving all students at a particular grade level the same test or other measuring tool, such as a writing assessment in which the student must write an essay or other piece to demonstrate proficiency. Students in every group (low-income, special education, Caucasian, African American, Hispanic, and other cultural groups) must meet all standards or they will not advance to the next level. The measures assess how far students have progressed in learning the knowledge and skills identified in the standards for each grade level. Although measurement tools are the same and the standards are common to a particular grade level, individual teachers can help students understand expectations in many different ways using a variety of strategies and materials tailored to student needs. A quick activity in "4.15 The Cookie Exercise" in the workbook helps workshop participants understand more about measuring success.

5. Accountability

Families and communities want to know if their schools are providing a good education for their children, preparing them to graduate, find a good job, or continue their education. They want to be sure their child is measuring up to standards and making progress. Families need to know how to read and interpret their children's *individual student report cards*. Today's student report cards hold valuable information about the child's personal, social, and academic progress.

Not only do families need to understand student report cards, they also need to learn to interpret, along with others in the community, *district* and *school report cards* so they can evaluate how well their district as a whole and school in particular are doing in teaching all children. Listening to families who have questions helps educators create discussion opportunities where families can talk about groups of students who are doing well, others who are struggling, academic performance trends over several years, and what their school can do to improve in areas of need.

6. Learning Styles

Helping families understand that children learn differently from one another can open doors for both adults and students. Children look at and operate in their worlds in unique ways depending on their learning style (or styles). Common learning styles are these:

linguistic, logical-mathematical, spatial, bodily-kinesthetic, musical, interpersonal, and naturalist.

Hearing the different ways people learn helps family members understand why one child responds better to written rather than auditory directions, or why another child prefers to draw a picture and another likes to build things. Families will also learn that no learning style is better than another and that students may use different learning styles at various times. Such understanding can help them support their children in new ways and celebrate unique strengths. "4.16 How Do I Learn: An Introduction to Multiple Intelligences and Learning Styles" in the workbook provides instructions for a workshop to help families understand those two concepts. "4.17 Learning Styles Self-Profile" is a companion handout to help participants identify their own learning styles. "4.18 Eight Ways of Knowing" identifies eight styles of learning and how students learn best in each.

Ways to Help Your Child Succeed

Once families understand the concepts around standards and measuring progress, they will want to know how they can help their child achieve those standards. Workshops give families valuable strategies and language to use in talking to their children. They also help engage families with teachers and others helping children within the school by providing the approaches and, often, the exact words to use to start a conversation with the teacher, principal, or other educator.

Communicating to families the following eight ways they can support success in school will help them assist their children, even without attending a workshop. School staff can highlight one approach a month to focus their parent education efforts.

1. Participate with confidence in family/teacher conferences.

    Some parents dread the family/teacher or student/family/teacher conference. For families who do not speak English, the thought of going to school to discuss their child's school performance is often terrifying. Yet a critical element in helping young people succeed involves successfully communicating with teachers about academic and other kinds of progress. Participating successfully in family/teacher conferences involves the parents preparing what they are going to say, how they are going to say it, and what they will do with the information gained from the conference.

A handout incorporating some simple steps and prompts about how to prepare for family/teacher conferences can be found as "4.18 Successful Family/Teacher Conferences" in the workbook. It can help prepare both family members and teachers to get the most out of the family/teacher conference.

2. Ensure regular, on-time attendance.

Students who are at school every day learn more consistently. Families can support their child in making regular, on-time attendance happen.

3. Model effective learning-oriented behaviors at home.

There are simple practices families can do at home to support learning: organize an appropriate place to do homework, have a family reading time, keep books for both adults and children visible around the house, encourage writing in journals or letters, tell stories to one another, and place limits on television and use of technology.

4. Praise learning.

Parents can talk about schoolwork and give praise for progress observed. They can encourage their children to think independently and discover answers on their own but should not do their children's homework.

5. Support positive test behaviors.

To help students prepare for tests, parents need to know when testing is scheduled, make sure their children get a good night's sleep, and that they eat breakfast. Parents can give students valuable pointers on test-taking, such as reading the directions carefully, watching their time, and answering the easy questions first.

6. Take the initiative to know the school and how your child is doing.

Families can stay informed about what is happening at school— activities, test-taking days, celebrations, family/teacher conferences. They can build relationships with the people who work at school and with other families. Concerned families do not wait for report cards or scheduled conferences; they ask immediately how their child is doing.

7. Help out at school.

There are many ways to have influence in the learning process at school including assisting children in reading or math classes, supporting the musical and sports programs, chaperoning, and helping with special programs and events. Families can volunteer in classrooms and on the playground or serve on committees, make decisions on councils or in parent clubs, or assist with translations for non-English-speaking families to support and learn more about the school environment.

8. Participate in study groups, dialogues, and other decision-making groups.

Families who voice their perspectives influence how their children and all students learn and succeed.

TAKEAWAY MESSAGES FROM THIS CHAPTER

- Student achievement is higher when families actively participate in family engagement programs linked to student learning and partner in school and district decision-making.
- Students, families, schools, and communities all benefit when families are engaged with schools.
- Families love their children and want to know how to help them succeed.
- Families can easily play a number of roles in their children's learning.
- Understanding and working to address a wide range of student and family needs is essential to improving academic achievement.
- Becoming culturally competent is critical for educators so they can help others bridge differences.
- While barriers often exist to successfully engaging families, a number of specific strategies can overcome the obstacles.
- Building the social and political capital of family members will not only increase their self-confidence and independence but will also promote more social and civic engagement.
- Families want and need to know about their children's schooling. Schools can help families understand the following concepts to enable them to engage more fully: current educational practices and systems in the United States; the benefits of engaging with school; state standards; measurement of student progress; accountability;

and various kinds of report cards (district, state, school, and student), and learning styles.

- Using practical strategies to make family/teacher conference less intimidating and more collaborative will encourage families to participate in them.
- Families often do not know how to contribute to their children's achievement, advocate for their children, or help them succeed at school. When schools take the initiative to share easy ways to connect with learning, everyone benefits.

HELPFUL RESOURCES RELATED TO THIS CHAPTER

- Donna M. Beegle's book *See Poverty . . . Be the Difference! Discovering the Missing Pieces for Helping People Move Out of Poverty* contains both insightful information and practical suggestions and activities to raise the level of awareness about living in poverty. Her inspiring personal story about emerging from poverty is in the Introduction. Available from Communication Across Barriers, www.combarriers.com. Beegle's website also contains other articles of interest in this content area.
- NSPRA's *Diversity Communications Toolkit* provides many examples from around the country of successful and new strategies for communicating with and engaging diverse populations in schools. Available at www.nspra.org.
- Anne Henderson's book *Beyond the Bake Sale* is full of suggestions for forming effective partnerships with parents and helping them engage with the school and their children's learning.
- The Harvard Family Research Project, located in the Harvard Graduate School of Education, provides the latest research-based information about engaging families, including its monthly *FINE Newsletter*. It also maintains a network (FINE: Family Involvement Network of Educators) for sharing. Many other resources are at www.hfrp.org.
- The National School Reform Faculty at Harmony Education Center is a professional development initiative focusing on increasing student achievement through collaborative learning communities. They provide workshops and materials on a wide range of topics about inequity in schools.

- Howard Gardner's book, *Frames of Mind: The Theory of Multiple Intelligences,* is helpful in articulating concepts about the variety of ways children learn. He and other research theorists have developed inventories to identify a student's most dominant intelligence and learning style.
- Practical approaches to helping parents understand and support their children's learning are at The Governor's Commonwealth Institute for Parent Leadership (GCIPL) at http://www.prichardcommittee.org/our-initiatives/cipl. GCIPL also provides training.
- Karen Mapp and Paul Kutter's 2013 research report, *Partners in Education: A Dual Capacity-building Framework for Family-school Partnerships,* presents a framework and its components for designing family engagement initiatives that build capacity among educators and families to partner with one another around student success. It includes three case studies.

Complete publication information for these resources is located in the reference list at the back of this book.

NOTES

1. Based on the work of Anne Henderson and Karen Mapp, *A New Wave of Evidence*; adapted by Kathy Leslie with permission from SEDL.
2. Based on Henderson and Berla's report, *A New Generation of Evidence,* 29.
3. Maslow, *A Theory of Human Motivation.*
4. Jerome Bruner included Demmert's quotation in *The Culture of Education.*
5. Paul Gorski cites many sources for the information in this paragraph in an *Education Leadership* article entitled, "The Myth of the Culture of Poverty."
6. Lyrics for the rap song "They School" (written by L. Alford, A Maier, V. Williams, and C. Gavin) can be found online on a 2000 Dead Prez album, *Let's Get Free,* at www.azlyrics.com/lyrics/deadprez/theyschools.html. (Last accessed June 16, 2014.)
7. Cohen and Prusak, *In Good Company,* 2001.
8. Anne Henderson and others, *The Case for Parent Leadership,* 40; used with permission of The Prichard Committee for Academic Excellence and KSA-Plus Communications.
9. Dufur, Parcel, and Troutman, "Does Capital at Home Matter More Than Capital at School?"
10. From Mapp and Kutter's online publication, *Partners in Education: A Dual Capacity-building Framework for Family-school Partnerships.*

FIVE

Facilitating Artfully

FUNDAMENTALS OF FACILITATING

Creating a new future that will lead to academic success for each student calls for facilitative leadership that engages stakeholders in deliberative processes in which many options are thoughtfully examined, wise choices are made, and decisions create sustainable futures that benefit students. The traditional model of hierarchal leadership is no longer effective in our complex, rapidly changing, and increasingly interconnected world. In a culture of engagement, the top-down leadership model, based on control, flips upside down. The power source moves from the top to the periphery, where leadership is shared and decisions are made closer to the classroom, families, students, and other stakeholders.

In this nontraditional culture, some of the most influential leaders emerge from among teachers, families, support staff, students, and other stakeholders. They are leaders who do not possess positional power but know how to empower others by creating structures to foster dialogue and inquiry where individuals share perspectives and uncover assumptions. As facilitators, they connect people and empower them to think creatively, suspend judgment, find connection in diverse perspectives, and use their intelligences to leverage new ideas and sustainable solutions. With good training and lots of practice, almost anyone can learn the necessary skills to become a successful facilitator. Depending on the scope and the politics of an issue, a facilitator may need more in-depth training and practice.

Those who successfully facilitate, guide, or coach groups know their inner selves well and possess excellent communication skills, political expertise, conflict management ability, knowledge of group dynamics, and democratic-process skills. Author Roger Schwarz explains: "Group facilitation is a process in which a person who is acceptable to the group and is neutral intervenes to help a group improve the way it identifies and solves problems and makes decisions to increase the group's effectiveness."[1]

This chapter defines the skills involved in facilitating effectively—the essentials for helping groups be successful in their deliberations and take meaningful action—and it provides practical ways to use those skills in real-life settings, both small and large. The fundamentals are approached in a linear way—from skills useful in forming and solidifying a group, to dealing successfully with inevitable conflict that will arise, to using protocols or structures to find common ground and take action, to involving a large number of participants in community forums for a variety of purposes.

Individuals can learn the skills and strategies required for good facilitation. "5.1 Everything a Facilitator Does" in the companion workbook, *The Politics of Authentic Engagement: Tools for Engaging Stakeholders in Ensuring Student Success* contains the full list of skills organized using an acronym—SAGE—representing the wisdom needed to be successful when easing the way for others as they grapple with changing their world. Useful as a memory tool for training others, it says the facilitator:

S *sees* opportunity in dialogue and leverages it to generate new thinking;

A *assures* that multiple diverse perspectives are heard, understood, and respected;

G *guides* participants through democratic processes including generative dialogue, inquiry, and careful consideration of the reasons for and against a course of action; and

E *exercises* mild control over the group, empowering them to think strategically and creatively together, make decisions together, and take action together.

The Politics of Facilitation Work

Realistically, facilitation work is political. Even though a good facilitator strives to remain neutral, s/he comes to the project with political perspectives and beliefs, a cultural identity, and values. A facilitator's opinions may, to a greater or lesser degree depending on how much the group is empowered to do its own work, influence the ideas considered, relationships built, and rules followed.

Facilitation work usually happens within a political context, including the politics of power, money, relationships, and education. Depending on the scope of the project, the facilitator may negotiate with several different political entities to ensure the fulfillment of the charge or purpose given to or developed by the group. The superintendent, school board, unions, teachers, parents, department of education, and state and federal government may exert some control over the outcome. Therefore, one of the facilitator's tasks is to clarify the group's boundaries—for example, the local, state, and federal laws within which the group must operate or any budget constraints or parameters.

When facilitators ignore politics, projects can fail: A group works for an entire year to develop a math curriculum that is scuttled when certain segments in the community rise up in protest because their views are not represented. A superintendent says he does not want to serve on the strategic planning team or know about the work until it is finished but comes in at the last gathering and rejects the framework. The union refuses to go along with the implementation of a safety program, although it declined to participate in the planning group. A team follows the charge of the board, does extensive research, and obtains wide approval for a revised report card, which the school board rejects.

The facilitator also deals with the internal politics of the group or groups with which s/he is working. Because the facilitator is present to guide the process rather than control the group, it can be quite challenging when group members confront the facilitator in uncivil or undemocratic ways. Keeping democratic principles in mind, the facilitator's role is to coach, probe, clarify, ask challenging questions, elicit thoughts and feelings of group participants, and prompt them to identify alternatives or options to address the issue and make choices for the common good.

The role is not to exercise firm control over the group, make final decisions, or force the group down a path they do not want to go. Though results are necessary, their character and detail should emerge from the deliberative process rather than be orchestrated by the facilitator. Demonstrating a sense of focus, inclusiveness, calm, and confidence as well as an attitude of listening and inquiry will contribute to making participants comfortable and willing to voice opinions and challenge old or conventional thinking.

Facilitation work is risky. Every facilitation project is different; a process workable with one group may not work in another group or place, and what works on one day may not work on the next with the same group. Human behavior is unpredictable. The facilitator cannot make participants be genuine, authentic, or honest. Facilitators must think on their feet, focus constantly, and respond to the group instantly. Depending on what surfaces during the meeting, the facilitator may change the process, time structure, or agenda. Good facilitators are courageous, patient, open, and comfortable with uncertainty and ambiguity—particularly difficult when the group wants a resolution immediately.

It may seem at times that the facilitator is doing nothing, but a good facilitator maintains what Otto Scharmer calls "an open mind, open heart, and open will every moment." He says this approach has three enemies, all within oneself: the voice of judgment, which shuts down an open mind; the voice of cynicism, which shuts down an open heart; and the voice of fear, which shuts down an open will. With an open mind, heart, and will, emptied of all biases, convictions, and ego, the facilitator listens for diverse points of view, contradictions, agreements, and insights. S/he creates space for silence and reflection, looks for invisible patterns, and feels for openings in the dialogue where new possibilities can emerge. Through appropriate protocols and processes, inquiry, surfacing dilemmas, and summarizing perspectives, the facilitator assists the group in assuming responsibility for their own work.

The group accomplishes a great deal as it takes ownership for the work, the choices made, and the ultimate outcomes. Effective facilitators guide in ways that enable participants to walk away saying, "We did it ourselves. We have responsibility for making sure our decisions are implemented and followed." This happens when the group controls the content and direction, and the facilitator assures that the group follows the agreed-to norms and processes. By observing the facilitator, many participants learn to be facilitative leaders themselves who go into the school or community and empower others.

* * *

For example, in one district several task forces called Tiger Teams (a military term for teams who quickly address and solve problems) were asked to think together and develop alternative ideas for addressing the loss of sports, music, drama, and other activity programs due to huge financial cuts. They developed many ideas including participation charges, scholarship programs for less afflu-ent families, fund-raising events, volunteer and partnership recruitment pro-grams to cover loss of paid staff, and an aggressive lobbying program to help decision-makers understand how their financial decisions were affecting the aca-demic success of thousands of children. After the school board accepted the plan, Tiger Team participants facilitated the empowerment of hundreds more people to raise money, lobby at the state capital, develop a scholarship program in each school, and recruit community partners and volunteers to coach activities and sports.

Facilitator Selection

The selection process for a facilitator working at any level in the course of a group's deliberations includes considering whether both the organization recruiting the facilitator as well as potential participants *perceive* the facilitator as trustworthy, neutral, and acceptable. In some cases, it means choosing an experienced professional outside of the or-ganization, while in others a trusted employee or stakeholder volunteer may be the right choice. Depending on the nature of the project, profes-sionals skilled in group process may be the best choice because they have expertise and skills in keeping a conversation moving, linking various perspectives, and confronting groups or individuals constructively as discussion unfolds, conflict emerges, or dialogue bogs down. However, funds are not always available to pay for someone with experience. Sometimes the best choice is to select an individual the group is more comfortable with, someone they know who may be representative of their race or culture, or who has a deep history and knowledge of the issue—someone they both like and trust.

Group situations vary and may include differing levels of facilitator expertise in the same project. There may be a need for more than one facilitator. For example, a district anticipating the need to engage the entire community in addressing a problem or setting new goals can hire an experienced facilitator to work with them in planning and conducting the overall process, and local facilitators to lead smaller group discussions supporting the larger project goals.

Group Processes

Once chosen, the facilitator can use the following set of introspective questions to think through and shape the elements of the project to meet the facilitation process's overall goals:

- What will I do to create a climate of trust and belonging?
- How will I help the participants see the big picture and know how their decisions may affect many others?
- What protocols and processes will I plan so participants thoughtfully engage with the issues and each other?
- How will I show and tell them I care about their well-being?
- How will I measure their level of satisfaction with my facilitation and the work in progress?
- How will I help participants understand their responsibilities to themselves, their planning group, and any subgroup to study the emerging issues more in-depth?
- What tasks and responsibilities will the participants assume for the group research, processes, and outcomes?
- How will I create conditions in which the participants become facilitative leaders themselves, able to take on responsibility for implementing the recommendations, plans, and ideas generated by their work?

Ensuring Balance in Points of View

The facilitator helps the school/district create lists of potential group participants who represent *all* segments of the population—socioeconomic levels, ethnicities, ability levels, gender, sexual orientation, age—and who have a stake in the outcomes. Without a broad spectrum of opinion and values, the conversation may be one-sided and fail to incorporate the diversity of needs and issues to place on the table for discussion and examination. For rich dialogue to occur and new ideas to emerge, a broad range of opinions and practices is included. Convincing organizations to bring in people with opposing viewpoints or values who may not support current or recommended practice may be challenging. Organizations may not want to include certain cultures because they have too few members. The facilitator stresses the importance of equity and the power in putting all perspectives on the table so new thinking can emerge. Depending on the issue, it may be appropriate to invite the larger community to observe the working group in action and even participate, if warranted, at a designated time during the meeting. The facilitator ensures observers understand and agree to the group's ground rules.

Creating the Environment

The facilitator is responsible for creating a warm and open environment, both physically and psychologically, so participants feel part of the group. Attending to the physical environment includes providing a circular seating arrangement, allowing participants to see eye to eye and hear one another. Peter Block, a facilitator who writes about designing physical space to support community, says not to use tables but put chairs as close as possible together in a circle and let people lean in together. If that is not reasonable or comfortable, round tables also allow everyone to sit at the same level, so they can see and hear one another clearly. Avoid seating arrangements in places such as classrooms, auditoriums, and conference rooms with rectangular tables. They enhance prestige, power, and control—all of which stop open dialogue.

Block makes two additional suggestions: (1) select rooms with a view so participants never forget they are not working in isolation but with a bigger world and (2) use movable chairs to support moving in and out of groups and going where one wants to focus while remaining connected to the entire group.[2] Attention to the light and temperature in the room, even the look of the walls, contributes to the comfort and willingness of those invited to share and talk together. Although educators meet and talk in schools or district offices, a site provided by a local business, community agency, or religious group might represent a more comfortable, neutral, and safe space.

Asking participants what needs to be in place for them to feel safe and have an open, candid conversation will increase their feelings of security. Good facilitators create environments in which participants talk about undiscussables. They believe every person in the room or on the team has something important to share. Often one of the facilitator's roles is to help people discover what they can offer.

The facilitator also needs to let people know and understand that s/he cares about each one of them. One way to do that is to make explicit every group member's starting points by surfacing their expectations, hopes, and fears related to the group's work. That means starting where participants are, not where the facilitator is. "5.2 Our Best Hopes and Worst Fears" in the companion workbook presents a group activity to elicit those starting points and make them visible within the room throughout the group's process.

Openings and Setting Ground Rules

A facilitation process may take place in one meeting or over several months. Setting the tone for dialogue and agreeing on basic ground rules early is important. The facilitator launches the group work by introducing him/herself or having someone from the organization do the introduction. The facilitator can then take a minute or two to communicate personal background information and facilitation experience. The key to the introduction is to build credibility but not to come across as the expert in the room. Others in the group then introduce themselves, perhaps through a grounding exercise like the one discussed below.

Depending on time constraints, the introductions may include exercises to identify participants' learning or communication style.[3] If this is a one-time meeting, the facilitator might ask people to introduce themselves by asking one of the following questions: What is the heart of the matter for you when it comes to the issue? What will you contribute to this process? What can you say about yourself that no one knows? In the first few moments, the goal is to create a warm, inviting climate and to get every voice into the room so participants feel comfortable speaking up and know it is okay to voice opinions. Good opening information also includes identifying the group's purpose and any charge given to it from the organization.

It is advantageous for participants to set their own ground rules, group norms, or operating agreements. Participants can identify what they need to have in place to feel safe, voice opinions without fear, and successfully meet the goals of their group process. They may also enjoy describing what drives them crazy in meetings. From this brainstormed list, a set of norms emerges. Those norms not only establish expectations about how participants will treat each other and make decisions together, but also help ensure a safe environment. In some cases, groups call the norms "conversation guidelines" to keep a friendly invitational tone about what is expected. They are especially helpful when differences in thinking generate heated discussion. While smaller groups can develop their own norms together, the facilitator of larger groups (such as in a community-forum setting) usually communicates a standard list of agreements that have worked well in similar circumstances and asks for agreement from the participants.

A facilitator might propose a short version of ground rules or operating agreements to include these elements:

- Agree to start and end times for meetings and finish on time.
- Honor silence and give people time to think.
- Listen without interrupting and refrain from side conversations.
- Consider differences as valid.
- Attack problems but not people.

Examples of a more in-depth list include these:

- We will remain open to influence and will not be judgmental.
- We will not criticize the views of others or try to persuade them.
- We will hold a space for different points of view and consider others' opinions carefully.
- We will listen intently to understand better.
- We will share "airtime" and participate within the time frames suggested by the facilitator.
- We will not interrupt except to indicate that we cannot hear a speaker.
- We will "pass" or "pass for now" if we are not ready or willing to respond to a question.
- We will be respectful and assume no one right answer but many perspectives.
- When we discuss our experience here with people outside the group, we will not attach names or any other identifying information to particular comments unless we have permission to do so.
- We will assume we all want the best for our children.

With either a shorter or a longer list, ask the group if any norms are missing. Suggestions can be added to the facilitator's or the group's original list. Then it is important to seek agreement *from each individual* about whether s/he can live within the final set of guidelines, indicated by a nod from each person. In large groups where participants are around tables, facilitators can ask if each person will abide by the agreements.

If someone does not agree, the facilitator asks the participant what it would take for him/her to agree and modifies the list until all can agree to the norms. Further, if a participant ultimately cannot agree to working constructively toward the charge itself, the facilitator can say, "You've been asked to be on this committee for the purpose of fulfilling this charge. If you believe you ethically cannot do this, then it is your responsibility to remove yourself from the committee."

Grounding the Group

The process of grounding a group helps the facilitator and participants know each other on a deeper level. It involves helping each participant listen with respect, establish verbal territory without being challenged, move from past to present to future thinking (a left-brain function), and express their feelings (a right-brain activity). Experiencing thinking and feeling with the group grounds each person.

Several questions create a grounding experience. The facilitator introduces the purpose of sitting in a circle and the notion of listening with respect to each other as each individual responds to the same key questions related to the task ahead. It is important that everyone experiences being heard fully with no judgments placed on their answers.

The facilitator can organize a large group into smaller circles of six to eight participants. The process might include asking members to state their names and what they do in the world, followed by their answers to these two questions: (1) What do you care deeply about—your passion—regarding children, school, and community? (2) What do you think about what you said and how do you feel about it? Including both a *thinking* question and a *feeling* question is important. Before posing the questions, writing them on a flip chart helps participants refer to them while they dialogue. Each person has up to three minutes to speak. In addition, the facilitator can ask participants to write their greatest passion on a Post-it Note and stick it on the large piece of paper displayed in the room labeled "The Passion Wall." Participants can view everyone's passions during the session.

If there is time, other questions can be asked that will lead to deeper thinking and feeling: What are your gifts and talents that might contribute to this process? What story do you tell about the challenges our school (district/community/education) faces? What are the reasons you are here today? (Not surface reasons, but the real reasons you actually came). What contribution will you make to this process? Questions are always followed by "What do you think about . . . and how do you feel about . . . ?"

After some time, listening with respect becomes a norm. After each person expresses an opinion, it is easier to speak again. When everyone has spoken in their group (there may be many small groups in the larger group), the entire group can share insights they have, such as something new they have learned or what surprised them as they listened to each other. The questions in the preceding paragraphs often generate new information and wisdom, which helps the group move forward. "5.3 Grounding the Group" in the workbook provides a grounding workshop activity. "5.4 Insight on Grounding" lists key steps, useful as a handout or presentation slide.

Using Effective Communication Strategies

Ensuring Effective Listening

> "If we try to listen we find it extraordinarily difficult, because we are always projecting our opinions and ideas, our prejudices, our background, our inclinations, our impulses; when they dominate we hardly listen at all to what is being said. . . . In that state, there is no value at all. One listens and therefore learns, only in a state of attention, a state of silence, in which this whole background is in abeyance, is quiet; then it seems to me, it is possible to communicate."[4]
> —Jiddu Krishnamurti, thinker and worldwide teacher, 1967

Listening deeply is the most important skill that facilitators and participants need to be productive and creative. However, studies show most people are poor listeners, with 75 percent of oral communication ignored, misunderstood, or forgotten. Respected author Will Schutz says at the lowest level of listening, people say, "I don't hear you," or "You are wrong," or "Let me tell you how it is." However, when there is a conscious intent to listen, people say, "Tell me more," or "This is what I hear you saying and feeling."[5] When listening attentively, one ponders what the other has said and wonders what the other is feeling. One does not think how to respond until the speaker has finished talking. In today's culture, the listener is usually thinking of a response while the person is talking, thereby missing the meaning of the words and the feelings behind those words. Robert Bolton in his groundbreaking book *People Skills*

identified three skills for effective listening: attending, reflecting, and following.

- *Attending skills* include the nonverbal signals listeners send to show
  they are paying attention to the speaker. Eye contact is the most
  important of these skills. Many people find direct eye contact difficult because it is intimate and because feelings about using it differ
  widely among cultures. Many Asian and Eastern cultures, for example, find it disrespectful to look directly into a person's eyes,
  especially one who is older, dominant, or of the opposite sex.
  Nevertheless, facial expressions and eyes reveal information about
  feelings and level of attention. Direct eye contact does not mean
  staring into the eyes of someone. It does mean looking softly on the
  speaker and occasionally breaking eye contact to look at gestures or
  body movement. Leaning slightly forward, facing the person directly with the body open—no crossed arms—and at a comfortable
  distance demonstrate alertness and openness to listening.
- *Reflecting skills* include paraphrasing content, reflecting feelings and
  meanings, and voicing summative reflections. Feelings are reflected
  both verbally and physically. Focusing first on the feeling words
  and observing body language builds the capacity to hear feelings.
  Then asking, "If I were having that experience, how would I feel?"
  makes it personal. Listening in this way does not involve trying to
  change someone's mind, but rather putting oneself in the other
  person's shoes.

  Reflecting meaning ties the feelings expressed to the content. Listening is a search for who a person is, both verbally and nonverbal-
  ly. Reflecting is restating briefly in your own words the feelings and
  meanings perceived to validate understanding and acknowledge
  the speaker's reality. It is discovering the essence of another person.
- *Following skills* include nonintrusive invitations to talk, minimal en-
  couragers, infrequent questions, and attentive silence. Minimal en-
  couragers keep the conversation going. Instead of asking questions
  when people are talking and sending a message of interrogation,
  using words like "Mm-hmm," "Tell me more," "For instance . . . ,"
  "Then . . . ," or "Oh, really?" "Yes, I see," "Right," "Sure," and
  "Darn!" suggest "Please continue, I'm listening and I understand."
  The following skill of silence—attentive silence where people can
  think—is one of the most powerful listening strategies.[6]

Following skills also include the facilitator or designee serving as a silent attentive recorder of ideas expressed. To acknowledge publicly the speakers in the room, the recorder charts the key ideas expressed by each individual *in the speaker's own words* on a flip chart or electronic device. If the recorder misses an idea, the facilitator can ask the speaker what s/he would like to have written. This focus on accurately recording each speaker's key ideas helps the note-taker and listeners remain silent and listen carefully without interjecting personal thoughts and biases.

Although the process of recording slows down the group, it also provides more time for participants to think and reflect. The facilitator does not have to record on a chart or other device. Any group member who can write legibly in the language of the group can be a note-taker, taking turns with others in the same circle and engaging more people in the process. If, however, any recorder has personal thoughts to add, another recorder needs to take over the note-taking role.

Sensing Opportune Timing

A good facilitator values time and manages it well. A sense of opportune timing means knowing when to stop, pause, or go on to the next issue; when to slow down the group; when to take time to reflect; and when to ignore the timeline and provide more time for discussion. Participants need opportunities to reflect and to work through issues and dilemmas. However, districts, schools, and communities often find it challenging to give groups the time they need to accomplish their goals.

Posing a question may be helpful in countering the concern that busy teachers, administrators, and stakeholders do not have the time to deliberate: How much time do you lose by *not* having these conversations? When an organization does take time to converse with its stakeholders and each other, people repeatedly say, "Thank you for taking the time to listen to me; thank you for letting us discuss this and work it out." It is often necessary to slow down to go faster. What are the priorities? When educators take the time to engage in deep conversation with themselves and with others, people are more likely to own responsibility for making their schools successful.

Facilitators have a sense of timing and sensitivity during conversations—knowing when to move forward and when to allow more time. Such sensitivity comes with practice and in being comfortable with silence—the amount of silence that provides enough time for people to discuss an idea, ponder statements, and integrate new ideas into their thinking before they are expected to respond or voice an additional thought. It also comes with the facilitator's learned ability to perceive when a group is leaning in a particular direction, when participants might be at a point of reaching consensus, and when to evaluate how the group feels about the progress made.

A facilitator thinks quickly and makes process adjustments to keep the group heading toward its objectives. Ultimately, the facilitator's sense of timing is important in moving the group, when they are ready, toward action steps, the stage in which people create concrete plans, seek agreements among themselves, and make commitments to each other for reporting results and implementation plans or perhaps engaging others in the implementation process.

Addressing Undiscussables

People do not feel safe talking about some subjects—the topic may compromise a group member's situation or safety. Sometimes feelings of risk can be unrealistic—based on a fear unique to an individual's life experiences. In either case, challenging issues impede dialogue if they are not on the table. Although dialogue time should not center on people or personal issues, sometimes participants do not feel they can continue a conversation unless they can deal with their concerns.

The facilitator and the school create a safe environment where people feel they can talk together. The facilitator helps the group walk the fine line between simply talking about personal issues and making visible personal concerns that significantly affect issues and looking objectively at the issue on the table. Participants must agree to hold conversations and information discussed in a group setting in confidence, never identifying anyone's name when they are talking about the issues arising in the group's deliberation. Further, the facilitator needs to underscore this agreement: Whatever is talked about in the parking lot outside needs also to be talked about in the room. Outside conversations destroy trust and the spirit of the entire effort.

Not identifying an elephant in the room can significantly impede progress. If a participant believes s/he cannot talk about something verbally, an "elephant box" provides a way to communicate the undiscussable. Placing a small box and blank cards on a back table enables anyone who feels reluctant to voice something aloud to write the concern or statement (anonymously or not) on a card and put it in the box. The facilitator reads those privately, learns about issues existing for one or more people in the room, and works to find ways to surface the issues within the larger conversation.

The facilitator works continuously to maintain an environment where group members can voice their own story about an otherwise undiscussable topic. When a participant expresses feelings in the context of a story, new pathways to dialogue often open because the speaker's courage and truth foster an attitude of understanding and patience in listeners. The listener's ability to suspend judgment while listening to the story of another can be powerful in making undiscussables visible and allowing them to be open for respectful exploration.

Using Questions in Group Process

Creating Well-Designed Questions

A core task in the facilitator's preparation involves designing questions that not only frame the issues clearly for the group and guide participants through the group's processes but also stimulate a sense of responsibility and commitment. Block says, "They are questions that take us to requests, offers, declarations, forgiveness, confession, gratitude, and welcome, all of which are memorable and have a transformative power."[7]

Group members may interpret questions in different ways. They can challenge the participant to think differently when s/he reaches inside to confront and address issues that matter. The facilitator asks questions to clarify, foster thinking, assess understanding, and seek information. Probing questions help people think and push them to process information in new ways. Clarifying questions help people define situations and issues. Other types of questions assess the validity of data or seek information. They push people to reexamine their own beliefs, help them focus, find their voice, and speak up.

Developing and asking the right questions to stimulate deeper deliberations is challenging. The best approach is to ask questions in continuing cycles of inquiry, depending on the participants' needs. Key attributes of provocative questions that stimulate thinking and cause people to question and feel deeply include these:

- They are open-ended to stimulate responses and dialogue.

- They are open to different interpretations so people come from their own experience.
- They are carefully prepared for unique participant groups and purposes.

One set of powerful questions useful at the beginning of a group's time together includes *expectation questions*, designed to surface each person's hopes and fears about the process.

- What does success look like to you?
- What commitment do you bring to this group to create this success?
- What do you think our greatest challenges will be?
- What gifts will you bring to the group when conflict enters?
- What are your hopes for this process? For our school? For teaching and learning? For our reading program (or whatever the issue is at hand)?
- What are you prepared to do to reach these hopes?

Surfacing perceptions of the problem, process, and potential outcomes up front begins the group process on a positive note and creates energy. It gives focus, sets a listening tone for the entire process, and lets people know where they are going. It also helps people hear there are diverse opinions in the room and that people have different hopes and dreams.

Using Questions to Frame the Issues

Sometimes a facilitation process informs the participants of the situation they will consider. Unlike traditional "sit and get" meetings in which people are told "the way it is," the facilitator of an authentic engagement process frames the issue by presenting options that address the situation, including pros and cons. The group can then suggest other options as well as pros and cons.

Framing an issue involves:

- Defining the problem broadly
- Receiving feedback from those who disagree
- Presenting a range of choices/options for addressing the problem
- Including arguments both for and against
- Asking the group to identify more options for solving the problem (working as one group or in small groups with chart paper)

- Asking the group to add to the list of pros and cons for each of the choices
- Laying out consequences, costs, and trade-offs together
- Being concrete and giving examples
- Emphasizing themes and underlying values versus the details

Within those steps, the skilled facilitator uses questions in varying ways at different points in a group's conversation. To begin any deliberative process, participants need to know clearly what the issues are underlying their charge. To explore the issue or the choices, ask the following questions:

- What do you know for sure?
- What do you think you know?
- What do you want to know?

Asking participants these questions engages them from the start, resulting in mutual understanding about the situation and a sense of responsibility and commitment. The facilitator or a person closest to the issue may also then provide more detail or answer questions. Tailored to the local setting, the following eleven *framing questions* help crystallize issues involved in any situation so the group can craft potential resolutions later:

1. What is the situation?

    - How would your colleagues describe it?
    - How would the principal describe it?
    - How would parents, students, and the district office describe it?

2. Why has the problem not been solved?
3. What do you think about the situation? How do you feel about it?
4. Who is responsible for the problem?
5. Does anybody make it worse?
6. How do you contribute to the problem?
7. If the problem were solved, what would it look like?
8. What is getting in the way of solving this problem?
9. What are the constraints within which everyone must live while seeking solutions (e.g., time, money, resources)?
10. What else do we need to know?
11. What do you need to help solve this problem?

Guiding through Questioning

One of the facilitator's tasks is to engage participants in identifying choices that may address the issue at hand. Once everyone has a clear idea of the big picture, the facilitator asks questions to uncover the dilemmas present in a situation and helps participants identify the pros and cons associated with different scenarios that address the problem(s). The facilitator's questions bring out additional details, uncover underlying patterns, and help the participants consider everyone's values and beliefs.

Probing questions raise awareness of the range of possibilities. They include questions designed to help understand another's point of view or explore potential solutions.[8] For example, the following questions help participants look at alternatives in solving problems:

- I wonder, what can we do to change this situation?
- How would you like it to be?
- What is the meaning of this situation in your own life?
- How could we change this situation so you could live with it?
- What would it take to move the current situation toward the ideal?
- What exactly needs to change here?
- How might those changes come about? (Name as many ways as possible.)
- How could you reach the goal? What are the other ways?
- How would your alternatives affect other people in this group? Other parents?
- What will the political effect be if you . . . ?
- What would need to change in order to implement this option?
- What would keep you from doing . . . ?
- What prevents you from getting involved?
- How can I support you?

Other probing questions can help participants understand their own perspectives and hesitations:

- In what ways is this situation (proposal/idea) a dilemma for you?
- In what ways is this dilemma important for you?
- If you could take a snapshot of this dilemma, what would you see?
- What have you done to try to remedy this situation?

To help participants clarify their thinking about data studied during the group process, these data questions are helpful:

- What do you see?
- Can you list your observations?
- What are your conclusions from what you see?
- What personal judgments might you need to reevaluate?

Each situation is unique. What is happening in the "now" will determine the questions to ask. Most importantly, the facilitator is responsive to the needs and issues of each participant and the group itself rather than selecting questions from a book and imposing them on a group.

MANAGING CONFLICT THROUGH ENGAGEMENT

The Nature of Conflict

Conflict is natural, and if it is not a conflict between egos, it can produce powerful energy that creates breakthroughs, generating new ideas and answers to stubborn problems. Many see conflict as bad and try to avoid it when, in fact, welcoming it and ensuring safety for full expression of differing perspectives is powerful and increases individual and group capacity. Conflict is not productive when people take it personally, start with the solution and not with the issue, do not value what someone else is saying, or attempt to persuade others to their point of view. Common causes of conflict are broken lines of communication and differences in values, roles, position/status, goals, or perceptions.

For example, the creationist clashes with the evolutionist. The traditional math proponent disagrees with the modern math advocate. The community is furious about a superintendent receiving a raise amid tightening budgets and reductions; the board wants to keep the results-producing, highly respected leader. Differences in values, status, and goals as well as communication breakdowns are all evident in these examples.

Conflict is normal, but it can only be *normalized* and addressed when it is acknowledged. Further, conflict *management* is dependent upon all parties recognizing their role in the conflict—because all parties in a conflict do carry some part of the truth.[9] The facilitator's responsibility is to create space in dialogue for all perspectives and for everyone involved in the conflict to express their part of the truth and suspend judgment long enough to listen deeply to all the perspectives. When participants are able to inquire into underlying assumptions and see the entire picture, the conflict most often dissolves because people understand each other. In a conflict, perception is equally important as the facts, and although facts may be open for debate, perceptions are not. When handled well, the challenge of conflict can be stimulating, fun, and restorative.

Handled poorly, conflict festers and escalates when one or more participants:

- Think they are going to lose and divide the world according to winners and losers
- Think they can avoid confronting the situation by avoiding it
- Think the conflict is about them and react personally to it
- Think they need to align with someone to resolve conflict rather than understanding the divergent points of view
- Are not clear about what the problem is because it is not fully visible on the table
- Do not understand the role each person plays in the conflict
- Are not clear about the boundaries and parameters within which they can operate in the group and do not know the constraints under which each person operates
- State the problem as someone's fault rather than a problem free-standing from blame

Fundamentals of Responding to Conflict

Facilitating groups is messy. The process is not linear. Engagement involves divergent pathways, disparate values, and multiple passionate human beings collaborating to accomplish a mutual goal. Below are thirteen considerations for a facilitator as s/he navigates conflict in a facilitation process.

1. Seeking first to understand should happen before seeking to be understood.
2. Managing a difficult person means managing oneself.
3. Knowing it is all right to disagree creates more authenticity.
4. Taking time-outs can lower the tension in the room.

* * *

I once worked with a group of districts from across the country when a discomforting incident arose between a union leader in a California district and a superintendent in a Kansas district. Each group had a team, including their union and administrative representatives. The California district was recovering but still angry and emotional from a teacher strike, and the team from Kansas had just ended their strike. The union leader from California passionately criticized administrators in general, after which the Kansas superintendent threw his pencil across the room at him because he had just quieted his group. Everyone started shouting at one another.

I attempted to calm the situation by changing subjects, but the high tension remained. I called for a break: "Let's take a time-out." Many teachers on every team came up to me with ideas about how to solve the problem. The conflict and anger eventually simmered down after the time-out. Participants came back to their tables and talked through a new question I posed about identifying the steps they would like to take to move forward. They were able to cooperate when they set the terms.

5. Allowing emotion validates participants. Authentic people show emotion; they cry and get angry. As long as they observe the group's operating agreements, including not attacking people but rather the problem, conflict can be managed. Creating space for divergent views, allowing time for reflection, and posing questions that empower people to value others' perspectives creates a place of respect and deep listening.

6. Identifying probable areas of agreement and summarizing the dialogue maintains clarity. One way to track and make the conversation visible is to maintain flip charts so everyone can see statements and ideas provided. It is helpful to note the points of agreement as they emerge, and identify points of hesitancy, areas of "still thinking," and topics of disagreement.

7. Using a "parking lot" chart keeps discussions on track if tangential issues arise. A flip-chart page or wall chart can serve as a place to park thoughts not on the topic, yet keep them visible until a more opportune moment arises to address them.

8. Confirming agreement verifies movement. The facilitator obtains confirmation from every participant by asking, "do you agree on

this point?" allows each to respond verbally or simply give a head nod.

9. Surfacing and recording points of disagreement as well as each participant's response assists the group in defining alternative approaches to the disagreements. Questions like "What would it take for you to reach agreement on this?" or "What has to happen for you to move off this point of disagreement?" are helpful in facilitating the conversation in a neutral way while gathering critical information about what is needed for consensus to be reached.

10. Identifying various options based on declared agreements enables participants to describe additional information or research needed. Volunteers from the group(s) can collect it before the next conversation. Putting choices on the table adds possibilities.

11. Setting next steps is important because it may be impossible to solve everything in one session or have the requested information on hand.

12. Presuming positive outcomes keeps group members hopeful and willing to continue.

13. Using advocacy and inquiry strategies helps participants state their thoughts but be open to new ideas.

Using several other quick and simple strategies *if further conflict arises* within the group during its process will keep the group moving:

- Reviewing the norms or operating agreements set at the beginning of the process to recenter people.
- Creating additional ground rules applicable for the moment.
- Paraphrasing frequently to clarify thoughts and feelings.
- Asking probing questions to prompt participants to delve deeper into the issues.

Advocates, Dissidents, and Activists

There are players in the political arena, advocates, dissidents, and activists, who can stir up conflict. Knowing how to respond to people in each category helps diffuse conflict.

Advocates propose what they believe in and use reason. *Dissidents* oppose one or many things by using logic and selected emotions. Some people say they are sour on everything. *Activists* want to get something done; they use logic and strategic actions. All of these groups can create conflict when they refuse to hear another perspective or compromise. The most effective way to work with each group is to use the strategies they employ: use reason with advocates; logic and selected emotions with dissidents; and logic and strategic actions with activists.

Zealots are single-minded, absorbed with one issue, egocentric, must be in charge, and want to moderate the enemy. It is best to leave zealots alone and isolate them by identifying other people to control them. The group has to control a zealot; the facilitator cannot.

Working with Polarities

A polarity exists when there is a division between two or more right answers that are independent of each other. For example, the conflict between individualism and collectivism is one such polarity. Both belief systems have value. It does not have to be one belief or the other; it can be both. It is possible to leverage the polarities to find new strategies. Using a visual framework with four quadrants can help a facilitator prompt thinking about the complexities of polarities. For example, one quadrant might represent the positive outcomes of individualism, while another the positive outcomes of collectivism. A third quadrant might represent the negative outcomes of focusing only on individualism and neglecting collectivism, while the fourth quadrant includes the negative outcomes of focusing on collectivism and neglecting individualism.

Some respondents considering the quadrant framework may say individualism protects freedom and fosters ingenuity, initiative, and innovation. Others may say collectivism provides equal opportunity, protects the marginalized, and leads to better thinking and innovative solutions to problems. Collectivists may believe individualism leads to mechanistic thinking, decreasing an ability to solve problems and implement sustainable solutions. Individualists may believe collectivist thinking causes socialism, heavy regulations, and excessive control, and stops imagination and creativity. As in evidence in the media, the negative outcomes often result in name-calling and demonizing of those who are entrenched in their views.

People steeped in their beliefs are less able to see the values of the opposite persuasion. However, when a facilitator asks participants to fill quadrants with their thinking, group members begin to see there are strengths and limits in each of the polarities. In this example, collectivists usually see the value in creativity and innovation while individualists see that certain populations do need support. Unsolved polarities result in stalled decisions and sometimes even war. Understanding and valuing the strengths of both belief systems helps participants see the big picture, avoid extremism, and create more inclusive solutions.[10] "5.5 Working with Polarities" in the workbook provides a sample quadrant framework for helping people understand how polarities may affect their perspectives.

Finding Common Ground

Common ground is an area of agreement found among diverse individuals or groups resulting from an honest and often heated sharing of ideas. Agreements are reached, sometimes very slowly and often only through skilled facilitation in a dialogue in which ideas and solutions are explored and pros and cons are raised. In general, it involves five stages:

1. Grounding the group
2. Exploring the situation or issue
3. Identifying the best and worst possible outcomes
4. Exploring several possible solutions
5. Identifying ways participants could support progress[11]

A facilitator's process of *grounding a group* provides an opportunity to know more about how participants perceive the situation under consideration. Sections earlier in this chapter offer suggestions on how to help a group find common ground. In addition, "5.2 Our Best Hopes and Worst Fears" in the workbook helps a group *create a positive working environment* to find common ground, and the grounding activity in "5.3 Grounding the Group" could be a beginning step in finding common ground.

The facilitator's awareness of their own feelings, their sense of the present moment within a group, and their ability to think of the past and the future at the same time are important attributes in helping people be present in the here and now—to let go of entrenched positions or opinions and consider what others are saying and needing.

"5.6 Finding Common Ground and Moving to Action" in the workbook outlines a process for moving a group through their thinking about issues and dilemmas toward the common ground existing among them and on to action.

Guiding the group to inquire more deeply about issues and possibilities helps people move through conflict and find sustainable solutions.

Facilitating the dialogue involves five steps. Practices, questions, or statements a facilitator can use are included in each step.

Step 1: Striving for inclusion by:

- Removing hierarchies
- Remaining neutral and empathizing with all perspectives
- Making room for all voices
- Finding the leader within each participant
- Honoring silence
- Maintaining the ground rule of only one person talking at once, without side conversations
- Ensuring there is enough time to work through any conflict

Step 2: Creating shared meaning by:

- Checking facilitator's own assumptions
- Withholding judgment
- Using phrases like "This is what I understand you are saying" or "What do you mean by . . ."
- Making visible the trade-offs and consequences for each party in the conflict so people can see and understand more clearly what others are giving up to reach compromise
- Clearly addressing wishful or compartmentalized thinking by helping people see the big picture and how things are connected; seeing that changing one part of the system has consequences for another part of the system

Step 3: Paying attention to *intention* by asking oneself:

- What do I want from this conversation?
- Am I open to be influenced?
- What are my interests?

Step 4: Focusing on inquiry by:

- Seeking first to understand
- Inquiring from a genuine desire to know and understand
- Using a "tell me more" prompt
- Avoiding blame and defensiveness
- Attacking the problem, not the people

Step 5: Exploring agreements and impasses by:

- Identifying explicitly where agreements exist and where they do not
- Asking questions like "How can we clarify or define differences?" or "Is there anything you cannot live with on this agreement?"
- Maintaining civility within the group's process by fostering restraint and awareness, and reminding participants that insensitive comments hurt.

Lessons Learned

Not all conflict is managed well or resolved. Every facilitator knows s/he may not be the best person for the task, or once into the process may need to resign because s/he cannot serve every member well for one reason or another. The best outcome of a difficult situation may be that the participants and the facilitator apply their learning at another time. The following example from a large, relatively new suburban high school illustrates a number of lessons learned.

*   *   *

It was a tough group of high school teachers—the members of a handpicked strategic planning team organized to address several issues in the school. From the beginning, some of the team members did not want me as a facilitator because they thought I was the principal's pawn. I attempted to separate myself from the principal and identify their issues, which included creating a staff decision-making model, determining a communication system between and among the professional learning communities, and developing a strategic plan for the school.

The principal who hired me wanted a strategic plan. However, team members pushed back. I conceded, asking them what they wished to do. Instead, they wanted a workable process for decision-making within their school neighborhoods and learning communities and were willing to work on developing it. I handed over the task to a number of volunteers on the team with expertise in decision-making models. They developed several options for consideration. Ultimately, everyone became engaged in the process. It took several months of investigating various proposals, receiving feedback from staff, and deliberating over the models' pros and cons. Different teams worked on other issues including investigating the best use of advisory periods and looking at the use of time.

Early in the process, I did a communication workshop with the group using some language the principal gave me to describe the school's issues. The language provoked anger and resentment among some teachers. It was not conducive to moving the team forward.

Lesson Learned #1: The facilitator needs to know information about the group s/he will be working with. Although it is time intensive, facilitators can gain the necessary background knowledge through pre-process interviews or surveys with team members. If money is not available to pay for this step, the facilitator should go ahead with the pre-work because it could save time and a great deal of grief.

Those who did not want me to be there were informal teacher leaders who had been running the school and thought they alone should continue to do so. They were successful in getting the principal dismissed about three months into the process. Others who were supportive of the ousted principal were very grateful I was there. Unfortunately, I did not acknowledge early in the process the situation would be unmanageable because I was not acceptable as a neutral facilitator to all parties.

Lesson Learned #2: The facilitator needs to be acceptable to all participants—those who select the facilitator as well as the group's members. Confirming that early is important, and removing oneself from a process may be necessary.

I thought we had identified all expectations clearly at the beginning of my work with the team. We established and agreed on norms and operating agreements. At each meeting, team members reviewed the guidelines as well as the group's purpose. However, one teacher continuously tried to dominate and not follow the agreements. Tension was mounting between him and his followers and me. Some group members warned me that there was an effort to force me out by undermining the team's work. In the middle of that contentious time, an interim principal came on board, asking me to continue. Although I did question my effectiveness, I continued.

Lesson Learned #3: The facilitator must not only *be* neutral, but also be *perceived* as neutral. Sometimes a person from outside the organization is the answer. At other times, a parent, student, or teacher can serve successfully, with the advantage that they know the culture well. The person selected to lead the group must meet the criteria for a successful facilitator: be neutral, know group processes, be able to step out of the picture and not push a personal agenda. When using an insider or outsider, it is the *perception* of the participants that matters. Although an insider may be able to speak and act in a neutral manner, if the team or participants *perceive* that the facilitator feels pressured to act according to district/ school desires or directions, the facilitator cannot succeed.

As the group moved toward final decisions and ending the process, a final disruptive episode occurred. Everyone on the team had agreed to the process established to control people who persisted in dominating conversations: You could talk twice and then everybody else had a chance to speak before you could talk again. When the dominant participant would not stop talking in a subsequent session, I reaffirmed the agreement: "You have had two opportunities to talk and now you have taken three, so we need to hear from other people." He said, "Are you telling me I can't talk anymore?"

"You can't talk until other people have talked."

He continued, "Are you saying what I'm saying right now, I can't say right now?"

When I said, "That's correct, you cannot," he threw his books down and walked out of the room.

We went on with the meeting and accomplished all we had planned for the day. After the session, the acting principal characterized the teacher as an immature rebel whom he would bring into line. However, after the teacher warned the principal the next day that if I returned, he would not participate, the principal called to say my work was finished.

Lesson Learned #4: Facilitators defeat the process when they get into a tug-of-war with a participant or take interactions personally. Asking the group what they want to do about the issue is one avenue to pursue, although in such a volatile situation, team members may have been intimidated enough by the dominating teacher to remain silent.

Lesson Learned #5: A facilitator removed from a process may move the team to a self-governing model if the organization sees merit in allowing the facilitator to provide positive closure.

It would have been better if I had been able to come back to validate the team and their work. I would have let them know they were doing well — that they had the capacity to finish the tasks themselves — and provided any final guidance requested to launch them on their way.

A facilitator should not play hero and protect group members without a voice. There are situations when a facilitator should consider resigning including when some participants on the team are consistently not abiding by agreements; when nothing seems to bring the disturbers to collaborate with the group; and when some of the participants are warning the facilitator that there is an effort by some to sabotage the process. The better choice is to tell the organization to seek another facilitator and step out of the group.

USING STRUCTURE AND PROCESS TO MOVE DIALOGUE TOWARD ACTION

Organizations have many different structures to promote democratic processes and to engage people authentically in dialogue around complex challenging issues. Below are a few of the processes that work well with schools.

The Study Circle

A study circle is a group of eight to twelve people who meet regularly over a period of weeks or months to address a critical issue in a democratic, collaborative way. Launched as a concept by Everyday Democracy, study circles take place all over the world in many different types of organizations. Participants examine issues from various points of view and identify areas of common ground. They emerge from the circle process with recommendations for action beneficial to the school and community. Topics tackled by study circles conducted around the country include youth mentoring programs, parent engagement for Latino families, safety in schools, and motivating students to take challenging classes.

Appreciative Inquiry

The appreciative inquiry process seeks what is good in an organization. Instead of looking at reasons for failure, it finds reasons for success by identifying stories of innovation, hope, courage, and positive change. Through inquiry, participants identify what they want the organization to be based on—what is working well now. Appreciative inquiry uses only a positive lens to determine action steps similar to those covered in this chapter.

Open Space Technology

Open space technology holds meetings for a group of five to one thousand or more people who care about a subject. It uses the principle of self-organization, thereby requiring little or no planning except to identify the purpose or theme. Participants—the more diverse the better—begin by sitting in a circle. The facilitator asks each person in the group to identify an issue connected to the overall theme they wish to discuss and for which they are passionate. The list of issues becomes the agenda and, depending on the size of the group, ranges from thirty to one hundred topics.

Those who offer a topic name are asked to come to the center of the circle—hence, the open space—write it on a piece of paper, state their name, and explain the issue to the entire group. These people, called conveners, post the topic on a wall with a time and place to meet and discuss the issue. Once the issues are posted, people go to the topic posting they are interested in and sign up. At the appointed time and place, the convener launches the conversation and takes notes. The facilitator usually compiles the notes into a report and distributes it physically or electronically to all participants. An open space process works best if it is a full-day event. However, in schools with limited time, it is possible to adapt the process to one-hour sessions, still using the principle of self-organization to identify and discuss issues. [12]

The World Café

The World Café is a "process designed to make visible and audible the collective intelligence of a living human system." [13] The event is set up and managed by the facilitator, who designs the questions, manages the time, and convenes the group in a large room with tables arranged like a café. Participants move from table to table, building on each conversation for several rounds of different questions. The steps and principles of the café process are as follows:

- Set the context by stating the café's purpose and process. Everyone arrives as equals and may begin by sharing his or her personal story.
- Create a hospitable space that is welcoming and looks like a café. Place tables around the room at which three or four people and a table facilitator can sit to converse. Cover the table with a paper tablecloth on which participants can write notes, draw, and doodle. Flowers on the table add ambience.

- Explore questions that matter. The thoughtfully planned questions should be open-ended, meaningful, follow a question sequence, and stimulate conversation in which anyone can participate.
- Encourage everyone to participate by talking, drawing, writing, and listening; listen for insights as they move from table to table and find patterns of thoughts and language; and connect diverse perspectives.
- At the conclusion of the event, the facilitator convenes the total group to share by making visible and audible the individual as well as collective insights and naming next steps together.

Community Forums

Unlike a summit, which is a meeting of top-level officials, a forum is a gathering where everybody is welcome and can speak up. Such a gathering may be the culminating event in a broad deliberative process or it may be a step within a planning process. In either case, stakeholders come together to talk about a particular question, issue or recommendation. A wide range of teachers, students, families, and community members listen, learn from, and influence one another in conversations in their group or groups. The rich data gathered form the forum's outcomes and may include a list of strategic priorities, final decisions on a direction to take, resolution on a tough single issue, and action steps, or anything else the community or schools desire. Another outcome is that those who participate are likely to assume responsibility for implementation because they have brought content, energy, and commitment into the work. The school board usually reviews the forum's work and incorporates the results into its policy-level decision-making process.

Holding a community forum often provides an antidote to skepticism for a school system. Inviting citizens to participate in discussions of urgent needs and issues not only builds stronger linkages between schools and communities, but it also contributes to more effective planning and enduring change. When people have a voice in the process, they will take greater responsibility for improving their schools. In addition to deepening links and broadening responsibility, other benefits from community forums may include:

- Improved learning and teaching
- Greater community trust in the schools

- Deeper parent/community involvement
- Increased resources
- More supportive legislative policy
- Stronger relationships with the media

A community forum is dedicated to improving schools and involves in-depth dialogue based on candor and mutual trust. An artful facilitator is key to establishing such trust, enabling the dialogue, and developing the linkages needed for plans and action to generate genuine progress. To that end, the process must be locally developed and based on democratic principles. It must involve face-to-face communication among as many voices as possible from all constituencies, including those of internal staff. There must be a mutual commitment to work at communicating and a willingness to tackle difficult issues. Although community forums vary in focus and setting, all proceed along a similar flow of processes. "5.7 Format of a Community Forum" in the workbook provides an agenda for a typical community forum, including instructions for facilitating each segment.

Community forums serve a variety of purposes. They can be used to: select a new superintendent, determine how best to use time in schools, develop system-wide priorities for a new superintendent, create a district's strategic plan, envision the design for a new school, determine where a school should be built, and identify what a district's constituents and staff believe students should know and be able to do and how progress should be measured.

Depending on the forum's scope and purpose, the event may extend over two days, an evening, or be conducted in a multiple-session format. Length can be adapted depending on purpose. Major elements important in creating a community forum are these:

- Decision to hold a forum

    An organization makes the decision to hold a forum when it may want to strengthen its community through dialogue, learn diverse perspectives on an issue, and/or capitalize on the energy and thinking of stakeholders planning together and generating new ideas. The decision is most effective when the school board decides to hold the event and it has the support of staff members and the community. However, it could be a self-organizing effort put in place by people who are interested in such an event or organized by a community group. Regardless of how the decision to hold a forum is made, if everyone works together, the forum has a good chance of success.

• Planning team responsibilities

The organization's first task in organizing a forum is to form a planning team made up of representatives from all segments of the community and district, and select a facilitator who will work with the team. The facilitator may also facilitate focus groups or gather other types of research to frame the process. The planning team's task, in coordination with the facilitator, is to plan all the elements of the forum: identifying and/or crystallizing the purpose, determining whom to invite and how, arranging for the location and any meals, developing background materials for participants so they come to the forum prepared, and identifying needed research and collection methods. The planning team also designs feedback loops, identifies questions, and selects the format for the final recommendations.

• Collection and analysis of data

The planning team collects research to develop questions to ask the forum participants. They also include a research summary in the participants' folders. Research may include data from a series of focus groups, surveys, and/or studies of model programs. The data provides the core information for the forum. Chapter 3, "Collecting and Using Stakeholder Research," describes how to conduct focus groups as well as how to analyze and use data gathered from participants.

• Planning and implementing the forum event

For forum participants to come informed and able to make sound judgments, they need background information about the nature of the event. A fact sheet can include demographics about the district, test scores, school improvement funding explanations, budget information, as well as neutral and non-advocacy summaries of the issues to be deliberated at the forum. It is important to provide the materials in the languages of the participants and arrange for translators to be available electronically or personally for each language represented at the forum. Such background information can be included as part of a written invitation to potential participants.

The entire forum group (which can be as large as five hundred to eight hundred people or more) needs to be pre-divided into smaller groups for everyone to be able to speak with others during the forum. It is best to assign a mix of the forum population to each table, creating conversation groups with diverse points of view: for example, a teacher, student, businessperson, social service worker, representative of the clergy, school administrator, and government representative.

Participants in the forum work in small groups of six to eight people with a "table facilitator." The lead facilitator trains each table facilitator prior to the forum. The table facilitator role includes greeting people at the table and helping everyone relax and learn who else is in their group. Facilitators are important in setting a conversational tone, sharing conversation guidelines, and ensuring procedures move smoothly. Their training often includes working with keypad technology—an electronic way to see immediate responses of each participant in the room.

"5.8 Community Forum Conversation Guidelines" in the workbook is a handout listing the guidelines for interacting within the table groups. Table facilitators review the guidelines with participants, asking each person to confirm their agreement. In the rare case where someone cannot accept a guideline, the table facilitator can ask for suggestions about what modification might make the guideline acceptable to the dissenting participant, and then raise a hand to seek guidance from the lead facilitator.

Each table needs a flip chart with appropriate markers for recording responses. Participants choose someone from the table to begin recording those responses, with the expectation that everyone who wishes has an opportunity to write content on the chart. The recorder writes feedback statements from table members on the flip charts and then each group shares with the full forum group. Non-English-speaking participants may write in their native language unless they wish a translator to record in English.

In addition to preparing the forum room with tables, chairs, and charts, the lead facilitator ensures electronic projection systems are in place; signaling devices can call the group's attention back to center; "parking lots" for extraneous items arising during discussion are available; name cards for participants are on tables; note-taking materials are within reach; keypad technology tools are working; and participant packets are completed. A complete list of materials and setup reminders is available in "5.9 Materials and Setup Tips for a Community Forum" in the workbook.

- During the forum event

    Although the lead facilitator initiates the event's processes, table facilitators ensure conversations at each table move well, asking probing questions only if interaction lags. The lead facilitator also listens and watches to see how the table dialogue is going. Generally, conversations will move to an intense level with much energy displayed, then drop for a bit. Though at times a conversation will be quiet for a while, it will usually pick up again shortly. The facilitator's sensitivity to the ebb and flow of sharing will preclude stopping a group before everyone is finished. When the energy in the room is low, it is time to wrap up discussion on the current question and move on. The lead facilitator circulating among the tables and asking if everyone has had a chance to talk can prompt those who have not done so to add their thoughts. Checking on each table honors both those who take more time as well as those who go quickly.

    "5.10 Keypad Question/Response Samples" in the workbook provides a model for the kinds of layered questions needed in pursuing information through an electronic keypad feedback process. "5.11 Guided Discussion Question Sets for a Community Forum" gives examples of useful question sets for facilitating a guided discussion with a large group of participants in Volume II.

- After the forum

    Table facilitators gather and turn in to the lead facilitator all notes and the flip-chart pages of statements from each table group. The lead facilitator uses those to create a summary of the information and responses gleaned through the forum process to include as part of the final project report for the organizers. The lists help generate major themes and recommendations to consider.

    Table facilitators also fill out feedback sheets to report overall impressions, key points made, areas of agreement and disagreement, actions or changes recommended, and points helpful in developing a strategic action plan to address the issues discussed at the forum. Table facilitator responses on this feedback sheet become part of the data considered in the overall decision-making and strategic planning to follow. "5.12 Table Facilitator's Feedback about Participant Input" in the workbook provides content for this feedback form.

TAKEAWAY MESSAGES FROM THIS CHAPTER

- Facilitating artfully engages a broad cross section of stakeholders in deliberative processes in which many options are thoughtfully examined and wise decisions are made creating productive, sustainable futures for students.
- The SAGE acronym captures effective facilitation practices: an artful facilitator *sees* opportunities; *assures* multiple diverse perspectives are heard, understood, and respected; *guides* participants through democratic processes; and *exercises* mild control, *empowering* the group to think strategically and creatively, make decisions, and take action.
- Empowering people to do their own work and manage themselves is the most important gift a facilitator can leave to an organization.
- Part of the facilitator's job is to invite the opinions of experts but *not* to depend on them — they can negate the voices of less confident or less influential group members.
- One tenet of selecting an effective facilitator is that the individual must be acceptable to everyone in the group.
- The facilitator needs to know well those with whom s/he will be working, by conducting preprocess interviews or surveys with team members.
- A facilitator defeats the process by getting into a tug-of-war with a participant or taking interactions personally.
- A skilled facilitator must be adept at listening, sensing the movement and perspectives of groups, and employ skills including using opportune timing, framing issues, posing appropriate questions, and managing conflict to move the group toward reaching its goals.
- Process structures such as study circles and open space technology help facilitators move dialogue forward in civil ways.

HELPFUL RESOURCES RELATED TO THIS CHAPTER

- Robert Chadwick's book, *Finding New Ground*, offers a transformative approach to resolving conflict. His ideas and strategies have influenced the author for years.
- Trevor Bentley's book, *Facilitation: Providing Opportunities for Learning*, contributes many strategies for facilitators, most notably in "letting go" and allowing the group to evolve in its thinking and understanding.
- A good resource for educators is R. Bruce Williams's *Twelve Roles of Facilitators for School Change*.
- Bens Ingrid's *Facilitating with Ease: Core Skills for Facilitators, Team Leaders and Members, Managers, Consultants, and Trainers* provides an abundance of protocols, processes, facilitation tips, and tools for facilitating or for training others to do so.
- *People Skills: How to Assert Yourself, Listen to Others, and Resolve Conflict* by Robert Bolton is an old book but incredibly helpful in building stronger interpersonal relationships.
- *Difficult Conversations: How to Discuss What Matters Most* by Douglas Stone, Bruce Patton, and Sheila Heen. This book and *People Skills* are both outstanding guides on how to have productive conversations even in the most difficult circumstances.
- Barry Johnson introduces the notion of polarity management in his book *Polarity Management: Identifying and Managing Unsolvable Problems*. He distinguishes between a problem to solve and a conflict to manage. He shows how to leverage dilemmas through polarity mapping and says either/or thinking *and* both/and thinking are needed.
- *Asking the Right Questions: Techniques for Collaboration and School Change*, second edition, by Edie L. Holcomb. This book presents questions as a road map, facilitation tips, and many tools to guide facilitators in making school change.
- Hammond and Mayfield's *The Thin Book of Naming Elephants: How to Surface Undiscussables for Greater Organizational Success* is an easy-to-digest book of suggestions for getting everything on the table.

Complete publication information for these resources is located in the reference list at the back of this book.

NOTES

1. Schwarz, *The Skilled Facilitator: Practical Wisdom for Developing Effective Groups.*

2. Peter Block, *Community: The Structure of Belonging.*

3. Samples of such tools are available on the Leslie & Associates website: www.leslieconsult.com.

4. Jiddu Krishnamurti, *First Public Talks.*

5. From Will Schutz, *The Human Element: Productivity, Self-Esteem, and the Bottom Line Management.*

6. Adapted from Robert Bolton, *People Skills: How to Assert Yourself, Listen to Others, and Resolve Conflict.*

7. Peter Block, *Community: The Structure of Belonging.*

8. Expanded from eight such practices of former NSPRA president Tim Hensley, assistant superintendent in Floyd County Schools (Rome, GA), included by Tom Salter in his article, "Become a Better Communicator through 'Intentional Listening,'" in NSPRA's *Principal Communicator.* Used with permission of the National School Public Relations Association (www.NSPRA.org).

9. Elements of this material were developed by Judi Smith for a workshop called "Principles of Conflict."

10. Gaskins and Kayser, "Systems Thinking in Action: The Power Is in the Connections."

11. Adapted from a process taught by Chadwick in his workshop called "Beyond Conflict to Consensus: Facilitator Training with Bob Chadwick."

12. Harrison Owen, *Open Space Technology: A User's Guide.*

13. Brown and Isaacs, *The World Café.*

SIX

Planning Strategically

CREATING SUSTAINABLE CHANGE
THROUGH STRATEGIC PLANNING

A strategic system-wide planning process and other planning projects offer multiple opportunities to engage stakeholders—employees, students, families, and community members—on many levels. When stakeholders are authentically engaged, a deep sense of responsibility for each child's education is instilled in them. To the extent that the associative, democratic principles outlined in chapter 5 are learned and practiced, stakeholders become well informed, think strategically, make decisions with sound judgment, and assume shared responsibility for implementation and successful outcomes.

Depending on how people are engaged, the level of stakeholder engagement in planning processes varies from a minimum to a significant amount of time. Stakeholders might participate in a focus group session or in a forum; may answer a survey, participate in an online conversation, or engage in an informal conversation about how to improve schools; or serve formally on an exploratory or strategic planning team. Deciding when and where to engage people is tricky. With too many people on a planning team, the process becomes cumbersome; with not enough people engaged, planners may not learn what they need to know to make good decisions. Implementation may falter because people have not had a say about actions affecting them in some way or requiring their implementation. Recruiting participants representative of the community's demographics—not just from the usual active, affluent, dominant race—is challenging.

This chapter builds a case for the importance of engaging stakeholders in planning efforts and describes how it can be done. It outlines the stages of the planning process and how to accomplish each step, with concrete examples of how to engage stakeholders, including staff members, students, families, and community in planning. Approaches unique to *strategic planning* and other discrete processes such as visioning for a new school are also included. How to develop a comprehensive family communication/engagement plan and a visioning plan is described in this chapter, and resources to help facilitate both processes are available within several tools in the companion workbook, *The Politics of Authentic Engagement: Tools for Engaging Stakeholders in Ensuring Student Success.*

Although this chapter provides an overview of planning, it focuses in most detail on those aspects of planning processes where *stakeholders may be easily engaged.* As defined in chapter 1, the term *stakeholders* includes anyone who has an interest in the organization—students, educators, families, community members, government entities, and other constituents. While in this chapter the organization referred to most often as doing such strategic planning is the school district, the concepts and strategies can also be used effectively at the school or even the county level.

Authentic Engagement in Strategic Planning

Authentic engagement in planning occurs when stakeholders say what they think, ask questions, give ideas, or say what is important and why in focus groups, surveys, forums, and other venues. It occurs when stakeholders learn, serve on planning teams, analyze the results of research efforts, and seriously consider the data as they strategically plan for the future for the school or district.

Deep authentic engagement of this nature by non-educators calls for educators creating conditions in which people have the opportunity to obtain necessary skills and knowledge. Training in democratic process skills that foster equity, transparency, shared decision-making, and collective thinking can be provided by school or district planners, along with information about many aspects of the education world. Issues must be framed free of bias for participants so they can see all sides of an issue and can challenge, discuss, and decide objectively. Plans developed by well-trained, informed stakeholders are richer, stronger, more imaginative, and challenging, and are more apt to be implemented and lived.

Strategic planning was the cutting-edge management tool of the 1960s. However, when it did not live up to its original expectations in the 1980s business environment, school districts and others moved away from it. Today there is a resurgence in strategic planning, but the plans are simpler and are focused on school improvement in teaching and learning. They are based on better data, more strategic thinking, and reflect the perspectives of the stakeholders. Still, many districts behave in unproductive ways:

- develop plans, put them on the shelf, and do what they have always done
- divorce the plans from the reality of what is happening in the trenches of teaching, leadership, and learning—the classroom, the real work
- do not engage anyone in their plan development and plan in isolation behind closed doors;
- develop plans only to legitimize what they are doing already
- try to control rather than create the future
- assume that the future is predictable
- blame demographics for student failure rather than looking at and improving teaching, learning, and leadership

However, when educators plan effectively through engaging others, they can expect meaningful outcomes such as:

- living documents adaptable to changing needs and conditions
- clear direction to guide the school board and staff in future decision-making
- increased understanding and support from constituents and staff for the district or school's mission, vision, and goals
- a workable plan that energizes the staff and community
- a high number of well-informed stakeholders
- increased commitment by stakeholders who have not previously been engaged
- a willingness on the part of everyone to embrace a new future

* * *

When first assessing an organization, I can tell almost immediately if a strategic plan is in place and if the planning process has engaged stakeholders at every level. Often in focus groups I ask about the purpose of the school or district. Sometimes I receive different answers from each participant; other times everyone answers the same using almost identical words such as, "We are working together to put student success first," or "We want every student to graduate," or "We educate students for leadership in a global society."

I then ask how they are doing that and, most often, they easily cite examples such as, "We have a new global education program," or "We just developed a parent liaison program." In those schools and districts, there is little or no evidence of silos—people working independently and sometimes against each other. Department and school plans, while reflecting local needs, align with the district's mission and vision. The school board makes decisions that are also aligned with the mission, vision, and priority goals. The board annually reviews the strategic plan to see progress and make adjustments.

Such districts and schools know where they are going and how they are going to get there. They struggle just like everyone else with issues, funding, and the unanticipated, but there is a focus on student success. Families, students, educators, and the community work strategically and continuously to help students improve and succeed.

At its best, planning is strategic—a road map for achieving goals that ensures the accomplishment of the vision and mission. Strategic planning identifies what is important and focuses all efforts to ensure success for each student. While plans differ and the processes for their development reflect the district's uniqueness, planning should build on what is already in place and working. A strategic plan must be flexible to respond quickly to trends, patterns, and emerging issues potentially preventing the accomplishment of the vision and mission. Planning never ends because there is a constant focus on how well the goals are being met and making adjustments, as needed. There are short and continuous improvement cycles allowing frequent mid-course corrections. Department plans focusing on specific issues and operations are aligned with the strategic plan's mission and goals.

Applications of Systems Thinking for Strategic Planning

Strategic planning and systems thinking are intricately linked. Planners who stay focused on the vision while grappling with challenges, studying results, and deciding strategy by looking at the interconnections and interdependencies of the components within the system are systems thinkers. The five key concepts of systems thinking introduced in chapter 1 are relevant to authentic engagement:

1. Schools as complex systems

   School systems include many linked components such as the district, a school, department, team, family, community, neighborhood, professional organizations or unions, and after-school programs.

2. Interrelatedness

   When an event happens in one part of the system, it does not occur in isolation. Learning what the underlying structures and patterns are is fundamental to resolving issues and making good decisions across the organization.

3. Pattern awareness

   Patterns and trends are always present throughout the entire system and its substructures. Many times those patterns and trends are not explicit but are revealed by analyzing related events that show the systemic behaviors and variables at work. For example, when a student fails a class it is easy to point blame at the teacher. However, a close analysis of patterns and trends such as financial support of the program, illness in the family, learning disabilities or other disabilities of the student, poverty, or any number of other factors or combination of factors may have contributed to the failure. To address the issue, all of these trends and patterns should be considered. To engage people deeply means making trends and patterns more transparent.

4. Mental models

   People behave based on mental models derived from their attitudes, beliefs, and values that influence the system. Discovering stakeholders' underlying attitudes and beliefs helps clarify rationales and promotes workable solutions.

5. Feedback loops

Feedback-loop processes help organizations get information through an interconnected set of circular relationships in order to see, analyze, and integrate patterns, trends, and perspectives that lead to an understanding of the whole system—the big picture. A feedback loop perspective uncovers the interrelationships between all events, illuminating the patterns and systemic structures more easily. When the big picture is seen and understood, problems are more effectively addressed and solved.

Systems thinking—the ability to understand how all parts of a school or district relate to, affect, and operate in concert with one another—is critically important in molding a strategic plan. It requires that planners see how the elements of an organization interact and how issues and events fit within the larger organization and its unique dynamics. Knowing how people's behaviors are based on their personal attitudes, values, and beliefs, compels planners to discover and honor those attitudes and their influence on the system. Decision-makers must have relevant data not only on the workings of the organization and how elements are connected and affect each other, but also data about how people think and what they value. A broad perspective is gained from studying the overall structure, patterns, and cycles within subsystems and their connection to the whole education system and its relation to societal systems. Strategic planning involves reflection in which planners intentionally review, reconsider, reconnect, and reframe what they learn from data collection.[1]

Whether a district or a school is developing a system-wide comprehensive strategic plan, updating and making relevant a plan already in place, adding a new section to a plan, developing an action plan, or developing strategies to address a particular issue, *it cannot be done in isolation*. A planning team looks at the set of relationships and interactions needed to create a solution or strategy. It studies every potential decision and the effect of each on the entire system and its subsystems.

Team members look at the implications of outside forces like potential budget reductions or new government requirements such as Common Core Standards. They conduct research through a variety of methods to determine what all people affected by the decision think, believe, and value. They scan the environment to see what the issues are and study other available research such as test scores and demographics so they know the context within which they are making decisions. They talk with people to determine the impact of a decision on their work or lives and, most importantly, on students.

STAGES OF CREATING A SYSTEM-WIDE STRATEGIC PLAN

There are many stages in a comprehensive strategic planning effort. One can easily bog down in the process or drown in too much detail. Designing a focused planning process starts with an assessment of available resources including time, personnel, and money. It includes deciding if the planning will be a renewal or updating of a current successful plan or a full-scale planning effort starting from scratch. Based on such an assessment, an organization may go through all the stages listed below or just some of them. Regardless, the stages can be shaped and modified to fit the unique culture and needs of the school or district.

Creating a realistic comprehensive strategic plan typically involves twelve stages:

1. Develop a communication and engagement plan.
2. Appoint and engage the strategic planning team.
3. Determine the most appropriate process.
4. Conduct and review research.
5. Discover or confirm the mission and create the vision.
6. Clarify the core values.
7. Identify strategic issues.
8. Develop strategic goals.
9. Determine strategies to support the goals.
10. Identify indicators of success.
11. Develop action plans.
12. Create a budget to support the strategic plan and the supporting action plans.

Definitions: This list defines terms used in the following pages to name some of the components of this framework and process.

- Action plan: a plan aligned with the strategic plan identifying the steps program directors, schools, work teams, school boards, and individuals will take to make the district or school vision, supporting goals, and strategies a reality.
- Core values: beliefs and principles that guide actions and are practiced daily.

- Indicators of success: quantifiable measures of progress toward the vision, a goal, or a strategy.
- Mission: the noble purpose of the school or district.
- Strategic: essential or highly important to an objective or plan of action.
- Strategic goals: statements identifying expectations or intended results.
- Strategic issues: priority issues that, if addressed, will close the gap between the desired future and the current reality.
- Strategic plan for a district/school: a road map showing what the school or district wants to accomplish, how it will do it, and how it will measure progress.
- Strategic planning communication/engagement plan: a plan identifying how to inform and engage stakeholders in the strategic planning process.
- Vision: a description of the organization's desired future, often expressed in the hopes for the school or district.

"6.1 Framework and Definitions for Strategic Planning" in the companion workbook is a handout of the twelve stages of strategic planning and definitions of terms for members of the planning team.

Criteria for Success in Strategic Planning: For everyone involved in the process, certain criteria ensure success for effective strategic planning. The criteria include:

- planning anchored in a rigorous needs assessment and solid research, including a thorough examination of student achievement data
- a focus on students and the systems supporting student learning
- operating agreements developed with everyone's input and agreed to by everyone
- clear roles in the planning process
- collective decision-making
- equal opportunities to speak
- excellent training in process, dialogue, and decision-making skills
- results-oriented communication/engagement plan
- a plan simple enough so everyone understands it

Stage One: Develop a Communications and Engagement Plan for Strategic Planning

Ideally, the organization already has a comprehensive communication and engagement plan in place that is current and strategic, not simply a list of communication and engagement activities. If not, the strategic planning effort will call for a comprehensive stakeholder communication and engagement plan. At a minimum, a communication/engagement plan for the strategic planning effort needs to be developed to inform stakeholders about the planning process and how they can be engaged.

The purpose of the communication and engagement plan is to support the strategic planning efforts and to ensure stakeholders have a role in the planning work and are updated throughout the process. The plan identifies the following information:

- who will be informed and engaged in each step of the strategic planning process
- what each stakeholder is to do to support the strategic planning process and its implementation
- the strategies identifying how people will be informed and engaged
- how the success of those strategies will be measured
- the timeline for planning and decision-making
- who will be responsible for implementing each communication and engagement strategy

"6.2 Communication and Engagement Plan for Strategic Planning" in the workbook is a template for the person or group responsible for communications and engagement planning within the context of strategic planning.

The public relations department or person responsible for communications/engagement in a school district usually works in partnership with the superintendent and the strategic planning team to develop the plan for strategic planning, capitalizing on known effective communication channels, and engagement opportunities. If there is no public relations department or other person responsible for this work, the strategic planning team may appoint a subcommittee or the facilitator to fulfill the responsibility.

Stage Two: Appoint and Engage the Strategic Planning Team

Selecting who will be on the strategic planning team needs careful consideration. There should be enough people on the team to provide different perspectives but not so many the process is difficult to manage. The team should be representative of the realities of the school or district. A working team of no more than thirty people can dig deeply into issues, study their interrelatedness, carefully consider different viewpoints, and make sound decisions after weighing all sides of an issue. While the planning team may be relatively small considering the large number of people affected by a school or district planning process, the design can and should include many other opportunities to engage stakeholders.

Ideally, team members would be reasonable people who can speak up, listen to others, focus on improving education for each child, and be good strategic thinkers. The following list of possible recruits includes a broad range of roles: board member, superintendent, business manager, curriculum director, communications/engagement director, human resource director, high school principal, middle school principal, elementary school principal, three teachers (one from each level of schooling), two support staff members, the mayor, a religious delegate, the police chief, Chamber president, two business representatives, two students, and five family members representing various ethnicities.

For *educators* involved or the *facilitators* they employ, both at the district and school levels, these attitudes or actions can impede successful planning:

- unwillingness to share all data
- unable to see assumptions, opinions, and recommendations of parents, community members, and others as valuable
- believing support staff and other non-educators have inadequate educational knowledge and are incapable of ever fully understanding the nuances of the education process
- giving an unclear charge to the planning team and community
- neglecting to identify or provide parameters for the planning process
- designing complicated processes that drain human and financial resources

For *stakeholders*, these behaviors or attitudes can be problematic:

- unwilling to be influenced
- only caring about one's own children
- having difficulty seeing the big picture or the entire system
- being unwilling to study the issues or read background materials
- being unprepared to participate effectively in meetings

Each school and district is different, but when the goal is to see "what is," spending thoughtful time in identifying all groups in the system and engaging them in the process on some level is critical to the overall success of the plan. In addition to reaching out to more visible constituents, it is important to make a special effort to engage reluctant or atypical stakeholders. Such groups may include non-English-speaking families, high-school dropouts, homeless families and students, preschool parents, parents and educators in private schools, senior citizens, apathetic stakeholders, and disenfranchised parents. Anyone can answer questions such as these:

- "What does student success look like to you?"
- "What are your greatest concerns about our school/district?"
- "What should students know and be able to do when they graduate?"

Diverse perspectives ensure greater success for the strategic plan.

The charge, including the planning group's purpose, must be clearly stated with the parameters outlined. The following example was given to the strategic planning team representing a school district:

* * *

Thank you for agreeing to serve on the District Strategic Planning Team. While your agreement represents a significant time commitment on your part, we feel certain you will enjoy the experience, grow and learn, and most importantly make a difference. Below is the charge to your team. We will answer all your questions and discuss this at the strategic planning team's first meeting.

- *Attend ten three-hour monthly meetings and one all-day retreat.*
- *Identify staff, student, family, and community issues preventing the achievement of our vision.*

- *Conduct and/or review available research to determine "what is" from study groups, surveys, focus groups, neighborhood meetings, and other processes.*
- *Based on the research, develop a five-year strategic plan to include a vision, mission, values, guiding principles, goals, strategies, and indicators of success. Make it a living document responsive to emerging issues.*
- *Serve on one of four exploratory teams—subcommittees of the planning team—to dig deeper into one broad issue. (Time commitment is ten to fifteen hours.)*
- *Participate in trainings on education issues, process skills, conflict management, understanding research, and strategic plan development. (Training incorporated into monthly meetings.)*
- *Make no final decisions without seeking opinions and ideas from all team members.*
- *Participate in the community forum as a table facilitator.*
- *Submit the plan and all background materials to the school board for approval.*

A newly formed team is ready to work once they understand and accept the charge to the team and determine their agreements about working together. For help in guiding team members in creating those operating agreements, see "5.8 Community Forum Conversation Guidelines" in chapter 5 in the companion workbook.

"6.1 Framework and Definitions for Strategic Planning" in the workbook can also be used as a handout for team members to outline the stages they will move through to create a strategic plan.

Stage Three: Determine the Most Appropriate Process

Schools and school districts do not all employ the same planning processes because each system must reflect the organization's unique needs and culture. For example, some districts may take up to a year or more to complete their strategic plan, while others spend a few meetings or a day or two to complete their work. Some want only a framework to identify the mission, vision, goals, strategies, and indicators of success while others want all of these elements and measureable action steps identified to the last detail. Some want to engage stakeholders in planning work on many levels, others only at discrete places. Some use planning templates predetermined by the state or prior precedent while others want to design a fresh approach. The planning team or the facilitator working close-ly with the superintendent, principal, or designee identifies the process best fitting the uniqueness of a particular school or district.

While analytical thinking is important in planning development, plan-ning itself is not a linear process. Many elements may occur simultane-ously; stages may not occur in the order listed in this book and some may not occur at all. The planning process is like putting a jigsaw puzzle together. People have their own special way to complete the puzzle. Some start by filling out the edges, others collect all the same colored pieces and place them, while still others look for recurring patterns. The road map presented here is a framework that can be adjusted to meet unique local needs.

"6.3 Road Map Planning Process" in the workbook is a diagram of a sample planning process. It includes all of the elements in a one-year planning effort. A blank version of this template can be created and filled in with steps unique to a particular school or district.

Stage Four: Conduct and Review Research

The strategic planning team begins its research almost immediately by reviewing available data related to the present status of the district or school. Environmental scans and situational analyses may include all of the following ways to gather data about what is currently happening: surveys, focus groups, interviews, community forums, examinations of past plans and reports, and a SWOT analysis identifying strengths, weak-nesses, opportunities, and threats. The planning team, the superinten-dent, or both determine the research needed, how to collect it, and who will conduct it (see chapter 3). Engagement work at a private high school in Texas, provides a good example of how several of these data-gathering strategies work together.

* * *

Driven by a strong mission and a desire for continuous growth, the high school committed itself to a strategic planning process that defined the school's goals and priorities based on thoughtful input from all of its stakeholders. In an eight-een-month planning process, fourteen focus groups provided input. Those homo-geneous groups involved parents, students, graduates, and other alumnae as well as their parents, volunteer leaders, faculty, business professionals, educators from outside the school, and nuns from around the United States. Participants were asked how the school was doing—what they thought was working well, what was not working, and what they saw as the challenges or barriers to success.

To assess patterns and structures in place and obtain a full picture of "what is," the school collected other information: (1) The Global Education Initiative; (2) the 2033 Vision Plan; (3) the 2011 Identity Assessment; (4) the 2009 Master Plan; (5) the 2015 Technology Plan; (6) the Communication Plan; (7) the 2008–2011 Strategic Plan; (8) student data on grades, scholarship history, college placements, and test scores; (9) volunteer activity; (10) organizational structure; and (11) other documents available pertinent to what was currently in place.

Technological Tools for Research

A number of technological tools are also helpful in the strategic planning and research processes. *Online surveys* are used to gather and analyze opinion data from a variety of stakeholders. *Keypad technology* described in chapter 5 for focus groups and community forums is useful in gathering data instantaneously from a large group of people, with immediate feedback available to participants in those groups. *Targeted e-mail alerts* allow planners to give stakeholders information on specific topics of interest and provide opportunities for input to their processes. *Strategic planning websites and blogs* provide these advantages:

- a virtual meeting place promoting communication among group members
- links to websites, further informing and assisting group members, staff, and community
- access to documents and files, offering sources of information for referral
- master planning-calendar information taking care of routine meeting needs
- useful communication tools offering opportunities for group members, staff, and community to consider and exchange ideas outside regular meeting times

The SWOT Analysis

One way to summarize findings and help participants or external stakeholders consider a large amount of information is to use a SWOT analysis, a tool that helps team members lay out conclusions about everything learned in the data collection process in a readily understandable, compact format. It pictures an organization at a strategic rather than operational level in each of four areas represented in its acronym:[2]

- Strengths—the organization's advantages upon which to build (e.g., a strong academic program, high test scores, strong family involvement)
- Weaknesses—the areas in which the organization could improve (e.g., declining test scores, decreasing family engagement)
- Opportunities—favorable conditions not in the school or district of which the organization can take advantage: outside funds, space, people, equipment, partnerships, prospects, etc. (e.g., improve attendance through linkages with families, incentives from businesses, grants for professional development)
- Threats—emerging situations or conditions that could challenge the organization (e.g., impending legislation, funding reductions)

"6.4 A SWOT Analysis Process" in the workbook provides a framework for creating the analysis.

If the planning team decides to host a community forum (chapter 5) in which a large number of people are recruited to participate , the responsibility for organizing this event may rest in this stage. Planning teams often hold a forum sometime after stage four and before stage eleven.

Stage Five: Discover or Confirm the Mission and Create the Vision

> "We would argue that it is impossible to develop a results orientation unless we are clear about the core of the enterprise (the mission), about the kind of district we are seeking to become (the vision), and about the attitudes, behavior, and commitments we need to promote, protect, and defend."
> —DuFour and Eaker[3]

Clarifying the Noble Purpose (Mission)

In this stage, the strategic planning team goes through a discovery process. It may not be explicit, but there is a mission already. It is present in the reason why the school or district exists. The mission is called a "noble purpose" because educating students is noble work. The answer to the question "Why do you educate students?" reveals the mission. If there is a written mission statement in place stating clearly why the school or district exists, it probably does not need to change unless it is too long and unclear. If it needs tinkering, changes need to be handled with caution.

For stakeholders to know and support the noble purpose of an organization, the mission statement must explain why the school or district exists and be clear, understandable, succinct, and easy to remember. It is the bedrock of the organization, yet may change if the reason for the school or district changes.

Samples of mission statements include:

- Devereux changes lives and nurtures human potential. We inspire hope, ensure well-being, and promote meaningful life choices.
- Hunter McGuire School, in partnership with its parents, seeks to instill in its students high standards for academic scholarship, integrity, leadership, and responsible citizenship.
- In partnership with home and community, Vancouver Public Schools provides an innovative learning environment that engages and empowers each student to develop the knowledge and essential skills to become a competent, responsible, and compassionate citizen.
- The mission of the Buckley Community School, where kids come first, is to partner with families to develop enthusiastic learners.
- At Woonsocket High School, our mission is to educate all students in a safe, supportive, challenging environment where they learn to be citizens of a culturally diverse society.

The term "noble purpose" helps planners as well as constituents understand how a mission is different from a vision. Stating both the words *mission* and *noble purpose* together in written materials or verbally reinforces the distinction — the mission is not the vision.

"6.5 Discover or Confirm the Mission" in the workbook presents an activity to help planners update or validate an existing mission statement or create a new one.

Identifying Hopes to Create the Vision

The vision of an organization—the description of its desired future—provides the benchmark or standard for evaluating the quality of the goals and strategies considered for implementation in the strategic plan. An effective vision pushes the organization into a new future. A district or school pusuing excellence creates a new vision about every five years. Stakeholders—everyone who has an interest in the school or district—are never satisfied with the status quo because they know there is always room for improvement.

In response to the unrelenting desire to make sure every child is successful, the strategic planning team imagines what is possible, then unites and focuses their energies on creating a vision requiring significant change and progress. The challenge for them is to create a compelling vision that will engage people's spirit and passion, inspire them to excellence, and invite them to meet lofty goals.

As a first step in creating the vision, planning team members make explicit their hopes for the organization, ideally in the first gathering of the group. The protocol positively engages team members who have just met each other, serving as a catalyst for engaging people's feelings in dialogue about their aspirations—their own hopes for students, families, and staff of the district or school. A good strategic plan contains analytical and systemic reasoning with great infusion of heart (feelings).

It is also wise for the facilitator to encourage the team to look back at those hopes throughout the entire planning process to reflect on how they align with those of the *larger community* as they uncover the perceptions of others during later research phases. Team members can then incorporate the desires of all the stakeholders throughout their process, the expressions of hope becoming an integral part of developing the vision for the entire system. "6.6 Identify Hopes to Create the Vision" in the workbook provides an activity for helping the team express their hopes and create a vision statement.

Stage Six: Clarify Core Values

Core values guide excellent schools/districts. Values are the beliefs and principles that guide actions and are practiced daily. They are not what the district aspires to—that is the vision. Rather, they represent the underlying principles people are committed to as they pursue the larger vision. Values may also describe the ethics of the district/school or how people treat one another. They express what is most important to everyone connected with the organization—its core ideology. For example, a district or school may have a core value saying all children can succeed, or acknowledging that all families desire the best learning environment for their children. Being aware of the core values helps everyone working to educate children act in ways that acknowledge those beliefs.

These examples of value statements are from two educational systems:

Devereux Schools:

- We support a respectful and integrated team approach.
- We foster personal and professional growth of our staff.
- We develop innovative and effective solutions.
- We partner with families and communities.

North Clackamas School District:

Achievement

- We will ensure each student possesses twenty-first-century skills to reach his or her potential to excel.
- We will direct our collective and individual efforts to that end.

Character

- Each student will be supported in the development of strong, positive character traits and caring relationships.

Community Engagement

- We will encourage everyone to participate in making key district decisions.

Diversity

- Each student will be treated with respect and given an equal opportunity to participate, learn, and succeed in a safe, caring environment.
- All students, staff, parents, and community members will value and embrace diversity as enriching our society and schools.

Relevance

- School learning and instructional approaches will be connected to the real world and will include practical applications in life and the workplace.

"6.7 Clarify Core Values" in the workbook suggests an activity to help the planning team compose or update a list of core values and beliefs.

Stage Seven: Identify Strategic Issues

Identifying strategic issues happens through a review of all available research: focus group results, interviews, a systems audit, historical documents, state or district student-assessment results, the SWOT analysis, and other accessible, pertinent information. The team should not be overwhelmed with research results but should have enough information to study the workings and issues of the organization deeply and broadly. The planning team's effectiveness depends on the willingness of the district to be transparent in providing information and research. From data collected, the strategic issues with the greatest possible impact on the district's ability to reach its vision emerge. Once those issues have been identified, synthesized, and prioritized, the strategic planning team organizes them into three or four broad categories for deeper study that will result in goal setting and strategy development.

"6.8 Identify Critical or Strategic Issues" in the workbook suggests a series of activities for the team to move through to help them define strategic issues.

When the strategic planning team wants to study one or more areas deeply, but is limited by time and people resources, they can organize what are called *exploratory or investigation teams* to further the research into discrete areas of interest. The smaller teams are most successful when all the members of the strategic planning team participate on the teams. Exploratory teams may include other stakeholders who are connected to the area of study by their work in the district, their expertise, or because the plan's implementation may have an effect on them. In addition, the teams may be enlarged to include others who know the issue well: parents, community members, students, teachers, administrators, other school staff or experts in related fields.

Exploratory teams are appointed and begin their work after strategic issues are identified and the strategic planning team has narrowed the focus to the primary areas (never more than three or four) needing further study. The deeper research of such a group may take three to four months to complete. They must talk with other people, conduct primary research, and synthesize their findings around the charge given by the strategic planning team.

*   *   *

For example, one school district that was engaged in a strategic planning process concerning its option schools organized exploratory teams to look more deeply at four areas in which the planning team was particularly interested:

> *Team One: Creation, Evaluation, and Termination of Option Schools*
> *Team Two: Exploring Learning Options for Struggling Students*
> *Team Three: Models of Delivery for Learning Options*
> *Team Four: Learning Options for the Future*

Each exploratory team's charge was to "thoroughly research and analyze one assigned area of focus and, based on their research and analysis, develop recommendations to guide the full strategic planning team in developing the master strategic plan." Exploratory team recommendations were expected to align with the core values and mission of the district.

Although critics of using such exploratory teams say they are ill informed, do not know the whole picture, and, therefore, cannot make valid recommendations; properly trained teams educated on the issue can dig deeply into the subject assigned to them and present a comprehensive, well-researched, and balanced report to the strategic planning team.

"6.9 Sample Guidelines for an Exploratory Team" in the workbook provides additional information about the charge, organization, and work of an exploratory team supporting a comprehensive strategic planning team.

"6.10 Exploratory Team Recommendations Model" in the workbook shows samples of the kind of report an exploratory team might make to the strategic planning team. Key sections of the reports are these:

- Team recommendations
- Supporting research
- Feedback incorporated
- Support for core values

- Support for equity
- Anticipated impacts on items such as budget, staffing, professional development, transportation, facilities, students, families and community, employees, boards, and all constituents
- Identification of potential losses and gains (trade-offs, pros and cons, all constituent groups)

"6.11 Processing Exploratory Team Reports with the Strategic Team" in the workbook helps the strategic planning team thoroughly understand and respond to exploratory team reports. Moderated by a facilitator, it includes structured processes for analyzing and responding to proposals and recommendations and generating new ideas in a respectful environment of listening. Those processes also enable the exploratory team to refine and extend their work.

What emerges from the data collected and analyzed is clear, relevant information and understanding about the organization's strengths and weaknesses. Analysis also points out priority issues; the culture; organizational structure; management practices; effectiveness of existing systems serving the organization and its people; information on what stakeholders think, value, and desire; and the overall success of the educational program. The entire set of data is foundational to the strategic plan. More about research can be found in chapter 3.

Stage Eight: Develop Strategic Goals

Not every strategic plan takes a goal approach. While some organizations design their plan using a strategic issue approach, others skip right to identifying strategies rather than goals and some use a scenario approach. The strategic planning team decides how they will design their planning process.

Strategic goals are statements of intended results. They identify expectations and say what stakeholders will do every day. They are concrete, identifying specific targets. They close the gap between what is desired—the vision—and what is the current reality. They should be challenging, yet realistic. Sample goals from several schools and school districts include:

- Technology is reliable, service is available, and instructional needs are satisfied.
- The district is fiscally responsible and efficient.

- Students develop relevant, transferable academic and life skills.
- Students have access to adequate school resources and support, making rigorous learning possible.

"6.12 Develop Strategic Goals" in the workbook describes steps for either an exploratory team or the strategic planning team to develop and prioritize goals.

Stage Nine: Determine Strategies to Support the Goals

Strategies breathe life into goals. Everything done throughout the process leads to this point. The strategies say how the vision, mission, and goals will be accomplished. Developing the strategies is the heart of the process and determines what people will be doing. For example, these sample strategies support a trust-building goal implemented by a school board after research revealed trust held by the community for the board had plummeted to 27 percent.

Goal: Trust will be built between the school board and the community.

Strategies to reach the goal include:

- Each board member will attend at least one city council meeting and one county commissioner meeting to learn the issues they are addressing, provide a short report on school district challenges and achievements, and report back to the board at a regular board meeting.
- The board will personally invite elected local officials to participate in all district planning meetings.
- Each board member will visit classrooms on a regular schedule at the invitation of teachers and/or principals.
- The board will host a community forum open to all stakeholders for the purpose of determining community educational priorities.

"6.13 Determine Strategies to Support the Goals" in the workbook provides a process and activities for identifying specific strategies to assist in reaching each goal.

Stage Ten: Identify Indicators of Success

Indicators of success are quantifiable measures of progress toward the organization's goals. They benchmark progress. The key question in establishing indicators of success is this: "How will you know you have been successful in moving toward your vision, living your mission, and reaching your goals?" The strategic planning team is responsible for clearly articulating these indicators so others throughout the organization can use them as standards to measure progress. The team bases their choice of indicators on the research they have gathered and on other existing school or district data. The team then analyzes each goal and brainstorms the quantifiable measures needed to indicate progress. Assessing movement against each indicator helps organizations assist implementers in areas of need, advance toward the goals, and adjust ineffective strategies.

These examples show indicators for two possible strategies:

Strategy A:

Each board member will attend at least one city council meeting and one county commissioner meeting to learn . . . and report back.

Indicator:

- Each board member attends two meetings.
- Evidence of increased trust is shown by a 2 percent increase in council funding and continuation of utility dollars.

Strategy B:

The board will appoint key communicators to assist them in communicating about priority district issues.

Indicator:

- Twenty-five key communicators attend an orientation meeting, learn of district priorities, commit to staying updated on district issues, and communicate those priorities in their day-to-day contacts.

Once indicators have been developed, the work of the strategic planning team is usually complete. The team presents their recommendations to the school board, which approves the plan because it has been kept informed and engaged along the way. The strategic planning team then directs the administration to implement and communicate the plan to all stakeholders in a simple, understandable format. The indicators of success will also be used at all levels as everyone across the organization creates action plans within their various spheres of influence to support the accomplishment of the strategic plan's goals.

"6.14 Identify Indicators of Success" in the workbook provides an activity to help the strategic planning team articulate the indicators so everyone is clear about where they are going and can better judge how to use the strategies to get there.

Stage Eleven: Develop Action Plans

An action plan is created on the front line to support successful implementation of the strategic plan. Within the organization, each school, department, program, or team constructs action plans aligned with the overall strategies and goals but tailored to unique responsibilities. Hopefully, people on the front lines have been engaged in the planning process in some authentic way through focus groups, exploratory teams, a forum, or personal dialogue with their colleagues about the elements directly affecting them. If they have been kept well informed about the strategic plan's elements and been offered opportunities to express their thinking, action planning will go much more smoothly.

Action planning can be launched with dialogue groups made up of individuals from across the organization representing major divisions who look at the implications and challenges of implementation with the goal of increasing understanding and commitment. They can serve as leaders and facilitators in the action planning process at the area closest to implementation of specific goals and strategies. To be consistent with expectations and actions in all areas, each action planning work team can use a master template developed by the organization or the planning team for each goal and strategy. When the strategies or action steps align with the school or district strategic plan, people must demonstrate how the steps identified for them as individuals or smaller units will lead to the fulfillment of the overarching vision and support the strategies and goals. Concrete action steps are best when they are as specific and doable as possible and fit easily into the daily routines of those implementing them. Stating each action step on the plan using a strong action verb will help implementers.

"6.15 Action Steps for Successful Implementation of the Strategic Plan" in the workbook provides action planning steps. It includes a template useful for implementers at all levels of the organization to show action steps, timelines, and persons responsible for aligning efforts with the comprehensive strategic plan.

Stage Twelve: Create the Budget to Support Strategic Plan and Action Plans

Sometimes the strategic planning team creates the budget, but it is more likely that the district finance department will have budget responsibility. Usually the budget director serves on the strategic planning team offering budget numbers when requested so members have at least ballpark estimates on the financial resources their ideas require. Further, an exploratory team considers their recommendations' budget implications. This stage is woven throughout the process so planning team members are aware of budget constraints but are not so focused on dollar limitations as to limit creative thinking and blue sky ideas.

Once the process is completed and accepted by the board, the plan is made visible. Districts communicate through a variety of mediums including videos, social media, printed booklets, speeches, news media, flyers, newsletters, posters, and banners stating the vision and mission. Some districts hold study sessions to review various components of the plan and identify ways to support the goals and strategies. Those responsible for the communication and engagement plan decide how best to communicate the work and results of the planning team.

OTHER APPLICATIONS OF PLANNING PROCESSES

While working through all twelve stages results in the deepest and most comprehensive strategic plan, there are occasions in which an organization may need to focus more planning attention on a specific area. Issues arise from time to time that call for planning on a less comprehensive scale than system-wide planning, or a single but more in-depth action plan may be needed to support the strategic plan. This smaller-scale planning may have many of the same stages but center on only one aspect of the district or school.

Three additional tools in the workbook capture processes helpful in alternative settings:

"6.16 A Decision-Making Process," developed by Beaverton School District, describes the steps anyone—a principal, department head, volunteer citizen managing a district, or school program such as a foundation or bond campaign—can take to engage stakeholders when issues arise. It is a circular process because all planning is circular. The tool gives facilitators and others a template for deciding next steps and mapping a pathway forward when confronted with an issue.

"6.17 Stakeholder Communication and Engagement Plan" is a template for developing a plan to inform all stakeholders about district or school information, issues, and needs, and engage them in work that supports teaching and learning.

"6.18 Visioning for a New High School" provides a vision-building process for leading a group through envisioning the possibilities of a new facility before it is built.

TAKEAWAY MESSAGES FROM THIS CHAPTER

Recommendations from this chapter for ensuring an effective strategic planning process include:

- At its best, all planning is strategic—a road map for achieving goals that ensures the accomplishment of an organization's mission and vision.
- Successful strategic planners must be systems thinkers who take into account all aspects of a *complex system* such as a district, school, or community by acknowledging and capitalizing on the *interrelatedness* of its elements; the *patterns* and trends in its movements; the diversity of the *mental models* shaping attitudes and beliefs of its stakeholders; and the ways in which the system can establish and honor *feedback loops* to keep communication open and flowing.
- Engaging stakeholders in planning processes is fundamental to identifying meaningful changes needed and implementing sustainable programs and practices to meet needs.
- The strategies and processes involved in strategic planning are applicable in many other school and district venues.

HELPFUL RESOURCES RELATED TO THIS CHAPTER

- Widely used by business, free examples of SWOT (strengths, weaknesses, opportunities, threats) analysis templates can be found and downloaded from www.swottemplates.com.

- For examples of strategic planning booklets and brochures, see www.leslieconsult.com.

Complete publication information for these resources is located in the reference list at the back of this book.

NOTES

1. From Cambron-McCabe and Dutton in Senge et al., "The Wheels of Learning: The Rhythm of Learning and Learning to Learn," in *Schools That Learn: A Fifth Discipline Fieldbook for Educators, Parents, and Everyone Who Cares About Education*, 93–98.

2. Many SWOT templates can be found and downloaded at www.swottemplates. com. Last accessed April 18, 2014.

3. From DuFour and Eaker, *Professional Learning Communities at Work*.

SEVEN

Reflecting on the Journey

Inspiring Change

VOICES OF HOPE

This chapter presents voices from the front lines where "engagement pioneers"—a parent, a school board member, two public relations practitioners, a school administrator, a business leader, and a futurist—provide experience-based perspectives on authentic engagement. They share a common belief that the success of schools hinges on the ability to tap the wisdom and experience of all stakeholders as they participate in a continual dialogue on how to help each student achieve success. Contributors wrote their own bios.

- Gary Marx, an author and international consultant/futurist, tackles head-on the challenge of moving away from polarization to engagement by "pooling our genius." He says even though we must be dragged kicking and screaming into a more civil future, our future depends on it.
- Sherre Calouri, a multi-term school board member, describes how school board leadership changes under a system of authentic engagement. While the role of the school board as the decision-making body may seem eroded when everyone from the classroom teacher to the local bank manager is involved in developing school district policy, Calouri illustrates how discussions with all these

people who hold many different opinions truly enrich the educational outcome for students.

- Janet Hogue, a parent volunteer, will not only share what she learned from more than twenty years of experience but also why it mattered. She describes her work lobbying the legislature for stable funding, leading bond campaigns, heading up a school district foundation to provide funds for classroom innovation, and helping others find meaningful ways to make a positive impact on student learning.
- John Boone, an economist and president of ProFocus, a technology staffing company, tells how a business organization can be engaged at the school level and make a significant difference for students working in partnership with the school and a teacher.
- Nora Carr, a school administrator and public relations professional, welcomes readers to the new online neighborhood and asks: "Is it a tool for connecting people and providing information, or a platform for authentic engagement, or both?" She will untangle the knotty issues relating to social media and demonstrate how this continually evolving medium can help ensure success for all students. Considering that moms with children under age eighteen are among the most prolific social media users, Carr's perspective is essential.
- Karen Kleinz, associate director of the National School Public Relations Association, leads you down the "insider's path" to the development of meaningful, inclusive, and relevant engagement processes. Her rich success stories from school districts are interesting, instructional, and inspirational.
- Sylvia Soholt, an educational consultant, challenges us to go beyond family and community engagement to explore the root causes of low student achievement. The questions she poses regarding the politics of community engagement implore us to expand our efforts to ensure that every student, in every school district, in every state, masters the knowledge and skills needed for a successful future.

The preceding chapters have stressed how varying perspectives enrich dialogue. The perspectives in this chapter provide hope. If all stakeholders listen, question deeply, think out loud about complex issues, are open to learning, surface and weigh multiple options, and move to action that supports student success, authentic engagement—while challenging and

time-intensive—can indeed result in stakeholders breaking through perceived boundaries to take individual and collective responsibility for
each child reaching his or her full potential.

PERSPECTIVES FROM THE FIELD

Perspective #1: Gary Marx—Engagement: A Ticket toward Common Ground[1]

Gary Marx, APR, CAE, is president of the Center for Public Outreach
in Vienna, Virginia. His focus is future-oriented leadership, communication, education, community, and democracy. As a futurist and leader in
education, Marx has spoken in all U.S. states, across Canada, and on six
continents. He has visited more than eighty countries. Marx's most recent
books include: *Twenty-One Trends for the 21st Century: Out of the Trenches,
Into the Future* and *Future-Focused Leadership: Preparing Schools, Students,
and Communities for Tomorrow's Realities.*

* * *

Some people have engaging personalities. Some organizations have engaging reputations. Then, there are the others.

So here are a few questions. How would people generally describe us,
as individuals and as education systems? Would they say we are open?
Welcoming? Interested? Forthcoming? Responsive? Standoffish? Protec-
tive? Closed?

Let's face it. We earn whatever reputation we have. The kicker is that
personal experiences tend to override what we say. We can write articles,
spin a sunny description on the website, speak at service clubs about how
much we welcome ideas, and even adopt an openness policy . . . all good
ideas. However, if we have a habit of hunkering down and defending
ourselves whenever someone shares a concern or putting people down
when they suggest how we can do even better, people will simply stop
believing us. When it comes to our pledge of openness, we end up cancel-
ing the message.

For the sake of stimulating further discussion, why don't we look into
just a few of the many faces of engagement?

- Are we listening?

This question is perhaps central to effective public engagement. No secret here; the best leaders are often the best listeners. With few exceptions, they are interested. We know that every encounter is an opportunity to learn something new or to clarify what we may not fully understand. Listen and learn.

How will people judge whether we're actually listening? Some of it is nonverbal. Do we pay attention, try to avoid distractions, and ask clarifying questions, so that we're sure we grasp what someone is trying to tell us?

Do we avoid a rush to judgment based solely on what we know at the moment? Granted, some ideas might not pass ethical muster. However, in other cases, our best response might be: "We need to think about this. You've shared an important point of view. Thank you."

Is what we've shared ever mentioned again? Do ideas from individuals and groups too often fall through the cracks, or do they become part of our thinking and conversations? Zealots will judge us on what actually happens, what changes, whether results match their particular expectations or demands. Many others want some kind of hint that, in our democratic society, their voices have been heard. "Here are some of the things people have told me that we've considered in making our recommendation." As a citizen, I translate that into, "I may not get the whole loaf, but my thinking, along with the thinking of others, has helped to enrich the process."

We all know the benefits of technology in stimulating communication and the sharing of ideas. Let's consider the other side. Do we isolate ourselves, on purpose, because we don't think we have time to consider any more ideas? Do we hesitate to take phone calls or sit down with people in person because we'd rather use texting or e-mail? That way, we can edit whatever we write before we send it? That kind of engagement, if used too much, can carry the seeds of our own destruction. Rather than having forthright exchanges, we end up being alone together. Later, we sometimes discover that we've blindsided ourselves.

- Who is engaging whom?

As an organization, such as a school system, we might very seriously discuss, "How can we engage parents? Community organizations? The business community?" How can we engage people who no longer, or who may not ever, have kids in our schools? Those are legitimate discussions, and we should probably have them more often.

Rather than focusing only on what parents need to know about schools, maybe we also need to be deeply interested in what schools need to know about challenges facing parents. Flipping the questions, we might also ask, "How can we be engaged with parents and other groups?" In a world of *us* and *them*, is it possible to be both at the same time? Think of it as two-way engagement.

- Do we want counsel or an opportunity to reinforce our predetermined point of view?

  We've all said it: "If this is going to work, then we need to bring people along with us." Most of us would agree that having broad understanding of where we're headed and getting people on board is a building block of our success . . . on behalf of those we serve. Some of us become captives of an idea or strategy we've hatched either on our own or working with a small group of like-minded colleagues. Moving into the more public sphere, we are convinced that all we need to do is sell the idea. Instead of a quick sell, people start asking questions and making suggestions. Rather than considering the possible answers and the wealth of thinking our constituents may be sharing with us, we go into a defensive position and sometimes even declare ourselves under attack. Why not build that counsel into the process rather than keep it at arm's length?

Case in point: During a two-year period, I was confronted with helping develop strategy for passing a bond election to build some new schools and upgrade a number of others—as well as a process that led to the closing (or combining) of eleven schools. Over many years, population patterns had changed. Where once there had been neighborhoods teeming with children, there were now older homes and empty nesters.

In preparation for these challenges, seasoned planners, demographers, designers, communication professionals, technology experts, transportation administrators, and curriculum and instructional leaders considered options for the future. Working directly with top officials, they advised on developing a proposed plan.

In each case, the board approved a series of recommendations for presentation to the community at large. Those proposals were not only shared with everyone internally and with the media, but we also took them directly to the community. We wanted everyone to focus their thinking on the actual recommendations rather than on rumor about what they might be.

Listening sessions were scheduled at every elementary school, with every advisory group and with most substantial community organizations. Meetings were held with individual reporters and editorial boards at their offices. Those who did briefings were thoroughly prepared to present the recommendations. All had the tools to support their presentations and facilitate responses. Recorders were assigned and prepared to collect questions, concerns, and suggestions for improvement. We took the same approach at meetings with mayors, county officials, business leaders, and others.

All of that information was collated and telescoped so that every concern or suggestion was addressed in some way during an open board meeting. Clusters of questions were stated in a way that encompassed what people had asked during the listening sessions.

The board responses? One general response ran something like, "This is something we need to pursue. Let's see how it might impact the recommendations." Another, "Good thought and good idea. It's likely beyond what we can do this time, but we need to be sure it's on the record for consideration in the future." A third, "We appreciate the thinking but we simply can't pursue it because of the need to make sure we maintain equal opportunity for all of our students." All of us wanted to know that the voices of our community were heard and considered by decision-makers in a public forum.

A Q&A brochure was developed and all of the questions and answers were printed in a two-page spread in a local newspaper. Today, they might also be shared online. Even responses to the Q&A contributed to a constructive public conversation. By the time the traditional finance campaign began, funded by contributions, community voices had been heard and had an impact on recommendations. Growing numbers of people and organizations didn't just consider it "someone else's plan" but "our plan." A poll, as we began organizing for the bond election, gave us a slightly greater than 20 percent chance of passage, but voters approved it by a margin of 60 to 40 percent. Three previous bond elections had failed, but despite that recent history, board members and educators felt strongly that they needed to demonstrate courage on behalf of children and their futures. Naturally, following school closings, we were taken to court. A judge noted, in his concluding statement, that the approach we used could be considered a model for making democracy work at the local level.

In the world of public engagement, the philosophical choice had been made. We were working on behalf of children and the community. We had what we considered very responsible positions, but we remembered at every turn that we were surrounded by a wealth of good thinking and commitment that spread across the entire community. Part of our responsibility was to capture that thinking and make it part of our own in shaping the future.

Engagement versus Polarization

We have a choice. We can succumb to narrowness or thrive with open-mindedness. Nonetheless, some people abandon the common good in favor of pure self-interest. However, most of us don't want that to happen. Democracy and our civil society are at stake. We do, after all, live in a networked world, held together by some modicum of collaboration. As for leadership, it's becoming increasingly lateral, while the predominantly vertical model is fading. Just because public engagement and collaboration are more difficult doesn't mean we should abandon them.

Our future depends on thinking together, pooling our genius. Yet, we have what often seem to be increasing numbers of people camping out in the extremes. The mood is often us versus them. Everything is black and white with no shades of gray. People in what are often called positions of partisan leadership take special pride in declaring polar opposites, despite the need for constructive exploration of issues and decision-making.

We hear a constant chorus singing the praises of teaching our students to think and reason, problem solve, and become increasingly able to guide us kicking and screaming into a more civil future. Those are the same skills all of us need to get past the divisiveness of polarization.

Some thoughtful observers are encouraged that members of the Millennial Generation often tend to see gridlock and suboptimal decisions as utterly disgusting. Concern is growing that we have multigenerational issues that need long-term attention. Among those issues are education, energy, the environment, and the economy—even war and peace. Since the world is moving faster than ever, every moment lost to entrenchment may take us even closer to the brink.

To loosely quote the late U.S. President James Madison, factions are part of the air that feeds the fire of democracy. We thrive on the sheer variety of our differences, but we desperately need to engage in pursuing a common good. The seeming inability or unwillingness to engage has come at a price. Public officials, shouting from their corners of the arena, have over time consistently lost our trust.

Since the extremes seem to be covered, there must be fresh ground. It's called *reason*. While turbulent times stir around us, we have an opportunity to bring people together to address the reasonable. Broad public engagement can help find a way forward, even as an abundance of people have declared their isolation from any ideas that are not their own. In some cases, people have developed a sense that, too often, those narrow views have been bought and paid for with earmarked campaign contributions or favors. Even lobbyists are looking for a new term to describe what they do.

In a nation that is becoming increasingly diverse, we should always consider that, if people don't feel their voices are heard, various groups will emerge to plead their cases. In several parts of the world, that conflict is fueled by tribe, race, ethnicity, religious differences, ideology, or other social and economic divides.

Our role, if we accept it, is to bring people together in common purpose around issues that are critical to our future. One way is to back off from today's polarizing issues. Instead, we can focus on massive trends that impact everyone. Together, we can consider their implications for education and for what our students need to know and be able to do as we move into a very different future. We might also think about their implications for economic growth and development and quality of life in our communities, maybe even in our country and the world. In the process, we might discover the benefits of a civic temperament.

A frequent question: Are we equipping our students to build and maintain an even more civil society? Do they develop a sense of empathy, understand the need for ethical behavior, respect differences, and grasp the idea of what it means to be civil? Do they practice conflict management, negotiating, and consensus-building skills? Do we emphasize civic education and the importance of public engagement and policymaking? Are today's students prepared to lead us toward the common good? That might lead to another question: What are the basics we all need to build and maintain a truly civil and democratic society?

Getting Connected to the Big Picture

I have spent a good part of my life urging all of us to see what we're doing within the context of a much larger, more complex world. All of us need perspective. Too often, the top of our desk becomes the world. We could work at what we have on our desks 24/7/365 for the rest of our lives, and we would likely never finish. Stuff keeps trickling or flooding onto our desks. The world might change around us, but some of us will respond by working even harder to do what we've always done. Sometimes, we gear up with new technologies to do even more efficiently what might have become obsolete. (Most of us have heard the war story about industrial plants that were destroyed but people came to work every day, putting in extra hours, even though nothing would ever again come off their assembly lines.)

In a series of books I've written, the most recent, *Twenty-One Trends for the 21st Century: Out of the Trenches, Into the Future*, introduces a number of massive forces that impact each of us and every institution. It's the environment in which we exist, with projections for what we might need to consider if we hope to thrive in the future. We address trends in areas such as aging; diversity; the flow of generations; technology; identity and privacy; the economy; jobs and careers; the environment; polarization; sustainability; poverty; personalization; ingenuity; the depth, breadth, and content of education; scarcity versus abundance; authority; and work-life balance, to name a few.

We are of this world, not separate from it. That's a good reason why we need to engage our staffs and communities in discussing the implications of these massive future forces for us in our personal lives, for our education systems, for businesses, for governments, and for everyone else. Those discussions are sometimes called *Community Conversations*. Often, they bring together up to 250 people from a diversity of organizations and walks of life, including educators and students. That group goes through an exhilarating process of thinking about the future.

We recommend that smaller groups get together as *Futures Councils* during the months and years that follow, to constantly spot trends, do research, and share what they learn for consideration by the organization. It is a fact that unless we develop shared *aspirations*, a constant flow of *circumstances* will drive our future. Leadership, coupled with foresight and courage by every member of the team, is the essential ingredient.

The truly dynamic organization is always focusing on today and thinking about tomorrow. Not by accident . . . but intentionally. A logical question is, "Where will we ever get the time to do that?" The answer, "Use some of the time, energy, and brain power we regularly spend defending the status quo and fighting any semblance of systemic change."

Another question might be, "I'm an educator. Why should I care about the economy? If I wanted to spend my time on the economy, I would have become an economist." Of course, we know that everything is connected to everything else.

In short, we need to engage with both people and ideas. What we so often try to avoid is the very thing that keeps us connected to a fast-changing world. As we move into the future, every institution will have to adapt and help lead us in new directions. No one gets a pass.

If These Kids Can Do It . . . So Can We

While visiting educators and students across Senegal in West Africa, I encountered a project in the northern town of Ross Bethio, near the Senegal River. This village is located in the Sahel. The streets are desert sand. For as long as anyone can remember, water for Ross Bethio has come from the river, along with a panoply of river-borne diseases.

A team of students, ages ten to fifteen, involved in *Project Citizen* decided to address that very issue. These young people identified issues their community was facing, sorted them out, and settled on the need for freshwater as number one. After doing further research, they sharpened their definition of the problem, then developed a strategy, a plan of action, and suggested public policy. In the process, they engaged with authority figures, such as the village elder, the imam at the local mosque, the rural administrator, the head of a nearby gendarme detachment, parents, and others.

One part of the plan was a demonstration or march. National media carried the story. Before long, these ten- to fifteen-year-olds had convinced the government that their community desperately needed freshwater. When the principal at the local middle school took me to the river to see young people ladling river water into barrels to take home, he proudly pointed upstream to a water tower in its final stages of construction. Many adults had long ago given up on the luxury of a freshwater tap in their town. However, these children engaged their community and solved a problem. Everyone who lives there is living a relatively healthier life. If those kids can engage their community in dealing with big concerns . . . so can we.

Making the Leadership Difference

We've discussed the need for leadership that is capable of engagement. All terrific leaders know that power shared is not power lost. It is power multiplied. Being interested, demonstrating a sense of duty to improve the lives of others and get a job done, coupled with the willingness to display courage and allow ourselves to be vulnerable, are often seen as signs of good leadership. Why vulnerability? If we seem to constantly protect ourselves from the ideas and concerns of those we serve, in essence, try to appear invulnerable, we distance ourselves from reality.

Of course, there are legions of possibilities for engagement. We've mentioned a few in this perspective. Others might include: online chats or webinars, surveys, parent report cards (allowing parents to give us feedback on how we're doing), listening sessions, think tanks and Delphi groups (structured feedback panel), and paying attention to ideas generated by advisory councils and a host of community organizations. To make sure the whole team is ready to reflect our commitment to engagement, we might want to do customer service workshops for all staff. Of course, Community Conversations and Futures Councils can be rallying points.

Our willingness to engage gives us an opportunity to generate the energy every organization and every person needs to be successful. We need to couple all of that energy and know-how with a demonstrated sense of empathy and a willingness to understand what it's like to walk a mile in someone else's shoes. In a highly diverse world, that also means cultural understanding, at least an interest in language skills, and expressions that reflect an appreciation for the enrichment that graces the community we serve with the arrival of students and families whose origins may be thousands of miles and oceans away. Servant leadership is essential, and one of the prime ways to demonstrate it is through community engagement.

Perspective #2: Sherre Calouri — The Role of School Boards in Parent/Community Engagement Programs[2]

Sherre Calouri was a member of the school board in Beaverton, Oregon, for seventeen years, serving three years as chair. Her professional career path took many directions, including several years as a teacher of the deaf and a few more as a journalist with a special interest in education. After retiring as a chief deputy sheriff, she spent a decade as public information reservist with the Department of Homeland Security. Currently she writes grants for a nonprofit that provides housing for farm workers. She holds a bachelor's degree in communications from Northwestern University and a master's degree in public administration from Lewis and Clark College.

* * *

School boards play a crucial role in the success of parent/community engagement initiatives. When board members enthusiastically encourage staff and administrators to build active, authentic engagement programs, the rewards are many, especially in the area of improving student achievement at all levels.

It only makes sense that all school boards would embrace parent engagement. After all, we want our parents to support their students and our schools. But we probably aren't nearly as eager to support parent involvement when it means they might disagree with us. If we decide to delegate certain decisions only to find out we don't like what they decided, what do we do then? We could try and explain why we don't like their decision, but sometimes they might be so adamant in their views that no amount of education or persuasion will move them to where we want them to be. It's easy to see why parent engagement is frequently messy and exhausting. It is much easier to just make decisions, then hunker down in the storm cellar when the angry winds howl, knowing that it will all blow over in time. Unfortunately, the hunker-down strategy works against our educational mission to help every child succeed in school. We simply can't justify that leadership model any longer.

It's not just parent engagement that matters. The entire community — businesses, churches, mosques, synagogues, city and county governments — must also be involved in school and student improvement. Many families and their children come to us with a variety of challenges including food and housing insecurity, lack of medical care, household and/or neighborhood violence, illiteracy, crime, and unemployment. We know these problems have a negative impact on student learning and we also know solutions require collaboration within the entire community.

So, where to start? The first step is to begin crafting a policy that reflects the school board and community's beliefs in the value of parent/community engagement. A written policy is vital because it lets your community know that parent/community engagement matters to school leaders.

While there are a number of sample policies to guide you in developing your own, the most effective process is one in which you engage your parents and other stakeholders in a discussion about parent/community involvement. What are their beliefs regarding the family's role in educating children? Do parents see themselves as the primary educators of their children or do they think that schools play that role? Do they believe that teachers should be partners with them in educating their children? Do teachers feel similarly as parents or are there big differences? Are school principals eager to work with parents on a successful program? What barriers do your parents and educators see in creating an active engagement program? Do community members want to be engaged? If not, why not?

Once your policy vision is documented, you can begin discussing how your board can include parents and the community in the board's work and decision-making. As you begin discussing strategies, you can use your policy to test whether or not the strategies meet the intent of your policy.

Here are some successful strategies you may want to employ:

- Host regular listening sessions.

    Listening sessions may be held to discuss a specific topic or routinely scheduled to provide a forum for parents and community members to meet with district or school staff and board members to talk about what's working and what's not. The key to successful listening sessions is "listening." This is not the time for speeches or telling parents what you want them to know. This is the time for you to understand what parents are telling you. It's a time to clarify what you think you are hearing and to ask for suggestions from parents as to how you can help them support their students' success in school. The more carefully you listen, allowing adequate time to clarify understanding, the far less likely you are to be blind-sided by Twitter screeches or Facebook slams.

Don't forget to hold listening sessions with students. What do students want from their parents and the community to help them succeed in school? It's also a good idea to encourage people who have publicly opposed school district policies or practices to attend these sessions. One way to quiet the din of disagreement is to invite opponents to participate.

Take your listening sessions into the community. If you hold all your meetings in a school building, you may miss involving parents who may not have transportation or child-care services to free them to attend a meeting, or they simply may not feel comfortable coming to school. Take your listening sessions to neighborhood centers or church recreation halls.

- Stage community forums.

There aren't many people in your community who don't have an opinion about their local schools. Just stand on a busy corner in your city, stop people at random, and ask, "What do you think about the schools in our community?" You'll get an earful. The community forum is one way to elevate street corner opinions from the backyard fence to the boardroom where educational decisions are made. The community forums differ from listening sessions in that they bring together parents, business leaders, members of the faith community, seniors, teachers, staff, students, and political leaders, all in one room, to discuss their school district's vision and strategic plan. The forum is more formal with invited participants to ensure there is a broad cross section of the community. There is usually a formal agenda that includes educating attendees regarding the status of the district, facilitated discussion groups, reports, and follow-up sessions.

- Provide opportunities for parents to learn skills that support their children's at-home learning and academic success in school.

When asked, many parents may tell you that they simply don't know how to help their children succeed in school. Some parents may have a language barrier or they may not understand what their student is learning. Other parents may be exhausted from working two jobs or caring for extended family and not have the time or energy to help their students. Teachers can guide parents into activities that will support their students and yet not require extensive time or knowledge. The research is clear on this issue: parents who acquire skills to help their children at home with schoolwork, or know how to get their student needed help, have a positive influence on their child's school performance. The outcome is worth the effort.

- Create an office of parent/community engagement.

When you commit staff to support your policy of parent engagement, you reinforce the importance of your vision. It may be tempting to create the office using volunteers, but professional staff working alongside volunteers are better able to develop and implement effective parental engagement strategies than are volunteers acting alone. An office of parent/community engagement will provide necessary continuity and commitment to implementing your policy.

What we know is that properly implemented community engagement collaborations strengthen schools and neighborhoods, improve student learning, and reduce the incidence of student problems. We also know that the community may view a poorly implemented policy as simply another reform effort that wasted time and resources with no positive results.

- Build collaborative partnerships within your community.

The basis of these partnerships is that they have a mutually held goal designed to solve a specific problem. For example, bullying is a problem in almost all school districts. Boards recognize that when students are victims or perpetrators of bullying, learning is compromised, not just for those directly involved but for the entire school. When the school environment is unsafe for some, it is unsafe for all. Schools today employ a variety of measures with some degree of success, but the most successful models are those that involve community partners—police, human services, parents, faith-based organizations, and youth groups—working collaboratively for a solution tailor-made for their community.

- Provide adequate funding for community involvement programs.

There is certainly a lot of truth to the fact that we fund what is important to us. Funding must be adequate and consistent. These programs require time to plan, implement, and evaluate. There are no magic answers that can be given to every school district. Make parent/community involvement a priority.

- Engage parents and community in solving problems that matter.

   Too many times we design parent/community engagement activities that require people to do something—staff the refreshment booth at the football game, plan the school carnival, or raise money to buy playground equipment. While these are worthy activities, they are not necessarily designed to solve problems that impact student success in school. Instead consider how your parents and community might help reduce the number of middle school students who have no supervision after school or increase the number of students who have books to read at home or address other local problems. When you begin to look at parent/community engagement as a resource for solving problems, those who work on the problem will feel like they are making a significant contribution.

- Show up.

   School boards, more than any other local elected officials, have easy access to their constituents. That access allows board members to be a sounding board for parents, business leaders, other government officials, and community members. Of course, access only happens if you grab it. The more you can encourage all board members to attend "other than school-sponsored" community meetings and events such as local service clubs, the more opportunities you have to listen. One school board member reported that she increased the amount of time she spent grocery shopping so she could talk to neighbors who inevitably asked her questions about schools. Another board member said that attending Chamber of Commerce meetings helped him educate business leaders on the fact that schools are an essential economic resource that needs to be nurtured. Communicate regularly with city and state office holders as to the status of education in your community and a list of unmet needs. Parent/community engagement volunteers can also be foot soldiers in helping to convince state and local office holders to fund public schools adequately.

- Gather data and assess your program.

   At budget time, some may consider the community/parent engagement effort to be icing on the cake, which is okay because there aren't very many cakes that taste good without icing. And that's what you need to explain. The "icing"—parent and community engagement—is essential to ensuring success for all students. The best way to tackle the "icing" discussion is to provide the data that prove your point. Ask your superintendent to develop an evaluation tool that will help your board determine how successful your program is. Make sure that data collection is more than a tally sheet of the number of volunteers and their hours. The evaluation must be qualitative as well as quantitative. It must provide you with information as to how participants viewed their experience, how it might be changed, etc.

As you work through developing policy and implementing your program, you will find a wealth of resources available. Everything you try may not work, but because you will be receiving continual feedback from your parents and community, your success ratio will increase with the increase in engagement. Of course, your key motivation for moving ahead is that parent and community engagement improves student success in school and life, and that's exactly why you serve on a school board in the first place.

Perspective #3: Janet Hogue—A Stake in the Outcome: The Importance of Civic Engagement to Public Schools and Democracy[3]

Janet Hogue taught biology at Sunset High School from 1979–1986. From 1993–2006, she was a leader on multiple Beaverton bond and school board campaigns. She co-founded and chaired a Beaverton citizen lobbying group focused on school funding and K–12 education issues. Hogue was hired as the executive director of the Beaverton Education Foundation in 1999 and served until 2006. In 2009, she retired from a three-year position as the Beaverton School District's learning options coordinator.

* * *

I became a professional volunteer in 1993 when the Beaverton School District presented the district's economic situation to many of us, asked for help, and provided training. My two daughters were in first and fifth grades in public school when I became embroiled in Oregon's struggle to stabilize public school funding. I spent years as an unpaid volunteer leading school bond campaigns and lobbying legislators. The catalyst for my involvement was Oregon's 1990 property tax limitation measure, Measure-5, which fundamentally changed how our schools were financed. It removed control from local communities and put authority for funding in the hands of our state legislature. The percentage of each property tax dollar allowed for education was capped and gathered into one pot that was divided equally across all school districts in the state. Unfortunately, the capped property taxes weren't enough to support education, and public schools were forced to compete for general fund dollars with other state services.

Between 1993 and 1995, as Measure-5 restrictions rolled in, our local school district lost one-third of its programs and staff, most of which was never regained. It was devastating to see our schools dismantled. While the district was losing staff and programs, it was also rapidly growing. From 1990 to 2001, the district grew by 29 percent, adding eight thousand students. Our schools were crowded, and our class sizes were skyrocketing.

The school district needed its parents to fight for education funding at the state level and pass bond measures to build new schools. Several of us who were the most passionate volunteered to lead the way. We built a powerful lobbying network of parents focused on school funding and K–12 education issues. As citizen volunteers, we coordinated rallies and citizen testimony, collaborating with teachers' unions and the school district to regularly testify in the Oregon legislature. We secured eleventh-hour educational funding that made a difference for our schools and those around the state. We conducted candidates' forums for legislative candidates and school board candidates.

Additionally, we led multiple successful school bond measure campaigns recruiting and establishing steering committees, initiating campaign fund-raising, analyzing polling data, and conceiving campaign strategies. We created collateral, directed mailings, canvassing, and phone banks. And between 1994 and 2006, we raised more than $520 million to remodel our old schools, build ten new schools, and upgrade technology.

It was an incredible effort that changed the face of our community. How did we do it? How does one quantify the essence of civic engagement and motivation?

Public Schools as the Foundation of Democracy

How did we inspire a community to fight for its schools? In 1993, during a failed sales tax campaign, I gave a speech about the value of public education. In it, I used a quote from then-governor of Colorado Roy Romer, spoken during an interview with David Brinkley in August 1993.[4] They were discussing the school choice movement and vouchers, and Romer was quoted as follows: "We ought to remember what the public school has meant to us—as the meeting ground for all kinds of Americans. When you encourage separate schools for Methodists, for Catholics, for Lutherans, when you divide youngsters by race or class or by their parents' view of Creation, you become less like America—and more like Bosnia. We ought to be careful where we go."

Obviously, there is a place and a constituency for private schools in America. But I fundamentally believed in the sentiment of unrestricted community implied by the term *public schools*. Our nation has made an investment in providing access for all children through our public school system, and they truly are the meeting ground expressed in Roy Romer's quote. At its core, I believed our democracy needed an educated citizenry to function, and public schools are the access to that education.

I must admit, however, that the original motivation for my activism was fear—fear that the instruction of my own two daughters would suffer because of the draconian funding reductions to education in our state. We looked at every private school in our area, and my children were accepted to several, but I couldn't shake my strong belief that public education was the foundation of our democracy. My husband and I made the decision to sink or swim with the public schools, and our lives revolved around the school funding issue. I eventually came to see the problem more globally. Every child became important to me. Every child was untapped potential. As parents, we were responsible to ensure that our children and *all* children were successful. Each child had worth and each child was important as a citizen in our democracy. We were accountable for keeping that democracy alive by educating its future citizenry.

- We are responsible for our democracy. It belongs to the people and requires an educated citizenry.
- The ideal worth striving for is that each child has worth and each child is important as a citizen and participant in our democracy.

- We engaged hundreds of people in our efforts, and they each had a stake in the outcome.

We held to these ideals and engaged citizens through teams at each one of our district's more than forty schools. We learned how to run a political campaign, and we recruited team leaders at every school who enlisted a cadre of parents willing to volunteer for lobbying and campaign efforts. We knitted the community together, engaging the Chamber of Commerce, business leaders, and the teachers' union. Each of the hundreds of volunteers, whether they were parents, grandparents, business leaders, or educators, had a stake in the effort. Each person engaged was a person on our side. Each individual was a voice for the cause. We all had a stake in the outcome. It was up to us to make it happen. And we did.

Parental Engagement in Public Schools

Parents can be engaged in their local schools in a variety of ways. Their motivations for engagement will vary. Some desire to advocate for their own children, while others enjoy the social engagement with other parents. Others become involved out of perceived need for their assistance or fear about the state of their schools. And some believe in the fundamental value of educating and caring for ALL children. It is important, if our democracy is to flourish, that we inspire parents, and all citizens, to think more globally, to see how all children must be successful for our country to thrive.

Many studies support the role of parental involvement in student success. Parents can be engaged, assisting the teacher at the classroom level, or commit to the school's parent/teacher organization. Most parent/teacher organizations have a fund-raising role and a function to bring activities to the school as a whole. As parents become involved outside of their child's classroom, they are more likely to see why promoting success for ALL students is important.

Parents working together created a safety net of community support for its teachers and students. It is important to engage as many families and parents as possible, including those who are disenfranchised and don't know how to become involved. Examples include new immigrants facing language and cultural barriers, families in poverty, and/or single parent families. Districts and school organizations must make the effort to communicate with these families, employing translators and counselors who work specifically to engage them. School and district activities that provide transportation, child care, food, and translators, and occur in schools, apartments, and community centers outside of regular school hours can overcome language and cultural barriers that hinder engagement.

The parent/teacher organization of one elementary school in our district sponsored a homework club for its struggling English-as-a-Second-Language students by providing funds they raised, supplemented with a grant from the local education foundation. The Homework Club delivered after-school tutoring and homework help in reading, writing, math, and science. Teachers and staff met twice weekly with students in the recreation center of the apartment complex where many of these students lived, giving assistance that helped them succeed in school. The program resulted in increased school attendance and academic success, and reduced the number of discipline referrals and incidents for these children.

The Homework Club became a part of their home community. Their parents also became engaged as they had access to teachers and translators and felt empowered to ask questions about how they could assist and support their children. Older students who graduated from the elementary school Homework Club returned to help tutor their younger friends and siblings.

Parents can also be organized across an entire school district in a variety of roles that benefit the success of all students in the district. These parents, in the course of their volunteerism, often become passionate advocates and parent leaders for public education. They bring a host of skill sets, perspectives, and backgrounds to the work that benefits the school district. They believe they are responsible for their schools and for fostering student success for all—they have a stake in the outcome. They are the face of their schools and community.

Some examples of work for parent leaders include:

- Serving on the school board,
- Serving on the parent/teacher organization board,
- Becoming an activist for lobbying and political activities including hosting candidate forums,
- Participating in campaigns to build schools or provide funding,
- Serving on an education foundation board, and

- Serving as a parent representative on district committees such as budget, strategic planning, textbook adoption groups, curriculum review, and boundary change task forces.

We have to remember that we are all connected and we *all* have responsibility for our democracy and for our society. We must aspire to a belief in the inherent worth and equality of each individual. Abraham Lincoln reminded our new nation, torn asunder by conflict and war, that we were "conceived in Liberty, and dedicated to the proposition that all men are created equal." If we can strive for that ideal, that each life is important, we can create a better future and a better country where everyone is engaged and everyone has a stake in the outcome.

Perspective #4: John Boone—A Business Perspective[5]

John Boone is the founder and president of ProFocus, a technology staffing company headquartered in Portland, Oregon. Before serving in that role, he was co-founder and CEO of Employment Trends, a highly respected staffing services company in Portland. The company garnered awards including the Inc. 500 and the #1 Best Small Company to Work for in Oregon. He holds a bachelor's degree with honors in quantitative economics and decision science from the University of California, San Diego.

* * *

Oftentimes we think the only way business can improve schools is by changing the overall system, such as educational curriculums, teaching standards, or testing benchmarks. Education is such a complex system that no one can tackle it alone. Even Congress, state legislatures, mayors, and local school boards are unable to solve all the problems. We can't wait for answers to act. We need to do something now, no matter how small. We can directly help students, even on a limited scale, if we act in partnership with teachers and schools.

My story is just one example of how businesses and business organizations can identify a problem, work with the teacher, and make a difference for students. When my children were in elementary school, there was a book fair in the library twice a year. Parents received notices informing them that if they wanted their children to buy books from the book fair "store," they should put money in an envelope and send it to school with their student. During the book fair, teachers would escort their children to the library to buy books.

I was surprised to see how excited my children were about this event. Our family had always valued reading and almost anytime one of the kids wanted a book we would buy it for them. But somehow the book fair offered something more. The kids talked with one another about their favorite books, they purchased the books by themselves, and they proudly showed their teacher which book they had selected. The experience seemed to be a lot more thrilling than buying a book with Mom and Dad.

My wife and I realized that some of our children's classmates would not feel that same excitement because their family simply did not have enough money. What would those kids be thinking and feeling? We were certain they would be sad, angry, and worse—maybe thinking reading was not important for them. We talked with the teacher about our concern. She agreed that it was a significant problem. She told us that over the years she had noticed behavior problems before, during, and after the book fair from children who could not buy books.

My wife and I decided to donate extra money for the kids who were unable to purchase books. Later the teacher told us about how our donation helped her students. She told us about a boy who was struggling to read and had never had a book of his own. He carried his book to school in his backpack every day and whenever he had free time in class, he took it out and read it, over and over again.

The next year we gave more money and the following year increased our donation. Finally, we decided there was so much need, not only at our school, but at other schools in our district, that I approached my Rotary Club with a thought . . . let's expand this idea to more schools. From that small beginning, "Books for Kids" was launched. Rotarians are not only involved in providing the funds to purchase the books, we also attend the book fairs, help students select books, and place "This Book Belongs to" stickers in the books along with the child's name. As of this writing, our Rotary Club has been running the "Books for Kids" program for nearly four years. We have provided approximately 1,500 books to approximately 975 children.

This letter from a teacher demonstrates how important our small contribution is to helping children achieve success in school:

"I just wanted to let you know how much I appreciate the money from the Rotary that has been given to students to purchase books. Last year, I had a student that would not read. He received money for the book fair and purchased a book. It was literally life changing. I couldn't get him to stop reading his book. In fact, he was supposed to go to another teacher for reading, but he kept forgetting because he was so involved in his book. Even though he wasn't following directions, I wanted to shout, 'Hooray!' So if you were wondering if the money makes a difference, oh, yes—yes, it does!"

There are many business leaders throughout our country who are making a significant contribution to improving student achievement through research, school improvement grants, scholarships for low-income students, and other programs. What's also important is that all of us can be engaged in some manner that may not be as time demanding but, nonetheless, can make a significant difference for kids.

Perspective #5: Nora Carr—Social Media: Communicating and Engaging in the New Neighborhood[6]

Nora Carr, APR, Fellow PRSA, is chief of staff for Guilford County Schools in Greensboro, North Carolina. With more than 72,300 students in 126 schools, GCS is the third largest school district in North Carolina. It also is one of the nation's most diverse, with students speaking more than 115 world languages and representing more than 95 different countries. A sought-after speaker with private and public sector experience, Carr writes frequently on communications, marketing, and public relations for a variety of professional publications and journals. She is a contributing editor for the *American School Board Journal*, serves on the editorial review board for the *Journal of School Public Relations*, and is a frequent contributor to *eSchool News*. During 2013–14, Carr served as president of the National School Public Relations Association.

*   *   *

Shifting Landscapes

With nearly three-fourths of American adults engaging in online networks, social media is no longer the purview of the young. While the always on, always connected Millennial Generation still leads all other demographic groups in technology use, even 65 percent of online adults over age sixty used social media sites by 2013.

These trends cut across income, education, gender, and racial lines, especially as cheaper and more powerful smartphones make Internet access nearly universal. In fact, women and Latinos outpace all but eighteen- to twenty-nine-year-olds when it comes to social media use, at 79 versus 90 percent. Similarly, Latinos and African Americans outpace all other groups in adopting mobile technologies, including smartphones. As Lee Rainie, director of Pew Research Center's Internet Project, notes in 2011, "new media are the new neighborhood." Engaging parents, educators, volunteers, taxpayers, and other key publics in the new online neighborhoods may require a shift in strategy and focus for many school officials. Knowing with whom to communicate, at the right time and in the right way, and with the right kind of experiences and information, underlies good public relations strategy.

Changing direction and adjusting organizational strategy in response to these interactions is the essence of Grunig's excellence theory of public relations and leadership, and what elevates effective two-way communication from a technical craft to a key management function and professional practice.[7] While school public relations professionals and educators have long sought to build important stakeholder relationships through more face-to-face and other interactive forms of communication, the pressure to share more and more information through an ever-growing number of tools and tactics has continued unabated.

Whether this outpouring of information and activity is changing hearts and minds is a matter of debate, which is why questions regarding the highest and best use of social media networks for school communications are so intriguing. Just because parents of school-aged children keep up with their friends and family through Facebook, Flickr, and Snapshot doesn't necessarily mean they want to confer with their child's teacher online about a troubling report card or discuss the impact of state budget cuts on class size with the superintendent. On the other hand, schools and districts without a strong social media presence leave themselves open to unanswered attacks and misinformation campaigns in one of the planet's fastest growing information networks. Clearly, as with other forms of communication, one size doesn't fit all.

Often lighthearted, always unfiltered and conversational, social media are by nature, social. They are more potluck supper than formal dinner party, more a friendly club for members with shared passions and hobbies than a trade association of experts or exclusive gathering for the moneyed elite. Social media are also highly personal, something many young employees have been chagrined to learn when the party shots and comments they post after a night on the town suddenly become fodder for parents' ire and local news stories. The anonymity and lack of civility on social media along with the rise of citizen journalists who don't know about, or feel compelled to follow, old-school news norms of fact-checking, balance, neutrality, and original sourcing also make the new media neighborhood feel more Wild West than suburban cul-de-sac. Some sociologists and psychologists worry that social media expansion is increasing social isolation, narrowing our perspectives and experiences rather than broadening them.

Yet, if social media can help mobilize the youth vote and elect America's first African American president and spark an Arab Spring of revolutions against oppressive regimes that continues to this day, then surely social media have a vital role to play in communicating with and engaging all those with a stake in one of our nation's most treasured democratic creations—the public school. This perspective explores the role social media play in this complex milieu and delves into the central question of whether social media are tools for connecting people and providing information, platforms for authentic engagement, or both.

Connecting in New Ways

Continuously shifting and evolving, social media use is becoming the new neighborhood, the virtual front porch, coffee shop, and playground where friends and family connect with each other, sharing daily anecdotes, photos, stories, trials and tribulations, often in mind-numbing, 140-character detail. Fueled by the Internet and mobile technologies, the new neighborhood features on-the-go and take-it-with-you communications, where a brief wait at a stop sign or in the drive-through window represents an opportunity to check in with friends and followers, and post new information. In this new neighborhood, the two main points of connection are smartphones and social media.

At the start of 2014, social media use was led by the behemoth Facebook, with somewhere between 800 million and 1.15 billion unique monthly users, followed by Twitter, LinkedIn, Google+, Pinterest, Tumblr, Flickr, VK, Instagram, MySpace (yes, it still exists.), Tagged,

Meetup, Ning, Meetme, and ClassMates, according to *Forbes* and *eBizM-BA*, As with other communication channels, however, demographics vary greatly in social media, so developing smart outreach and engagement strategies requires a deeper understanding of what each site has to offer and why.

Moms with babies, toddlers, and school-aged children, for example, rank among social media's most prolific users. A white paper published by Experian Marketing Services in 2013 indicates that moms with young kids (MYKs) visit social media sites more than three times each day, leaving a trail of posts, comments, photos, quiz answers, and other social media interactions behind them. In fact, according to the 2010 Census, slightly more than 30 percent of U.S. households included moms with children under the age of eighteen.

Women, mothers in particular, also tend to drive the decision-making processes regarding home purchases, apartment rentals, and school selections. Parents of school-aged children also have the most at stake in district decision-making processes regarding boundary changes, student assignment issues, transportation policies, budget allocations, capital improvement campaigns, and tax referendums. Research also shows that Latino audiences, another priority group for many public schools, led the United States in social media and mobile communications use. Clearly, figuring out ways to connect with these priority groups through social media isn't a matter of if, but when and how.

While it always pays to do statistically valid research at the local level, national data can point educators in the right direction. The Mosaic Group USA, for example, in a 2013 study, found that families with young children use the following sites the most: Facebook 70.4 percent; YouTube 15.1 percent; Twitter 2.2 percent; Pinterest 1.0 percent; Google+ 0.9 percent.

Social Media versus Face-to-Face Strategies

While the rise of social media and the 140-character message are shifting the communication landscape, these newer technologies aren't obliterating more traditional approaches. Within the hierarchy of effective communications established by decades of research, one-on-one, face-to-face engagement still reigns supreme. One-to-one conversation and dialogue is followed by small group interactions, large group interactions, and other two-way communications where the facial expressions and body language that comprise 80 percent of human expression and meaning are included. While social media and other emerging information communication technologies (ICTs) are creating new opportunities to share information, converse, and interact with parents, students, teachers, and other important stakeholder groups, an online relationship typically is not as robust as one that includes human interaction.

The real value of social media and other ICTs, however, may lie in the ability to connect school officials with individuals who don't have the time or interest in traditional public engagement activities. Given the often frenzied pace of modern life, on-the-go platforms like social media are being used to engage citizens in setting budget priorities and parameters, redrawing school boundaries, and other important district-level decisions. These new technologies enable schools and districts to create branded social media–type sites focused on critical issues or decisions that need to be made.

By including infographics, polling, online surveying, photo sharing, document sharing, and other interactive tools in smartphone-friendly formats, these engagement sites help break down complex issues in an easy-to-understand and easy-to-access manner, prompting greater awareness, better citizen input, and better public decision-making. When new topics or issues emerge, school officials can use the system to notify participants that new conversations are taking place, thus encouraging an ongoing relationship. From a district perspective, using automated software to create compelling infographics, translate content in multiple languages, frame critical issues, generate new ideas, sort conversations by topic, generate reports, analyze data, and identify trends adds even more value and insight. These tools also typically include links to the major social media sites, spreading the conversation further.

Social Media Concerns

Despite the possibilities, enthusiasm, and growth in this sector, social media and other ICTs are not a panacea. Without clear, published guidelines and careful monitoring, well-meaning efforts to engage students, parents, and other constituents in many districts can backfire, creating embarrassing posts, negative news stories, student discipline issues, and employment concerns. Yet schools and school districts without a strong social media presence may simply create a vacuum that others will fill, often with misinformation and negative news.

School communication, grassroots mobilization, and employee, parent, and public engagement are by nature contact sports. E-mails, "likes," "favorites," "retweets," instant polls, and other technology tools aren't going to replace human interaction. As anyone who has managed a school bond campaign understands, survey data doesn't always guarantee consensus or a positive outcome at the polls. Consensus, input, and majority votes don't always yield the best public policy decisions.

Social media will never replace courageous community conversations, leadership, and public policy decisions that focus on what is good for children, no matter the opposition. Social media may help increase transparency, engage more people in public decisions, and get more diverse voices to the table, but only if school officials work hard to make that happen. Finding common ground for common schools among increasingly diverse and often divided electorates and communities represents the single most pressing challenge confronting public education today in democratic societies.

Engaging citizens in meaningful ways in the work and decisions of civic institutions like public schools remains a challenge, especially when nearly 70 percent of U.S. households (2010 Census) no longer have school-aged children, and when demographic shifts mean that today's schoolchildren no longer look, dress, or sound like the majority of citizens whose taxes support them. Bridging these gaps in experience, perspective, age, economics, ethnicity, gender, race, and other demographic-driven realities is a daunting yet critical task.

Perspective #6: Karen Kleinz—Keeping Public Education Strong: Public Engagement Makes a Difference[8]

Karen H. Kleinz, APR, associate executive director of the National School Public Relations Association (NSPRA), has over thirty years' experience in public relations, working in the private sector as well as public education. Since joining NSPRA in 1998, Kleinz has led the Association's public engagement efforts and has represented NSPRA in collaborative partnerships with the Annenberg Institute for School Reform, the Everyday Democracy, the Deliberative Democracy Consortium, and the Kettering Foundation.

* * *

Most of us have experienced a major "aha!" moment at some point in our careers, when something connects and resonates so powerfully that we are inspired to change our way of thinking or approach to how we do our jobs. For me, that was the day in 1996 when I received a copy of *Is There a Public for Public Schools?* as a membership bonus item from the National School Public Relations Association (NSPRA).

This little seventy-seven-page book (now well-highlighted and dog-eared), written by Kettering Foundation President and CEO David Mathews, truly changed the way I saw my role as a school district community relations director. Like Dorothy stepping out the door of her tornado-flung house into the new Technicolor world of Oz, this book opened the door to the concept of public engagement and the relationship between the community and schools as being integral to the success of our public schools. It introduced me not only to a new way of thinking about how to connect with stakeholders, but I also discovered a new set of skills to learn—facilitating dialogue and deliberation, framing issues, planning forums and study circles, and promoting choice work and the value of engagement to skeptical district administrators.

Eighteen years later, this book continues to remain relevant. For me, one line still drives how I think about the role of the school communicator—*"What a school does makes little sense unless we know how its mission relates to the community's educational goals and public purposes."* If we cannot connect the dots for our publics so that they understand the intrinsic value of public education and the myriad ways that it impacts the quality of their lives as well as community life, and at the same time meet their basic expectations of the schools, then we are not doing our job very well.

The work of public engagement is work that is easy to get passionate about. It is endlessly interesting, energizing, and rewarding. It can build ownership and a sense of responsibility for the schools among varied stakeholder groups, parents and nonparents alike. It allows all voices to be heard, not just those who are loudest and most demanding. It can introduce different points of view in a setting that often allows for those "aha!" moments among stakeholders who otherwise would never interact. It embraces the diversity of human experience and weaves it into a tapestry that is stronger, more vibrant, and better able to support the needs of all students in our schools.

At the same time, it is challenging, labor-intensive, and time-consuming. Getting public engagement right, and realizing useful outcomes, takes patience, planning, detailed coordination, skilled facilitation, broad outreach, commitment, and courage to embrace change—things sometimes difficult to come by in school systems. It is not a course to embark upon unless you are willing to listen, deepen the dialogue, expand participation to include all voices—from the most active and informed to the disenfranchised—and find common ground on which to act collaboratively.

A Look Back

As an NSPRA member my entire career, both as a school district communications professional as well as a staff member, I have seen NSPRA and NSPRA members in the vanguard time after time as "early adopters" of public relations trends and strategies. This was especially significant when it came to embracing the concept of authentic public engagement.

NSPRA members leading the way twenty years ago included three key individuals: author and NSPRA past president Kathy Leslie, APR, and her vision for engagement in the Beaverton (OR) School District; and past president Jennifer Reeve, APR, and her colleague Jane Urschel, PhD at the Colorado Association of School Boards, with their innovative efforts to introduce public engagement processes to school board decision-making around the state.

Recognizing that public engagement in its truest form is, in fact, the highest level of public relations practice (focusing on the public RELATIONSHIPS that drive our work), NSPRA executive director Rich Bagin, APR, reached out to Dr. David Mathews at the Kettering Foundation which resulted in NSPRA members receiving free copies of *Is There a Public for Public Schools?* This was quickly followed by collaborations with the Annenberg Institute for School Reform and the Study Circles Resource Center (now known as Everyday Democracy) and NSPRA offering a series of Public Engagement Academies around the country to introduce members and educators to this powerful process.

For many school public relations professionals, this was their introduction to the world of public engagement, and it ushered in a new era for NSPRA and school communication. This is not to say that there was an immediate sea change in how school district communication programs were structured or major decisions were made. Like most major shifts in practice and behavior, it took over a decade before real changes were noticeable in most school systems.

Defining Engagement

One of the first big hurdles to overcome was differentiating between "engagement" and the more traditional parent/community "involvement" programs. Certainly there is a place for both in the schools, but initially it was difficult to explain that authentic engagement is much more than asking people to volunteer in or partner with their schools with a specific outcome in mind. It requires creating opportunities for citizens to take part in a deeper dialogue about issues impacting schools, their values and expectations for education, and their role in decision-making for change and improvement.

As the term "public engagement" emerged in the education vernacular, it was used in many different ways, and for a while was co-opted by some who latched on to it as the newest buzzword and used it interchangeably with "involvement." This caused some confusion and lessened the impact, while frustrating those of us who were striving to implement authentic engagement processes.

It has taken a solid decade for the concept of public engagement—in its authentic form—to really take hold as a core component of an effective communication program in school systems. As interest ebbed and flowed, NSPRA continued to advocate for the power of engagement in building community support and ownership for the schools, and today our National Seminar program is packed with examples of successful engagement programs in school systems across North America.

Challenges Continue

Although public engagement is a proven component of all successful outreach efforts to connect the schools and community, it is not as simple as just implementing a process. We face challenges from multiple societal stressors—people are overwhelmed and over-communicated-to in today's mobile tech world, so it's difficult to capture their attention; in the majority of families both parents work, leaving little free time for commitments outside the home; race and ethnicity, inequities and inequality, and economic disparities present huge barriers to engagement efforts, particularly around student achievement.

In order to be successful, public engagement processes have to be meaningful, inclusive, and relevant to the personal concerns of those you are trying to engage, as well as to the community at large. As Mathews insightfully pointed out, "Issues that we might be tempted to see simply as problems within schools need to be reframed to embrace the larger context of community concerns." Successful schools and thriving communities are integral to each other, and truly effective engagement efforts recognize this and address issues in concert, not separately.

Sustaining ongoing engagement is also a challenge. Initial efforts (i.e., forums, town halls, study circles) can be very successful, drawing a large number of participants, but unless substantive and tangible outcomes are realized (and communicated) related to the issues stakeholders care most deeply about, numbers will quickly drop off and interest will dissipate. Environment also plays an important role. Convenient locations and times, a warm, welcoming atmosphere, a family-friendly venue, and sensitivity to cultural issues and the concerns of those whose personal experiences cause them to feel intimidated and out of place, all play a role in ensuring success.

Engaging to Make a Difference

The willingness and determination to enlist stakeholders in tackling the toughest problems—those without clear or easy answers or solutions—is a hallmark of successful engagement programs. And although it can be challenging to get our stakeholders to actively engage in education and recognize and accept their responsibility for helping all children succeed, it is possible and definitely worth the effort. The examples included here offer a brief description of just some of the variety of engagement programs possible. Each has successfully addressed specific needs and interests of the school district and the community in supporting student learning and achievement.

Success Stories

Study Circles Program—Montgomery County (MD) Public Schools. Montgomery County Public Schools (MCPS), headquartered in Rockville, is the largest school district in Maryland and the seventeenth largest in the United States, serving over 151,289 students. It is also one of the most diverse, with students from 157 countries, speaking 138 languages. Even though it is considered one of the nation's premier school systems, with ample funding and excellent teachers and curricular program, the achievement gap between white students and students of color was pronounced. In order to address this gap, in 2002 MCPS implemented Study Circles, structured conversations about how race and ethnicity affect student achievement.

Starting in one school, the program has since expanded to schools and neighborhoods across the county, and engaged thousands of MCPS employees, students, and parents in dialogues designed to address the racial and ethnic barriers to student achievement and parent involvement. The program now has a staff of four who work not just with parents and the community, but also with students, and provide training for staff Professional Learning Communities and Instructional Leadership Teams.

Over the years, these Study Circle dialogues have: improved the understanding and awareness of racial and ethnic barriers to student success, helped teachers develop awareness of the effect of unintentional stereotyping and facilitated behavior changes, encouraged the emergence of knowledgeable student leaders, developed discipline plans to ensure students of color receive fair treatment, and created new support systems in multiple languages to encourage parent involvement.[9]

100 Percent Graduation—Clarksville-Montgomery County School System (TN).   Clarksville-Montgomery County School System (CMCSS) in Clarksville, Tennessee, is the seventh largest district in the state, serving over 31,000 students, and the second largest employer in the greater county area, next to the Fort Campbell Army Post. In 2004, the graduation rate in CMCSS was 76 percent. The first step in addressing the problem was to profile the high school dropouts and correct assumptions as the profile changed over time. Focused interventions and student personalization was key. But once the district had maximized available resources, it looked to the community—not for financial support, but for voice and influence. In 2008, a group of influential community leaders were asked for their opinion on where the bar should be set for the district's graduation goal. Their answer: 100 percent.

While the goal was intimidating, CMCSS district and community leaders embraced the challenge and developed the "100 Percent Graduation Is Clarksville's Business!" campaign. The graphics staff at the local newspaper created the campaign logo. Signs were installed at entry points to the city with the logo and slogan. Businesses, large and small, signed on and a list of nonfinancial commitments was developed that businesses and organizations, including the city council and county government, could sign professing their partnership. More than one hundred businesses and organizations signed on to the 100 Percent Graduation Project, and every community partner received a logo decal to place on their door.

Partnerships took on a variety of forms, such as the manager of a local fast-food restaurant creating a study area for student workers and requiring them to bring in their progress reports for his review. (He cut their work hours if grades dropped—an effective incentive!) The project committee has hosted a student leadership summit, coordinated school tours to highlight education successes and challenges, appeared at community events and at civic group meetings, and shared their strategies with other communities. The result? The graduation rate steadily increased over the years and in 2013 reached 94 percent.[10]

Critical Conversations—Harlem Consolidated School District 122, Machesney Park, IL. A key goal in the Long-Range Plan for Harlem Consolidated School District 122 (HSD 122) is defined as: "The District will engage with parents and community at large in meaningful ways that will positively affect student achievement." Since 2011, this goal has taken the form of an ongoing, sustainable collaboration dubbed "Critical Conversations."

HSD 122 serves over 7,600 students K–12 and draws from three suburban municipalities. Every month, representatives from twenty-five different community groups meet with district staff for lunch and conversation that allows the group members to hear about and discuss district initiatives and needs. From classic "adopt a school" partnerships to efforts that focus on meeting the needs of families and neighborhoods in specific attendance areas, the emphasis is on the local school and community and the deep, caring relationships that result.

Opportunities for larger community collaboration also have flourished, with village government officials tapping in to the Critical Conversations group for resources that help community residents in general. For over forty years, HSD 122 offered a high school construction class where students built and sold a home. With the decline of the housing market, the district could no long afford to offer the program, but thanks to Habitat for Humanity, a member of the Critical Conversations group, students are now building a home in conjunction with the Habitat team.

From donated classroom space and materials for a preschool program to a joint-school district early reading initiative, to family fun nights in community venues that focus on student learning, creative engagement

programs abound in HSD 122, making a difference for the entire community.[11]

*FUTURE FOCUS. Educate. Collaborate. Communicate—Naperville
(IL) School District 203.*   Naperville School District 203 is among the
top ten largest school systems in Illinois, serving over 18,000 students in
preK–12. In 2013, district leaders convened a district-wide community
group to study and comment on the promise and opportunities facing
District 203. The volunteer-based community engagement program
brought together members of the community (families, residents, and
staff) to study and deliberate issues important to future planning and
decision-making.

This engagement effort, which facilitated a deliberate exchange of ideas and prioritization of community values, led to the development of
Future Focus 203, a strategic planning process designed to:

- Invite and engage the community in District 203 planning and decision-making;
- Define priorities and opportunities for improvement to inform strategic planning; and
- Build an ongoing process for strengthening trust, communication,
  and collaborative efforts with the full community.

A unique component of this community engagement process was the
involvement of Naperville Community Television (NCTV) as the district's media partner. Throughout the process, interviews were conducted with District 203 leaders and members of the Future Focus Facilitating Team. NCTV captured the critical elements of the story about the
community's values and priorities, and created a documentary to capture
the energy, enthusiasm, and thoughtful participation of community
members in making important decisions about their schools.[12]

Building Community and Creating Advocates

Public education is under fire from numerous adversaries today. As
political and competitive business interests look to dismantle public
schools and privatize education, it is imperative that we connect our
stakeholders and our schools in ways that create strong bonds that link to
the future of the community as a whole. Finding ways to overcome the
challenges of engaging those who are disconnected, distracted, disinter-
ested, and in some cases uneducated and wary of institutional authority

of any kind, will not be easy. If we are to sustain a thriving public education system, we must create advocates for our students and our schools. We must open the door to citizens and give them a real voice so they know and feel that their participation matters—and that they truly "own" their schools.

When we welcome and engage everyone—parents, staff, students, and citizens—as equal partners in education, we change not only the conversation but the outcomes. Instead of treating our stakeholders as "customers," we must encourage their participation in ways that allow them to take responsibility for ensuring that all students are successful and that public education continues to be a key component of civic infrastructure in our nation.

Perspective #7: Sylvia Soholt—Improving the Odds of Success for Our Country's Children [13]

Sylvia Soholt of Soholt Strategic Communications works with school districts, state departments of education, universities, and foundations to build support for high-quality K–16 education. As owner of Sylvan Sanctuary on Vashon Island, Washington, she supports guests in their quest for creativity while managing and restoring a four-acre forest and providing sanctuary for rescue dogs.

* * *

My perspective on engaging families in their children's education has been informed by conversations with parents, students, educators, taxi drivers, and hotel desk clerks in forty states. Listen in on some of these conversations and you might learn why I have become agitated about our attempts to improve the odds for all of our country's children.

- An African American mother is describing the conversation with her son's school principal, who has called to tell her that her son is being suspended from school. "He wants me to come pick up my child, but I can't leave work and will be fired if I do. So he tells me he's going to send him home in a police car. And I say, 'Don't you send my son into my neighborhood in a police car with everybody watching.' But he does," she says, crying. "That's what he does."

- In separate meetings, parents and then their school principals are shown a variety of free materials that can be used to explain what students are expected to learn in their schools. The parents want all of it. A school principal says, "Our parents don't need this stuff. They can't read it."
- Asked why parents have not turned out in large numbers to learn about school choices, an administrator sighs, "It's a lot easier not to care about something when you know it's not very good. Caring creates heartache."
- My young adult taxi driver is asking me what I know about the schools in his city. I ask him where he went to school. I say, "I know that if a computer breaks down in your school that it will stay broken, and if it breaks down at _____ High School, it will get fixed right away." He laughs and says, "You know a lot about the schools here. I guess that's just the way it is."

As I said to him, it doesn't have to be. But the prospects for changing the way it is for parents and students in our lowest-performing schools aren't especially good. When I began working in 1983 as a champion of public education, a presidential commission had declared the nation at risk because of the failure of its schools to educate students. *It's political*, I thought. Thirty years later, the effort to ensure our graduates in every state have mastered a curriculum that prepares them for college—if they want to go there—is viewed as subversive. Parents threatened by the consolidation of their suburban schools with city schools dispatch legislators to the state capital to change the law. It's still political—and self-serving. Somehow that pernicious gap in the achievement of students with means and those without still persists.

So, will it help students and schools do better if their families are more engaged? Yes, it will help, as you have learned from this book. But it won't be enough. It will only be enough when we are all invested in the success of those children most likely not to succeed. How likely is that to happen? Please tell me it could.

NOTES

1. This perspective was submitted by Gary Marx, APR, CAE, and it is used with his permission.

2. This perspective was submitted by Sherre Calouri and is used with her permission.

3. This perspective was submitted by Janet Hogue and is used with her permission.

4. From an interview of Roy Romer by David Brinkley, 1993.

5. This perspective was submitted by John Boone and is used with his permission.

6. This perspective was submitted by Nora Carr, APR, and is used with her permission.

7. From James and Larissa Grunig's model of public relations in *Excellence in Public Relations and Communications Management.*

8. This perspective was submitted by Karen Kleinz, APR, and is used with her permission.

9. More information about the study circles used in Montgomery County can be found at www.montgomeryschoolsmd.org/departments/studycircles/. Last accessed April 19, 2014.

10. More information about this increase in graduation rate project can be found at www.cmcss.net/programs/100pctgraduation.aspx. Last accessed April 19, 2014.

11. More information about these critical conversations can be found at www.harlem122.org. Last accessed April 19, 2014.

12. More information about the Naperville project can be found at www.naperville203.org/community/FutureFocus.asp, including a trailer to view at nctv17.com/videos/futurefocus.php. Both sites last accessed April 19, 2014.

13. This perspective was submitted by Sylvia Soholt and is used with her permission.

Reference List

Abowitz, Kathleen Knight and Steven R. Thompson. *Publics for Public Schools: Legitimacy, Democracy, and Leadership.* Boulder, CO: Birkenkap & Company LLC, Paragon Publishers, 2013.

Annenberg Institute for School Reform. *Reasons for Hope, Voices for Change: A Report on Public Engagement for Public Education.* Providence, RI: Annenberg Institute for School Reform, Brown University, 1998.

Argyris, Chris. *On Organizational Learning.* Cambridge, MA: Blackwell Publishers, 1992.

Bai, Matt. "A Turning Point in the Discourse, but in Which Direction?" *The New York Times Reprints.* Edited by Director Terrence Malick. January 9, 2011. http://www.nytimes.com/2011/01/09/us/politics/09bai.html? (accessed January 10, 2011).

Baldwin, Christina. *Storycatcher: Making Sense of Our Lives through the Power and Practice of Story.* Novato, CA: New World Library, 2005.

Baldwin, Christina and Ann Linnea. *The Circle Way: A Leader in Every Chair.* San Francisco: Berrett-Koehler Publishers, Inc., 2010.

Beegle, Donna. *See Poverty . . . Be the Difference! Discovering the Missing Pieces for Helping People Move Out of Poverty.* Portland, OR: Communication Across Barriers, 2006.

Bens, Ingrid. *Facilitation at a Glance: A Pocket Guide of Tools and Techniques for Effective Meeting Facilitation.* 2nd ed. Salem, NH: Goal/QPC, 2008.

———. *Facilitating with Ease: Core Skills for Facilitators, Team Leaders, and Members, Managers, Consultants, and Trainers.* 3rd ed. San Francisco: Jossey-Bass, 2012.

Bentley, Trevor. *Facilitation: Providing Opportunities for Learning.* Edited by Roger Bennett. McGraw-Hill Training Series vols. Berkshire, SL6 20L, England: McGraw-Hill Publishing Co., 1994.

Bernays, Edward Louis. *Propaganda.* New York: Horace Liveright, 1928.

Block, Peter. *Community: The Structure of Belonging.* San Francisco, CA: Berrett-Koehler Publishers, Inc., 2008.

Bohm, David. *Thought as a System.* London: Routledge, 1994.

Bolton, Robert. *People Skills: How to Assert Yourself, Listen to Others, and Resolve Conflicts.* New York: Touchstone, 2009.

Brown, Juanita, David Isaacs, and The World Cafe Community. *The World Cafe.* San Francisco, CA: Berrett-Koehler Publishers, Inc., 2006.

Bruner, Jerome. *The Culture of Education.* Cambridge, MA: Harvard University Press, 1996.

Bryk, Anthony S. and Barbara L. Schneider. *Trust in Schools: A Core Resource for Improvement.* New York: Russell Sage Foundation, 2002.

Buffalo Public School 80. "Parent Report Card." Buffalo, NY, unknown.

Cambron-McCabe, Nelda and Janis Dutton. "Wheels of Learning: The rhythm of learning and learning to learn." In *Schools That Learn: A Fifth Discipline Fieldbook for Educators, Parents, and Everyone Who Cares About Education,* by Peter Senge, Nelda

Cambron-McCabe, Timothy Lucas, Bryan Smith, Janis Dutton, and Art Kleiner. New York, New York: Doubleday, 2000.

Center, Allen H. and Patrick Jackson. *Public Relations Practices: Managerial Case Studies and Problems*. 8th ed. Upper Saddle River, NJ: Pearson Prentice Hall, 2008.

Chadwick, Robert J. "From Conflict to Consensus: Facilitator Training with Bob Chadwick." Breckenridge, CO: AASA National Academy for School Executives, 1996.

———. *Finding New Ground: Moving Beyond Conflict to Consensus*. Terrebonne, OR: One Tree Publishing, 2012.

Chizhik, Estella and Alexander Chizhik. "Resistance Theory." *education.com*. 2009. http://www.education.com/reference/article/resistance-theory/ (accessed June 20, 2014).

Clark, Susan and Woden Teachout. *Slow Democracy: Rediscovering Community, Bringing Decision-Making Back Home*. White River Junction, VT: Chesea Green Publishing, 2012.

Cohen, Don and Laurence Prusak. *In Good Company: How Social Capital Makes Organizations Work*. Boston, MA: Harvard Business School Press, 2001.

Dalton, Bev, Jennifer Freeman, and Tom Hiter. "Learning Styles Self Profile." The Prichard Committee for Academic Excellence, 1997.

———. "How Do I Learn? An Introduction to Multiple Intelligences and Learning Styles." The Prichard Committee for Academic Excellence, August 29, 1997.

DuFour, Richard and Robert Eaker. *Professional Learning Communities at Work: Best Practices for Enhancing Student Achievement*. Bloomington, IN: Solution Tree Press ASCD, 1998.

Dufur, Mikaela J., Toby L. Parcel, and Kelly P. Troutman. "Does Capital at Home Matter More Than Capital at School?: Social Capital Effects on Academic Achievement." *Research in Social Stratification and Mobility*, 2012.

Easton, Lois Brown. *Protocols for Professional Learning*. PLC Series vols. Alexandria, VA: Association of Supervision and Curriculum Development, 2009.

Edmonds District Teaching and Learning Department. "The Cookie Exercise." Edmonds, WA: Edmonds School District, 1998.

Epstein, Joyce L., Mavis G. Sanders, Beth S. Simon, Daren Clark Salinas, Natalie Rodriguez Jansorn, and Frances L. Van Voorhis. *School, Family, and Community Partnerships: Your Handbook for Action*. 2nd ed. Thousand Oaks, CA: Corwin Press, Inc., 2009.

Falconi, Toni M. "Engaging (and Grilling) the Social Side of James Grunig." *prcommunications*, October 2008. http://www.prconversations.com/index.php/2008/10/engaging-and-grilling-the-social-side-of-james-grunig (accessed March 11, 2011).

Faust, Drew Gilpin. "150 Years after the Gettysburg Address Is Government by the People in Trouble?" *Washington Post*. Washington, D.C., November 15, 2013.

Fromme, Cathy. "The Importance of Trust in Schools." 2004.

Gardner, Howard. *Frames of Mind: The Theory of Multiple Intelligences* 3rd ed. New York: Basic Books, 2011.

Gaskins, Russ and Cliff Kayser. "Systems Thinking in Action: The Power Is in the Connections." *Pegasus Annual Conference*. Indianapolis, IN: Pegasus, 2012.

Gorski, Paul. "The Myth of the Culture of Poverty." *Educational Leadership* (Ed Leadership) 65, no. 7 (April 2008): 32–36.

Grunig, James E. and Larissa A. Grunig. "Models of Public Relations and Communication." Chap. 11 in *Excellence in Public Relations and Communications Management*, edited by James E. Grunig. Hillsdale, NJ: Lawrence Erlbaum Associates, Inc., 1992.

———. "Public Relations Excellence 2010." *PRSA International Conference.* Washington, DC: Institute for Public Relations, University of Maryland, 2010.

Grunig, James E. and Todd Hunt. *Managing Public Relations.* New York: Holt, Rinehart, and Winston, 1984.

Hammond, Sue Annis and Andrea B. Mayfield. *The Thin Book of Naming Elephants: How to Surface Undiscussables for Greater Organizational Success.* Bend, OR: Thin Book Publishing Co., 2004.

Harvard Family Research Project. www.hfrp.org (accessed February 4, 2015).

Henderson, Anne T. "Engaging Families to Improve Student Achievement." Canby, OR, March 5, 2004.

———. *Beyond the Bake Sale: The Essential Guide to Family/School Partnerships.* New York: The New Press, 2007.

Henderson, Anne T. and Karen L. Mapp. *A New Wave of Evidence: The Impact of School, Family, and Community Connections on Student Achievement.* Research synthesis; Annual synthesis 2002, National Center for Family and Community Connections with Schools, Southwest Educational Development Laboratory, Austin, TX: Southwest Educational Development Laboratory, 2002.

Henderson, Anne T. and Nancy Berla. *A New Generation of Evidence: The Family Is Critical to Student Achievement.* Research synthesis, Center for Law and Education, Washington, DC: Center for Law and Education, 1994.

Henderson, Anne T., Bonnie Jacob, Ada Kernan-Schloss, and Bev Raimondo. *The Case for Parent Leadership.* KSA-Plus and Prichard Committee for Academic Excellence, 2004.

Henderson, Anne T., Lidia Krivov, and Kathy Leslie. "Strategies to Reach the Hard-to-Reach." Beaverton, OR: The Chalkboard Project Running Start Initiative, 2007.

Holcomb, Edie L. *Asking the Right Questions: Techniques for Collaboration and School Change.* 3rd ed. Thousand Oaks, CA: Corwin Press, 2009.

Isaacs, William N. *Taking Flight: Dialogue, Collective Thinking, and Organizational Learning.* MIT Center for Organizational Learning's Dialogue Project. Boston, MA: MIT Center for Organizational Learning, 1993.

———. *Dialogue and the Art of Thinking Together: A Pioneering Approach to Communicating in Business and in Life.* New York: Random House, Inc., 1999.

Jackson, Jackson and Wagner. *What We Do and Why It Works.* Seigel Web Development and Consulting, Inc., 2006. http://www.jjwpr.com/about_jjw/index.htm (accessed June 20, 2014).

Jackson, Patrick, interview by unknown. *Untitled* (unknown date).

Johnson, Barry. *Polarity Management: Identifying and Managing Unsolvable Problems.* Amherst, MA: HRD Press (Human Resource Development), 1996.

Justice, Thomas and David W. Jamieson. *The Facilitator's Fieldbook.* New York: AMACON, American Management Association, 1999.

Kessler, Rachael and Mark Gerzon. "Forms of Discourse." Unknown date.

Kleiner, Art. "The Continuum of 'Systems Thinking'." In *Schools That Learn: A Fifth Discipline Fieldbook for Educators, Parents, and Everyone Who Cares About Education,* by Peter Senge, Nelda Cambron-McCabe, Timothy Lucas, Bryan Smith, Janis Dutton and Art Kleiner, 78–80. New York: Doubleday, 2000.

Kleinz, Karen, interview by Kathy Leslie. *Associate director, National School Public Relations Association* (April 23, 2010).

Kober, Nancy. "Why We Still Need Public Schools: Public Education for the Common Good." Washington, DC: Center on Education Policy, 2007.

Krishnamurti, Jiddu. *First Public Talks*. Saanen: Talks and Dialogues, July 9, 1967.

Krueger, Richard A. and Mary Anne Casey. *Focus Groups: A Practical Guide for Applied Research*. Newbury Park, CA: Sage Publications, 2008.

KSA-Plus Communications. *Reporting Results: What the Public Wants to Know*. Arlington, VA: KSA-Plus Communications, 1999.

———. *Twelve Things Parents Should Know About and Expect from Their Schools*. KSA-Plus Communications, n.d.

KSA-Plus, and Center for Parent Leadership. *The Case for Parent Leadership*. Lexington, KY: Center for Parent Leadership, February 2004.

Leedy, Paul D. *Practical Research*. New York: MacMillan Publishing Co., Inc., 1980.

Leighninger, Matt. *Planning for Engagement: Why, What, Who, and How?* NSPRA1005. 2010. National School Public Relations Conference session.

———. *The Next Form of Democracy: How Expert Rule Is Giving Way to Shared Governance—and Why Politics Will Never Be the Same*. Nashville, TN: Vanderbilt University Press, 2006.

Leighninger, Matt and Peter Levine. "Education in a Rapidly Changing Democracy: Strengthening Civic Education for Citizens of All Ages." *The School Administrator* (American Association of School Administrators) 65, no. 9 (October 2008): 25–28.

Leslie, Kathy. "Community Relations: Engaging the Public." Chap. 14 in *School Public Relations: Building Confidence in Education*, by NSPRA, edited by Kenneth K. Muir, 119–134. Rockville, MD: National School Public Relations Association, 1999.

———. "The Wisdom of Authentic Engagement." Acceptance Speech, NSPRA President's Award, National School Public Relations Association (NSPRA), San Antonio, TX, 2000.

———. "ABCs of Community Involvement." Beaverton, OR: 2001.

———. "Handouts for OKSPRA Workshop." *OKSPRA Workshop*. Oklahoma City, OK: 2003.

———. "Is Your Secondary School Open to Partnership with Parents?" *Partnering with Your School: How to Help Your Child Succeed*. Salem, OR: The Chalkboard Project, 2006. 2.

———. "PRSA Speech." Salem, OR: 2006/7.

———. "Running Start: Trainers Guide for School Training Workshops." The Chalkboard Project, January 2008.

———. "Communication Skills for Administrators." Unpublished. Portland, OR: 2009.

———. "I Used to Believe." *National School Public Relations Association*. September 2010. http://www.nspra.org/e_network/75thanniversary_essay_september_2010 (accessed January 28, 2011).

———. "A Focus Group Script for Students." North Clackamas, OR: North Clackamas School District, 2013.

———. *Redefining Involvement: Research-Based Strategies for Engaging the Hard-to-Reach*. PowerPoint Presentation. Portland, OR: The Chalkboard Project, n.d.

Leslie, Kathy and Anne T. Henderson. "Engaging Families to Improve Student Achievement." Canby, OR: March 5, 2004.

Leslie, Kathy and Sherre Calouri. "Running Start: Trainers Guide for Parent Training Workshops." Portland, OR: The Chalkboard Project, November 2007.

Mapp, Karen L. and Paul J. Kutter. "Partners in Education: A Dual Capacity-Building Framework for Family–School Partnerships." *SEDL Advancing Research Improving Education*. SEDL in collaboration with the U.S. Department of Education. 2013.

http://www.sedl.org/pubs/framework/FE-Cap-Building.pdf (accessed April 16, 2014).

Marx, Gary. *Future-Focused Leadership: Preparing Schools, Students, and Communities for Tomorrow's Realities.* Association for Supervision and Curriculum Development (ASCD), 2006.

———. *Twenty-One Trends for the 21st Century: Out of the Trenches, Into the Future.* Bethesda, MD: Editorial Projects in Education/Education Week Press, 2014.

Maslow, Abraham H. "A Theory of Human Motivation." *Psychological Review,* 1943: 370–396.

Mathews, David. *Is There a Public for Public Schools?* Dayton, OH: Kettering Foundation Press, 1996.

McDonald, Joseph P., Nancy Mohr, Alan Dichter, and Elizabeth C. McDonald. *The Power of Protocols: An Educator's Guide to Better Practice.* New York: Teachers College Press, Columbia University, 2003.

Meier, Deborah. *The Power of Their Ideas: Lessons for America from a Small School in Harlem.* Boston, MA: Beacon Press, 1995.

MetLife Foundation. *MetLife Survey of the American Teacher: Past, Present, and Future.* Online, MetLife Foundation, n.d.

Mitchell, Ted and David Hammarstrom. "Press Room at MetLife." *MetLife.com.* February 25, 2009. http://www.metlife.com/about/press-room/index.html?compID=12296 (accessed January 17, 2011).

Muir, Kenneth K., ed. *School Public Relations: Building Confidence in Education.* Alexandria, VA: National School Public Relations Association, 1999.

National Center for Education Statistics. "Digest of Educational Statistics, Enrollment in Educational Institutions, by Level and Control in Institution." Table, National Center for Education Statistics, U.S. Department of Education, Washington, DC: 2009.

National Governors Association Center for Best Practices and Council of Chief State School Officers. "Frequently Asked Questions: Overview." *Common Core State Standards Initiative.* 2012. http://www.corestandards.org/resources/frequently-asked-questions (accessed February 7, 2013).

National School Public Relations Association. *Diversity Communications Toolkit.* www.nspra.org (accessed February 5, 2015).

National School Reform Faculty. www.nsrfharmony.org (access February 5, 2015).

NBC News. *Meet the Press.* New York, January 9, 2011.

Owen, Harrison. *Open Space Technology: A User's Guide.* San Francisco: Berrett-Koehler Publishers, Inc., 1997.

Payne, Ruby K. *A Framework for Understanding Poverty.* 3rd ed. Highlands, TX: aha! Process, 1996.

Payne, Ruby K, Philip E. DeVol, and Terie Dreussi Smith. *Bridges Out of Poverty: Strategies for Professionals and Communities Workbook.* 3rd ed. Highlands, TX: aha! Process, Inc., 2006.

Prez, Dead. "Let's Get Free." *Let's Get Free.* Comp. A. Maier, V. Williams, and C. Gavin L. Alford. 2000.

Prichard. "The Question Formulation Technique." The Prichard Committee for Academic Excellence.

———. "Governor's Commonwealth Institute for Parent Leadership." The Prichard Committee for Academic Excellence. www.prichardcommittee.org/our-initiatives/cipl (accessed February 5, 2015).

Public Agenda. *Helping All Students Succeed in a Diverse Society: A Public Agenda Citizen Choicework Guide.* New York: Public Agenda, 2005. www.publicagenda.org.

Remen, Rachel Naomi. *My Grandfather's Blessings: Stories of Strength, Refuge,. and Belonging.* New York: Riverhead Books, 2000.

Richardson, Joan. "11 Questions to Ask Before You Launch a Research Project." *Tools for Schools.* National Staff Development Council: 9, no. 1 (August/September 2005).

Romer, Roy, interview by David Brinkley. *This Week with David Brinkley.* ABC News. August 29, 1993.

Russell, Jeffery and Linda Russell. *Strategic Planning Training.* Alexandria, VA: ASTD Press, 2006.

Salter, Tom. "Become a Better Communicator through 'Intentional Listening'." *Principal Communicator* (National School Public Relations Association), December 2011: 1–2.

Sarason, Seymour B. *The Predictable Failure of Educational Reform: Can We Change Course before It's Too Late?* San Francisco: Jossey-Bass, 1990.

Satir, Virginia. *The New Peoplemaking.* Palo Alto, CA: Science and Behavior Books, Inc., 1988.

Scharmer, Otto and Katrin Kaufer. *Leading from the Emerging Future: From Ego-Systems to Eco-Systems Economies.* San Francisco: Berrett-Koehler Publishers, Inc., 2013.

Schmoker, M. J. "Tipping Point: From Feckless Reform to Substantive Instructional Improvement." *Phi Delta Kappan* 85, no. 6 (2004): 424–432.

Schutz, Will. *The Human Element: Productivity, Self-Esteem, and the Bottom Line Management.* San Francisco: Jossey-Bass, 1994.

Schwarz, Roger M. *The Skilled Facilitator: Practical Wisdom for Developing Effective Groups.* San Francisco, CA: Jossey-Bass, 1994.

Senge, Peter. "Creating Desired Futures in a Global Economy." *Society of Organizational Learning (SOL) Journal* (Society of Organizational Learning) 5, no. 1 (Fall 2003): Reprint.

Senge, Peter M., Art Kleiner, Charlotte Roberts, Richard B. Ross, and Bryan J. Smith. *The Fifth Discipline Fieldbook: Strategies and Tools for Building a Learning Organization.* New York: Doubleday, 1994.

Senge, Peter M., Nelda Cambron-McCabe, Timothy Lucas, Bryan Smith, Janis Dutton, and Art Kleiner. *Schools That Learn: A Fifth Discipline Fieldbook for Educators, Parents, and Everyone Who Cares about Education.* New York: Doubleday, 2000.

Sergiovanni, Thomas J. *Building Community in Schools.* San Francisco: Jossey-Bass, Inc., 1999.

———. *Leadership for the Schoolhouse: How Is It Different? Why Is It Important?* San Francisco, CA: Jossey-Bass, Inc., 1996.

Shaffer, Carolyn R. and Kristin Anundsen. *Creating Community Anywhere: Finding Support and Connection in a Fragmented World.* New York: Putnam Publishing Group, 1993.

Simon, Judith Sharken. *Conducting Successful Focus Groups: How to Get the Information You Need to Make Smart Decisions.* Nashville, TN: Turner Publishing (formerly Fieldstone Alliance), 1999.

Smith, Ed. "The Wheel of Learning in a Community." Portland, OR: Ed Smith, 1990s.

Smith, Judi. "Principles of Conflict." *Principles of Conflict.* Portland, OR: 2000.

Smith, Ronald D. "Pioneers in the Development of Contemporary Public Relations." *Buffalo State Communications Department.* Updated Fall 2010. http://faculty.buffalostate.edu/smithrd/PR/pioneers.htm (accessed January 13, 2011).

Stiehl, Ruth. *Fundamental Process Patterns That Distinguish Organizations as "Living" Systems*. Unknown: The White Water Institute, 2011.

Stone, Douglas, Bruce Patton, and Sheila Heen. *Difficult Conversations: How to Discuss What Matters Most*. New York: Penguin Books, 2010.

The Partnership for Kentucky Schools. "Is Your School a Welcoming School?" *Is Your School a Welcoming School?* The Commonwealth Institute for Parent Leadership, 1998.

U.S. Department of Education. "Parental Involvement: Title I, Part A—Non-Regulatory Guidance." *www.ed.gov*. U.S. Department of Education. April 23, 2004, http://www.ed.gov/programs/titleiparta/parentinvguid.doc (accessed February 9, 2013).

Williams, R. Bruce. *Twelve Roles of Facilitators for School Change*. Arlington Heights, IL: IRI/Skylight Training and Publishing, Inc., 1997.

Woods, Lutricia. "No Child Left Behind . . . Engaging Parents." Parent Leadership Associates, The Prichard Committee for Academic Excellence: 2003.

Index

About the Authors

Kathy Leslie, APR, specializes in community building, social research, conflict mediation, facilitation, strategic planning, systems thinking, and public engagement strategy development.

Leslie is president of Leslie Consulting & Associates, a company she founded to support educators in their quest to build trust and strong alliances with their communities. She is the past board chair of the White Water Institute, a nonprofit organization that uses a river experience to apply principles of living systems to human systems to guide and navigate change.

Leslie has been a teacher at all levels of education from preschool through university, a public relations administrator in three school districts in the Northwest—Gresham, Spokane, and Beaverton—and an independent senior consultant for KSA Plus Communications.

Leslie is past president of the National School Public Relations Association and has received the NSPRA President's Award for her lifetime contributions to the field of educational public relations.

Leslie has facilitated workshops, consulted, and given speeches in communications and engagement strategies internationally and in nearly every state for educational organizations, government agencies, and private sector businesses. She has written for national educational journals and co-authored the NSPRA workshop kits *Lighting the Fire: A Process for Building Staff Morale and Excellence; Staff Recognition: Unlocking the Potential for Success*; and *Team Building 2000: Managing Change Together*. Leslie co-authored Chalkboard Project's *Running Start: Reaching the Hard to Reach, a Tool Kit for Parents and Trainers of Parents*. She periodically serves as an adjunct professor of communication strategies and systems at Lewis and Clark College.

Leslie holds bachelor's degrees in communications and education, a master's degree in business, and certification in educational administration.

Leslie and her husband have eight adult children in their blended family and twelve grandchildren. Leslie is a world traveler, having visited seven continents and more than seventy countries. She enjoys conversations, hiking, whitewater rafting, golfing, and swimming. She lives in Beaverton, Oregon, and can be reached at kathy@leslieconsult.com.

Judy Taccogna, EdD, brings practical experience as a teacher, counselor, elementary school principal, and district administrator. She has also served as the education director at Search Institute, a national research organization in Minneapolis, Minnesota. She has contributed writing and editing to two previous books and a number of newsletters. *Global Oregon* represented a collaborative writing project among teachers throughout Oregon to produce an economics textbook for high school students under the auspices of Oregon State University/Western Oregon University School of Education. *Powerful Teaching: Developmental Assets in Curriculum and Instruction* was a project that brought together twenty-four educators who were applying Search Institute's developmental asset model to learning in classrooms and schools. She holds bachelor degrees in education and literature, a master's degree in counseling and guidance, and a doctorate in educational leadership, administration, and supervision.